*Farmstead windmill on refurbished homestead owned by Sheila Pauls, 2001, Arcadia, WI, by Barbara A. Pauls, her mother.*

## The Farm
### *Yvonne Klinkenberg*

Rolling hills, fields unplowed.
Unseen birds, singing loud.
A farmhouse, century-old, close to the road,
Sign in front: "I've been sold."
Through the eyes of two in love—
they see things we can't dream of:
The empty barn, soon to see
a herd of cows, maybe thirty-three.
From its loft flies what looks like a white dove,
being a sign of Good to those in love.
The house stands empty, but soon will ring
with music, which those two will bring.
By the woods, blackcaps doth grow;
the sweetness of jelly they will know.
The low-slung branch will hold a swing
when their boy turns two, come this spring.
Yes, the farm that sits close to the road,
to this young couple, it's been sold.

*To God Above; to the courage, dignity, disagreeableness, sweetness, humor, and strength of the American people; to our friends and families, everywhere and always; and to our enemies, who, we hope, will also become our friends and families ...*

"The Lord is my shepherd." —23RD PSALM

"Find the good and praise it."
—ANNA MUKTEPAVELS-MOTIVANS

"I've come not to stroke you, but to challenge you."
—SIDNEY POITIER

"It is dearness only that gives everything its value."
—TOM PAINE

"They did it because no one told them that they could not."
—SEAN NIESTRATH

"I am not an American—I am **the** American."
—MARK TWAIN

"They died together, a band of courageous brothers and sisters on September 11th... God bless them, God bless us all, and God bless America."
—ALICE HOGLAN, MOTHER OF MARK BINGHAM

"[T]hey slipped the surly bonds of earth, to touch the face of God."
—RONALD REAGAN VIA PEGGY NOONAN
VIA JOHN GILLESPIE MAGEE

"Tear down this wall..." —RONALD REAGAN

"And you that ask forgiveness of your Lord, then turn to Him..." —HOLY QURAN

"Love your enemies, bless them that curse you, do good to them that hate you, and pray for them which despitefully use you, and persecute you."
—JESUS CHRIST IN ST. MATTHEW'S GOSPEL

"We have to use 9/11 as a huge wake-up call."
—RAYMOND KELLY

"The only thing we have to fear is fear itself."
—FRANKLIN DELANO ROOSEVELT

"You have to be ambitious about an idea to preserve it—Liberty, for instance."
—WILLIAM F. BUCKLEY JR.

"In order to do the toughest thing there is to do in sport—hit a baseball properly—a man has got to devote every ounce of his concentration to it."
—TED WILLIAMS

"We're cursed with being reasonable."
—NORMAN LEAR

"Patriotism is interesting.... We [Americans] are very good at war, and we don't like it; that combination is our saving grace.... 'Hang onto your lights, America—they're the only lights left in the world.'"
—ROGER ROSENBLATT

"Courage is not just one virtue; it is the culmination of all virtues." —DEENA BURNETT, WIFE OF TOM BURNETT

"[G]iven a chance, people will make friends across, around, over and under all the natural and man-made barriers, which separate them."
—DWIGHT D. EISENHOWER

"Sow an act, reap a habit. Sow a habit, reap a character. Sow a character, reap a destiny."
—PHILLIPINE SAYING

"In America, we never stop kicking it."
—SAMUEL L. JACKSON

"I love being a salesman ... I can't imagine full retirement. I like people, and I'd like to continue as long as I can." —BILL PORTER

"Don't give up!" —JIM VALVANO

"Let's roll!" —TODD BEAMER, HUSBAND OF LISA BEAMER

FRONT COVER:
Main photo: Fourth of July fireworks, July 4, 1999, La Crosse, WI, by Gerald A. Bonsack.
Left inset: Mobile Vietnam War Memorial Wall, 2002, Arcadia, WI, by Steve Kiedrowski.
Center inset: "Lady Liberty," 2002, New York, NY, by Barbara A. Pauls.
Right inset: Bald eagle flying over fishing boats, 2000, Seward, AK, by Denise Havlik-Jensen.

BACK COVER, FROM UPPER LEFT CORNER MOVING CLOCKWISE:
The young men of autumn, Aquinas Eighth Grade Football Team, 2001, Onalaska, WI, by David J. Marcou.
World Peace Flag, designed by Jim Brush, Empire Screen Printing Company, 2001-02, Onalaska, WI.
*Air Force One* taking off in the rain, early November 1992, La Crosse, WI, by David J. Marcou.
U.S. flag with the sun shining through it, 2002, Riverside Park, La Crosse, WI, by Steve Kiedrowski.
Burning World Trade Center tower, September 11th, 2001, New York, NY, by Rick Wood, courtesy of the *Milwaukee Journal Sentinel*.
First Congregational Church of Lebanon, CT, designed by the great American Revolutionary War artist John Trumbull and built in 1804-07, by Grant Huntington, courtesy of the Town of Lebanon, CT.
Mississippi River sunset looking west toward La Crescent, MN, July 4, 1999, by Gerald A. Bonsack.
Big Indian statue created by Anthony Zimmerhakl (1956-60), 2002, Riverside Park, La Crosse, WI, by Steve Kiedrowski.
The Stevens Family: (Back, L-R) Mark Jr., Mark Sr., Anthony Michael; (Front, L-R) Marissa Paige, Roberta H., 1997, San Diego, CA, courtesy of the Stevens Family.
Canadian farmstead, 1990s, by Frances (Nina) Valiska.
Tulips whose bulbs were purchased by the photographer in Holland on holiday in 1998, Arcadia, WI, by Barbara A. Pauls.
Sam Besl in U.S. flag necktie on the night of his graduation from Aquinas Middle School, June 3, 2002, by David J. Marcou.

*"Loveall" headstone, 2000, Arlington (Virginia) National Cemetery, by David J. Marcou.*

# America's Heartland Remembers
*Words and Pictures*
*Before, During, and After September 11th, 2001*

Edited by
David J. Marcou and Barbara A. Pauls

Published by The Writers' Collective

Copyright 2002, David J. Marcou and Barbara A. Pauls for this complete book; the copyrights to individual items within this book are retained by their creators and/or by those creators' legal representatives. This book is made possible by a grant from the Sept 12 Guild.

**Production Staff:**

*Publisher:* The Writers' Collective
*Projects Director:* David J. Marcou
*Editors:* David J. Marcou & Barbara A. Pauls
*Typist:* Matthew A. Marcou

*Designer:* Sue Knopf
*Publicist:* Steve Kiedrowski
*Printers:* Fidlar-Doubleday, with assistance from Royal Graphix of La Crosse

ISBN#: 0-9716734-3-8

# Acknowledgments

*"With malice toward none; with charity for all..."*—ABRAHAM LINCOLN

I would like to thank here my parents (David A. and Rose C. Marcou), my son (Matthew A. Marcou), the Marcou families of Wisconsin and Washington, D.C. (including my brothers, Dennis, Dan, and Tom, and my sisters, Diane, Lynn, and Mary, and their families), the Hilbert families of Wisconsin and Connecticut (especially Greg Hilbert and his family), the Sondelski family of Chicago, the families of (Pope) John Paul II, George W. and Laura Bush, of . . . David W. Johns, Ron Kind, Jennifer Shilling, Mary Eisenhower, Sue Knopf and Jim Rothwell, Margaret and Cy Brom, Raymond L. Burke, John Paul, Monica Muskat, Ed and Zita Pretasky, Kathy and Cal Grise, Larry and Debbie Muskat, Ray and Bev Muskat, (Mr. & Mrs.) Ray Kline, Michael David, (Mr. & Mrs.) Calvin Lawrence, Dan Balaban, Yi Do-Sun and Ms. Lee, William and Carla Johns, Charles and Christine Freiberg, (Bert's widow) Sheila Hardy, Charles Keeble, John and Judy Whale, Charles and Elizabeth Erven, Bob and Peggy Beyer, Roger and Charlotte Grant, Patrick and Jo Anne Killeen, Robert and Loraine Mulock, Mary Ann Grossmann, David and Rosalee McCullough, Tony Boullion, Joe and Julie Besl, Mark Sr. and Roberta H. Stevens, Sean and Rebecca Niestrath, Betty Slate, Mary Lewis, William Medland, John Havertape, Richard Ruppel, Raymond Schoen, Linda McAlpine, Susan Webb, Richard Dungar, as well as the families of my son's mom, of Tony Skifton, of Mother Teresa, of Anne Frank, of ... Art Kiedrowski, Jim and Luciel Marcou, Jim and Alice Long, Joe and Cleone Muskat, Bob and Rosemary Trowbridge, William G. Blair, John Hansen, Charles Gelatt, Ron Wanek, Jim and Cindy Brush, James Cameron, Tom and Sue Elsen, Art and Mary Hebberd, Larry and Sydney Wangelin, Frank and Mary Devine, Joshua Swanson, (Mr. & Mrs.) Werner Engel, Richard Hannagan, Esther M. Jackson, Jon Walton, Lee and Sue Gilbert, Bob and Sibyl Floyd, Emma Raith, Ruth Simons, Jim and Madge Gustafson, Don La Fleur, Bill Croasdale, Josie Broadhead, Bjorge Olson, (Mr. & Mrs.) Robert Funke, and all my other family and friends, including all the contributors to our books, my teachers and students, our employers, and the publishers, printers, sellers, and, of course, the buyers and readers of all our books. Also, I thank God for reading, writing, photography, computers, and last, though not least, design, sales, libraries, and churches.
—*David J. Marcou*

I would like to thank my children, who are precious beyond words. My daughters, Sheila and Lisa, my sons and their wives, Todd and JoAnne and Ted and Annette. My priceless grandchildren, Derek, Hayley Myre and the new baby, who have brought great joy and laughter into my life and who have inspired stories, including the Sam and Doofus stories. My best friend, Jeanne Roets, who has been with me through thick and thin, and all my other family and friends, who are what life is about, and who also encouraged me to put my thoughts on paper.

I thank you for the most priceless gifts that you have all given me—your love and friendship.
—*Barbara A. Pauls*

# Contents

The Farm, *Yvonne Klinkenberg* ............................................. *i*
Preface, *David J. Marcou* .................................................. *ix*
Introduction: Effects of 9/11, *La Crosse Mayor John Medinger* ............... *xi*

## PART I: BEFORE SEPTEMBER 11TH, 2001

### SECTION 1: AMERICA'S HEARTLAND REMEMBERS

Ellis Island, *Barbara A. Pauls* .............................................. 2
It Took Courage to Enlist, Then Die for His Country, at Age 53, *David J. Marcou* ... 3
Our Priceless Gift: Music, *Helen Bolterman* ................................. 6
The Story of Flax: An Excerpt from *Anna's Story*, *Anna Muktepavels-Motivans* ..... 8
The Month of June, *Anna Muktepavels-Motivans* ............................. 10
Welcoming Strangers, *Robert Cook* ........................................ 10
The Immigrant, *Ursula Chiu* .............................................. 12
Visiting Grandma, *Karmin Van Domelen* .................................... 13
Integrity, *La Vonne Woodhouse Mainz* ..................................... 14
Jennifer's Story: Growing Up Hmong in America, *Jennifer (Choua Yang) Xiong* .. 15
America's Melting Pot, *Doris Kirkeeng* ..................................... 18
An Excerpt from "My First Long Train Ride Alone," *Sam McKay* .............. 19
Stirring Up, *Sharon Swenson Schmeling* .................................... 21
Cookbook Memories, *Barbara A. Pauls* ..................................... 23

### SECTION 2: NATURAL AMERICA

Moon Dance: A Frog Surveyor's Rhapsody, *Jim Solberg* ....................... 24
Trees: Nature's Wonder, *Helen Bolterman* ................................... 26
On the Trail of the Trailing Arbutus, *Jim Solberg* ............................ 26
When the Waters Rise, *La Vonne Woodhouse Mainz* .......................... 29
A Simple Affair, *Mark D. Smith* ........................................... 32
Life, Like Nature, *Barbara A. Pauls* ........................................ 33
A Gentle Giant, *Ursula Chiu* .............................................. 33
Let It Snow, Let It Snow, *Aggie Tippery* .................................... 37
To the Rescue? *Mark D. Smith* ............................................ 38

### SECTION 3: GROWING UP IN AMERICA

Anna Li, *Betty Holey* ..................................................... 40
Birthing Creates, *Barbara A. Pauls* ......................................... 41
Sister Janet (a.k.a. Elaine McNally) and the 50-Year-Old Secret, *Mary Lou Ryan* . 41
Born a Girl, *Mary Claire Fehring* .......................................... 44
The Significance of the Year 1914, *Mary Claire Fehring* ...................... 45
Inner Child, *Barbara A. Pauls* ............................................. 46
Growing Up in Mississippi, *Anene Ristow* .................................. 48
Mercy from the Bride of God, *Sue Silvermarie* .............................. 51
Michael's Story Quilt, *Nelda Johnson Liebig* ................................ 52
Baby Boomer Bandit, *Terry Smith* ......................................... 53
Life in a Small Country School, *William Kulas* .............................. 56
Fatherless, *Barbara A. Pauls* .............................................. 58
Challenge Academy Deserves to Be Saved, *Doris Kirkeeng* .................... 58

A Child's Soul, *Barbara A. Pauls* .................................... 60
Emily, *Evelyn Wilhelm* .................................................. 61
Brick by Brick, *Nelda Johnson Liebig* ............................... 61
We Wrap the Arms, *Barbara A. Pauls* ................................ 63
Building a Cathedral, *Robert Cook* ................................... 63

## SECTION 4: HUMAN INTEREST STORIES

Finding the Right Puppy: An Alaskan Malamute, *Joyce Crothers* .............. 65
If It Is Truly Love, *Barbara A. Pauls* ............................... 67
Surviving on the Power of Prayer, *Steve Kiedrowski* ................ 67
To Live for Those Who Love Me, *Barbara A. Pauls* ................... 70
Some More Equal Than Others, *Robert Cook* .......................... 71
The Family of Humanity, *Robert Cook* ................................ 72
Bobby L. Lyons, *Sam McKay* ............................................ 73
The Polish Prince, *Steve Kiedrowski* ................................. 75
Variations in the Key of English, *William Kulas* .................... 77
Too Often, Reality, *Barbara A. Pauls* ................................ 79
The Mysterious Boat, *Doris Kirkeeng* ................................. 79
The Mall is Always Greener on the Other Side of the State, *Aggie Tippery* ...... 81
"Too Old" to Learn, *Anene Ristow* .................................... 82
Spirit of Ettrick Boy Lives On, *Steve Kiedrowski* ................... 84
A Letter to My Californian Family, February 2002, *Lucinda A. Gray* ........ 87

## SECTION 5: HOLIDAYS & SEASONS IN AMERICA

A New Awakening, *Helen Bolterman* .................................... 89
Gardening Is Forever, *Robert (Bob) Smith* ........................... 90
The Olympics and Gold Medals, *Robert Cook* .......................... 92
A Summer Remembered, *Mary Claire Fehring* ........................... 93
When Autumn Has Me Spellbound, *Donna Huegel* ........................ 96
First Hunt, *Evelyn Wilhelm* ........................................... 96
Cantigny Day, 1938, *Sam McKay* ........................................ 97
World War II Memorial, *David J. Marcou* ............................. 99
Christmas Joy, *Yvonne Klinkenberg* ................................... 100
Swedish Christmas, *Mary Lou Ryan* .................................... 100
Gifts in Life, *Lucinda A. Gray* ....................................... 102
Wisconsin Winter, *Yvonne Klinkenberg* ................................ 104
Give Me Forty Acres and I'll Turn These Skis Around, *Donna Huegel* ........ 104
Winter Sense, *Lucinda A. Gray* ........................................ 106
The Disappearance of Minnesota, *Joyce Crothers* ..................... 106
In Praise of Winter, *Joyce Crothers* ................................. 107
Easter, *Yvonne Klinkenberg* ........................................... 109
The World Celebrates, *Doris Kirkeeng* ................................ 109
A Promise, *Barbara A. Pauls* .......................................... 110

## SECTION 6: AMERICANS AT WORK AND PLAY

Cracked Skin and a Note Make Hand Cream a Hit (or, No-Crack Hand Cream:
   How Great Thou Art) *Rick Romell* ................................ 111
Ordinary, Humble Work, *David J. Marcou* ............................. 114
A Well-Earned Tribute to Public Servants, *Doris Kirkeeng* .......... 115

Memories of a Milkman, *Steve Kiedrowski* .............................. *116*
One U.S. View of Seoul: Namdaemun, *David J. Marcou* ................... *119*
Boxing: The Ancient Art of Pugilism, *Steve Kiedrowski* .................... *119*
Muhammad Ali: Champion, *David J. Marcou* ............................ *122*
From the Series *Syracuse West,* "Part II: Recruitment," *Jim Rodgers* ........... *122*
Connecticut and the Leaf Peepers, *Nelda Johnson Liebig* .................. *126*
Between the Lines, *Jim Rodgers* ...................................... *127*
Blue Laws, *Ida Hood* .............................................. *128*
Regis Takes the Trophy, *Virgene Nix Oldenburg* ......................... *129*
A Good Day to Greet a Friend, *Yvonne Klinkenberg* ...................... *129*

## PART II: DURING SEPTEMBER 11TH, 2001

### SECTION 7: EYEWITNESS

Eyewitness, *Charles Nierling* ......................................... *132*
Midst of Silence, *Lucinda A. Gray* .................................... *135*
My City—New York, *Charles Nierling* ................................. *135*
Tragedy, *Blaine R. Thorson* .......................................... *140*

### SECTION 8: HEARTLANDERS' IMMEDIATE RESPONSES

Trapped, *Mark D. Smith* ............................................ *141*
September 11th and Photos in My Mind, *Karmin Van Domelen* ............. *142*
The Immediate Effect 9/11 Had on Me, *Joyce Clason* ..................... *144*
The Sky Was So Blue, *Sharon Swenson Schmeling* ....................... *145*
September 11th, 2001, *Joyce Crothers* ................................. *147*
Two Days to Remember, *Aggie Tippery* ................................ *148*
How September 11th Changed Our World, *Helen Bolterman* .............. *149*
Twin Towers Retrospective, *Mary Lou Ryan* ............................ *151*
September 11th, 2001: A Poem, *La Vonne Woodhouse Mainz* ............... *152*

## PART III: AFTER SEPTEMBER 11TH, 2001

### SECTION 9: HEARTLANDERS' CONSIDERED RESPONSES

American Heroes, *Mark D. Smith* ..................................... *154*
Letter to the Editor about Transplant Patients and September 11th, *Jim Solberg* *156*
The World After September 11th, 2001, *Bernard McGarty* ................. *156*
New Thoughts, *Donna Huegel* ....................................... *159*
Thoughts, *Alice Cook* .............................................. *161*
My Special Place, *Anna Muktepavels-Motivans* .......................... *161*
At the Edge of Life or Death, *Terry Smith* .............................. *164*
Harp of Hope, *Steve Kiedrowski* ..................................... *166*
Christmas 2001, *Donna Huegel* ...................................... *168*
First Year of New Millennium Was Great in Hokah, *Aggie Tippery* .......... *170*
And Now Every Day is Flag Day, *La Vonne Woodhouse Mainz* ............. *171*
Remember, *Terry Smith* ............................................ *172*

### SECTION 10: REVIEWS (BEFORE & AFTER 9/11)

Bridging the Gap, *David J. Marcou* ................................... *173*
The *Spirit* of America in a Book, *Aggie Tippery* ......................... *174*

To Love—Or Not, *Barbara A. Pauls* .................................... 177
Great Day Coming: Civil Rights before the Movement, *David J. Marcou* ...... 177
In Vietnam He Took His Stand, *David J. Marcou* ........................ 179
At Centennial, Steinbeck's Easy Reading Still Draws, *Geeta Sharma Jensen* .... 180
Heart Home, *Barbara A. Pauls* ........................................ 183

## SECTION 11: AMERICA'S HEARTLAND REMEMBERS (AGAIN)

Wings of Freedom, *Terry Smith* ........................................ 184
Safe Harbor, *Barbara A. Pauls* ........................................ 186
A Balanced Reassessment of the Life of the Late Junior Senator from Wisconsin
   *David J. Marcou*. .................................................. 186
The Adventuresome Summer of 1941, *Sam McKay* ...................... 188
The Red Cake, *Anene Ristow* ......................................... 190
Jeanne, *Barbara A. Pauls* ............................................. 192
My Son, My Friend, *Barbara A. Pauls* .................................. 193
The Rocket Scientists of Butterfield Valley, *Tom Tippery* ................. 193
The Soda Fountain in Fountain City, *La Vonne Woodhouse Mainz* .......... 194
The Carpenters, *Barbara A. Pauls* ..................................... 196
My Latvian-American Mother, *Anna Muktepavels-Motivans* ................ 196
Bedtime for an Old Woman, *La Vonne Woodhouse Mainz* ................ 197
Grandpa's Corncob Pipe, *Robert (Bob) Smith* ........................... 197
The Whale House, *Jim Solberg* ........................................ 198
Ode to Archie, *Barbara A. Pauls* ...................................... 200
Forgotten Heroes, *William Kulas* ..................................... 200
A Thankful Gift to a Pastor, *Yvonne Klinkenberg* ....................... 202
World Peace Flag, *Steve Kiedrowski* ................................... 202
**Author Biographies**................................................ 204
**Over Lake Arbutus, Forever,** *Mark D. Smith* ........................ 212

*All uncredited stand-alone epigrams were written by Barbara A. Pauls.*

*Fireworks over Grandad Bluff,
New Year's Eve, 1991,
La Crosse, WI, by John Leisgang.*

# PREFACE

## David J. Marcou, Projects Director and Co-Editor

This book relates to memory and American history, from the American Revolution through the present day, but especially to the time just before, during, and after the terrorist attacks of September 11th, 2001, at the World Trade Center in New York City, the Pentagon in Washington, D.C., and part of the Pennsylvania countryside. As journalist-historian Paul Johnson has written, "[A] journalist cannot divorce himself from history even if he wishes... The more he tries to understand the present, the further he is driven to probe into the past . . ." September 11th has many antecedents—direct and indirect—and our book sheds light on key parts of our group's history, and American history—the American "story," in fact.

This book is a literary-photographic anthology, and our group has the complex instincts and experiences to create worthwhile books of this type, this being our seventh, to help readers understand the region we live in (America's Heartland), and America more generally as well. The group of adult students and other, more professional, writers I've directed since 1993 in producing anthologies has learned why and how books get published. Our sixth book, *Spirit of America: Heartland Voices, World Views*, has even won a national award—the First Annual Spirit of America Award, which will be presented to us in October 2002 in Kansas City by the Sept 12 Guild. The present book's publication was initiated by that organization in conjunction with The Writers' Collective, a relatively new organization that exemplifies what actress Sissy Spacek said at the recent Spirit Awards Ceremony for independent filmmakers: "It's not the size of the dog in the fight; it's the size of the fight in the dog."

*Spirit of America*, a coffee-table-style volume, is equal parts literary and photographic. *America's Heartland Remembers* is a bit more literary in focus and smaller physically than *Spirit of America*, but it is equally readable and relevant. *Heartland* contains quite a few photos, but our writers have learned to do what my former teacher in London, John Whale, advised in his book *Put It in Writing:* "Think in pictures." Since I've been trained in both writing and photography and have taught in both areas, I feel strongly that words should often be linked with pictures. What Mr. Whale meant, though, is that words themselves can create great pictures in the mind. We've depicted our stories in two ways here—with word-pictures and with photographs.

Thus have we tried to tell our stories of why and how America is remembering its collective past again, especially relating to events and people just before, during, and after September 11th, 2001. Although American writers and their subjects—including countless ordinary people who have done extraordinary things, like police officers, firefighters, and military personnel—have matured a great deal in the last 225 years, we've still got more growing up to do, as Bernard McGarty would attest to, and our collective memory can help us do that. Read his essay "The World after September 11th, 2001" to understand that lesson better. Or read Charles Nierling's accounts during and right after September 11th to see the range of dreams a native Heartlander can feel after becoming a New Yorker. Or read Steve Kiedrowski's, Jim Solberg's, Nelda Liebig's, Robert Cook's, or Barbara Pauls' work, for instance, to begin to see how we Heartlanders feel, think, and remember. And also read Terry Smith's "Baby Boomer Bandit," Jim Rodgers' "Recruitment," Mark D. Smith's "A Simple Affair," and Aggie Tippery's "The Mall Is Always Greener . . ." to chuckle a bit with us, too.

Then read the dozens of other equally superb and honest writings, and you will see the big picture clearly, about how and why America and her friends—great as we can be—still can remember and mature further, and are doing so again in the world we live in. While there may have been lulls in our nation's growth since World War II, we have a National Purpose again. Our

Founding Fathers suggested what that concept can mean, and it is up to all Americans to reclaim their ideas and actions, to make a better country and world. No one in life—except Jesus Christ and his mother, Mary—is perfect. We can all use some "work." Our own group will be indebted, then, to whoever guarantees us more, decent work. America, our group, our subjects, and our readers must remember again both triumphs and tragedies—in fact, all of life's journey. This memory should come from the Heart—Land.

"Milwaukee Nighthawks," 1991, Milwaukee, WI, by David J. Marcou.

Limner of Mark Twain, The American, 1981, Hannibal, MO, by David J. Marcou.

Picture of Vietnam War hero and La Crosse native Terry Payne in front of Vietnam War Memorial Wall, 2000, Washington, D.C., by Matthew A. Marcou.

# INTRODUCTION

# Effects of 9/11
## *La Crosse Mayor John Medinger*

I was in giving a pint of blood at the local Red Cross when I heard the news. Immediately, I had to find a TV set, because it was something you had to watch. It was an exceedingly frightful and shocking day. I think people here were very overwhelmed by the impact of the violence and death, but frankly, I think people were anticipating even more terrorism—that more was imminent.

But to our credit, that very night, September 11th, we had an ecumenical service at St. Joseph the Workman Cathedral in downtown La Crosse. The church was packed. We had many, many ministers of different faiths leading us in song and prayer, and it was a short, but important, respite from a horrible day. Then, upon leaving the Cathedral, I drove by gas stations where the lines to buy gas at exorbitant prices were incredibly long. People were panicking, which filled me with fear again.

The American and world responses at the time were very good; we were as united as I've ever seen. But now, today, the coalition against terrorism is being fractured. And that frightens me. We've got second-guessing and partisanship, and our foreign allies are questioning us. I think the Administration needs to be totally honest with us and rise above any partisanship. Both sides need to do that. The President hasn't really explained the real cost of war in human terms and the sacrifices that are required, and we need to learn about that as a people, too. We just went through another Memorial Day, and we talked a lot about what we went through in New York City and at the Pentagon. But our Washington politicians keep telling us we need to get back to a normal existence—and we're at war. I'm perplexed by this, if indeed we are at war. And it's obviously a unique war, because we're not at war with any particular country, but—with a few exceptions—against a nameless, faceless group called "terrorists."

President Bush was in La Crosse on May 8, 2002, and talked about what young people could do to help their country. And he asked them to go into education and to help an elderly neighbor. But he never talked about the real cost of war; he didn't talk about a draft, and he didn't really talk about young people dying for their country. When I graduated from Aquinas High School in 1966, all the boys knew that if they didn't go to college, they would either have to volunteer for, or be drafted into, the military. So people then knew that sacrifice for your country had a potentially high cost. Two of my classmates, Terry Payne and Russ Haas, and my best friend's brother, Mark Jacobson, were killed in Vietnam. And those were real sacrifices—not just cutting somebody's grass because you're a nice guy, but giving the ultimate sacrifice for your country.

It's just a strange war that we're in now—as long as the economy stays good and the war doesn't directly affect us, then we're all for it. So far, the government hasn't really asked anyone to make any sacrifices. They haven't even asked us to pay higher taxes for a war effort. In fact, they promise us a tax cut. It's going to be hard to defeat terrorism, because although we may be able to get rid of Osama bin Laden and Sadaam Hussein, there's someone being born every day who's going to hate America for one reason or another.

On the optimistic side, we have to be prepared to control terrorism, but also to show America's best side, which represents an eternal desire for peace and justice.

But I'm in politics because I'm an eternal optimist, and I remain one.

—*The day after Memorial Day, 2002*

*Stained glass window, 1990s, Cathedral of St. Joseph the Workman, La Crosse, WI, by David J. Marcou.*

# PART I

# BEFORE SEPTEMBER 11TH, 2001

"I still believe that people are really good at heart."
—Anne Frank

*Matt (L) and Dave Marcou in front of White House, 2000, Washington, D.C., by Joy Marcou.*

# SECTION 1
# AMERICA'S HEARTLAND REMEMBERS

*Ellis Island during research relating to the author-photographer's ancestors, New York City, 2000, by Barbara A. Pauls.*

## Ellis Island
### Barbara A. Pauls

I stood in the doorway of the immense room I was about to enter as a tourist in the year 2000—and not as an immigrant arriving a hundred years ago.

I rented a headset for the walking tour, heard the voices and cries of many people, and imagined myself in their shoes—shoes worn and full of holes. I wore all the clothes I owned. I felt tired, sick, and dirty from being on a ship for weeks, in cramped, primitive quarters.

Now I had to look healthy to stay in this country of hope and freedom. Healthy, or have a chalkmark put on my clothes and be sent to the infirmary—or wait to be put on the next ship back to a country of no hope.

Lines and lines of benches filled with people. Old, young, men, women, children, and babies. All sizes, shapes, and ages. The men and fathers had made the decision to immigrate to the new country, in hopes of being able to provide better for their families. The women were afraid, but still hoped to have food for themselves and their children. The children, whether trusting or not, had no choice for survival except to trust that what was happening was for their good.

Better here than in a country where the potatoes rotted and turned black and where we watched each other starve and die. An old land with war after war. An old land with tyrants, dictators, and serfdom. No more. All are equal here. To have the freedom to work with the sweat of our brow and make something of ourselves. To have a chance. Even to have the chance to makes choices was a mental taste nothing could compare to.

Looking at the statistics showing how many emigrated from so many different locales—Britain, Ireland, Poland, France, Italy, Germany, Austria, Spain, Switzerland, Russia, Asia, Africa, Australia, Canada, Latin America, and all of the other places—was amazing!

We heard the taped stories of immigrants, thankfully preserved for generations of us to hear. We were grateful for the hardships they endured. "My baby was sick. My husband was chalked; he had a bad cough. How could the children and I stay if he was sent back. Waiting for someone sick to get better . . . or not. Then what?"

Today, the infirmary is sad to see. It has not been restored yet. Broken windows look forlornly out over the ocean. Inside, flaking, peeling paint covers walls, ceilings, and part of the floor. Old beds, boards, and miscellaneous items rust and decay. This was once the home and hope of the sick.

Thank you, Grandmothers and Grandfathers, for having the courage to come here. Thank you for digging out stumps and rocks with your bare hands until they bled. Thank you for persevering through the years of trying to provide food, clothing, and shelter—the bare necessities of living—for your large families in the days of no birth control; regardless, the hands and bodies were needed to farm, work, and survive.

Thank you for surviving hunger, cold, sickness, despair, and poverty. Thank you for the hardest part of all: shutting off your feelings and emotions to survive what you had to, many times at the expense of your happiness.

Thank you for having had the conviction that, with your sweat and blood and every beat of your heart, you had a chance for a better life here than you did under suppression and oppression.

Thank you, because without you, I would not be able to say, "I am proud to be an American, in the Land of the Free." We can be hurt physically and mentally, but our freedom is something that is an intangible spirit. Try to destroy and take our freedom, and the intangible becomes the tangible Spirit of America, in all its many forms.

# It Took Courage to Enlist, Then Die for His Country, at Age 53

*David J. Marcou,*
*with the assistance of Charles and Christine Freiberg, Norman and Marion Freiberg, Joyce Russell Morman, Vanetta Hosford Warren, Louis Marchetti, Edgar E. Ladu, the* **Wausau Daily Herald,** *and other friends and relatives of the William G. Blair family.*

**Author's Note:** *William Gibson Blair was the great-grandfather of Charles Freiberg's mother, Marion Morman Freiberg, and was a Union nurse during the U.S. Civil War. Blair reportedly died following wounds sustained at the Battle of Shiloh, in Tennessee, and the sketchy account of his demise makes for intriguing reading. His fate may have been very much like the fate of too many troops in that war, with no clear records of his sufferings or his death. However, he did show great courage in enlisting in the Union war effort at the age of 53, leaving a successful* business and a happy enough, if at times tragic, family life. Blair entered the Union Army in early 1862 and apparently died that same year, reportedly of infections and dysentery. Any excerpts from original documents published here use original spellings, punctuations, etc., to suggest the context of the time.

William Gibson Blair was born in Glasgow, Scotland, on August 12, 1808. His wife, Sarah Cornelia McBride, was born in New York State on July 12, 1818. William and Sarah married, and he worked as a millwright in Galena, Illinois, where one of their children, Lucy Philena Blair, was born. The couple had three children by 1852, when the family moved to Mosinee, Wisconsin, and purchased the Fall City Inn (also called the Fall City Hotel and the Fall City House), on the east side of the Wisconsin River, opposite Mosinee, from George Kollock.

The Blairs' hopes that Fall City would become a booming metropolis were dashed when a bridge was built nearby, opening traffic to both sides of the river, reducing the former importance of Fall City, where the main road had been. Still, the Fall City Hotel did not go under; in fact, it thrived, being a popular resting place for teamsters and other travelers.

More children were born to the couple, eight in all, but three of them died early on, and two smaller boys drowned in the river on July 23, 1860. Only three of the eight children reached adulthood, not an atypical result in that place and time.

Despite the loss of five children, the Blairs proved to be a successful, business-oriented family. But when the Civil War began in 1861, fifty-three-year-old William felt the call to service. He volunteered for the Union Army in December of that year at Plover,

William G. Blair, circa 1860. In the background is a form documenting interment of his body in the Nashville National Cemetery, Nashville, TN.
Both are courtesy of the Charles and Christine Freiberg family.

Wisconsin, and mustered in at Milwaukee the next month. He wrote to Sarah in January, 1862: ". . . You have heard that now I belong to uncle Sam and the colnel has put me in the hospitle as one of the head nurses which I find a laborious business but I have good warm quarters and have no other duties to do but oversee other workers. Here the soldiers are better cared for than half of them would be if they were to home with ingnerent nurses and fool doctors." Private Blair goes on to write about the various illnesses that had troops laid up—from measles and mumps to "deptheria" and typhoid fever. After adding news about the death of someone he knew, Blair noted that two of the unit's four preachers did not stand muster and went home; that a doctor declared him "spry enough for a boy of 21"; and that he must tend the sick, because "some of them will have no one to wat on them except me." He closes affectionately, invoking the Lord's blessing.

On April 6, 1862, in Tennessee, a border state, Blair was wounded in the arm in the Battle of Shiloh, or Pittsburgh Landing, in which Union Commander Ulysses S. Grant claimed that his men had given a "surprising surprise" to the Confederate Army, whose commander, General Albert Sidney Johnston, was killed by a stray bullet. The next day, the Confederates retreated to Corinth, Mississippi, and the Union forces won a pivotal victory. More than twenty-three thousand casualties were endured by the two sides.

The Blair family has a copy of a letter dated May 30, 1862, from one L. Butterfield, who signs himself "Friend." It reads in part: "Madam Blair, your husband Mr. Blair has arrived from Macon, Ga. this day and is well with the exception he is suffering from the wounds on his arm received at the battle of Shilo. He looks thin for want of something to eat as he has had nothing but parch corn for a week." He went on to write about Blair's being placed under a Dr. Mack's care and being given some money.

But William Blair would not be coming home. Chronic diarrhea set in, and Blair died on July 7, 1862. In a letter dated February 25, 1865, D. A. Barnes (or Burns), another family friend, wrote to Mrs. Blair, who had asked him to find her husband's grave, that he had gone first to U.S. Hospital #3, in Nashville, and was told it had not opened yet when William Blair was supposed to have been hospitalized there. But as it had been a Confederate hospital first, only passing into Union hands when the latter Army crossed the Tennessee River after the Battle of Shiloh, the Union forces had not officially made it a federal hospital until August 1862, thus Mrs. Blair's difficulty in finding her husband's grave. Barnes then wrote: "After searching some time I found Mr. Blair's grave in the U.S. cemetery on the south side . . . Mr. Blair's grave is the 18th (counting from the north end) of the 20th row (counting from the west side). The grave is in a pleasant part of the cemetery . . . . The board at the head of Mr. Blair's grave is marked: '"W. G. Blair, Co. E —18th U.S. WIS."' The U.S. citation was not part of the official unit designation. The undertaker said that at the time, there were 12,000 buried troopers in that city alone, a larger number than the U.S. Army contained live before the war began.

As for S. Cornelia Blair, William's widow, she carried on as keeper of the Fall City House and did not "lose the saddle." She received a widow's pension of eight dollars from the government and went on to successfully bid on and buy some seventy lots, sixty-eight of them in the old Fall City plot, at a total of $1,967.98—and thereafter put much of this land into crops. All three of the surviving children married, and two of them had children.

*The salt in our tears heals the wounds of our soul.*

Lucy Philena Blair, who married Frederick Henry Morman, a druggist, had nine children. Her sister Helen Mar Blair and Helen's railroad-worker husband, Orvando Hosford, had seven. When the Morman couple married, they bought land on Forest Street in Wausau, where they built a log cabin in the woods and later built a fine three-story building. And there, on Forest Street, in 1922, relatives visiting Aunt Lucy Philena and her daughter Mary Ella found a tall, spare, old lady with bright eyes and a keen mind, who playfully remarked that the best antiques in the house were her children.

Far away, Lucy's father rested in his grave, perhaps somehow knowing that the country he died for would be a good home for many more "antiques" to come—his immediate offspring and the other descendants of the family he loved, the "business" that meant the most to him and Mrs. Blair, even at age fifty-three. As Charles Freiberg, one of his descendants, has said, "If you need a lead-in for this story, it could be about how a successful businessman with a family, at the time when he might have thought of retiring, volunteered for the Union Army. It's like guys our ages (fifty-two and fifty-one), going to Afghanistan to fight in that war. And he gave his life for his country."

## Our Priceless Gift: Music
### *Helen Bolterman*

One of life's most priceless gifts is music. It is available to everyone—rich or poor. Music is there for us through happy times and sad times, from birth, childhood, adulthood, and beyond to the grave. It radiates from churches, cathedrals, mosques, and synagogues for every worshiper on bended knees. It is a part of the marriage ceremony, the baptism of our children, and the farewells to our loved ones. From the simple nursery rhymes set to music to the classical melodies of Beethoven, Mozart, and Tchaikovsky, music is ours to cherish.

I have always loved music, from the time my mother sang lullabies to me as an infant, through my growing-up years, and on to the present. I recall memories as a young child when my sister Clarice, being the eldest, was the recipient of piano lessons, and my oldest brother, Charles, took lessons on the violin. As the younger sibling, my formal music lessons would come later, but I recall the pride I felt when I mastered the simple tune of "Peter, Peter, Pumpkin Eater" and a few phrases of "Old McDonald" that my sister taught me on the piano. When our family moved from Fond du Lac, Wisconsin, to La Crosse, Wisconsin, during a time our country was experiencing a depressed economy, our piano, not being a priority, was sold.

Radios in my growing-up years were our family's tie to the outside world and my source for music. As a teenager, the "Hit Parade" was popular and a great favorite of mine. It was where Frank Sinatra (Old Blue Eyes) got his start. He was the heartthrob of many in my age group. In my high school years, the musical giants Tommy Dorsey, Glenn Miller, Guy Lombardo, Sammy Kaye and Lawrence Welk were the rage. Ballrooms flourished throughout the country. It was at the Triagon Ballroom in Chicago that I, as a young adult, and several of my friends danced to Tommy Dorsey's band during a weekend trip.

During my senior year in high school, war was declared between Japan and the United States following the surprise bombing by the Japanese at Pearl Harbor. Some of my classmates enlisted for war service, while others were drafted later to serve their country. Patriotic songs popular then were "White Christmas," "I Left my Heart at the Stagedoor Canteen," "White Cliffs of Dover," "I'll Be Home for Christmas," and "When Johnny Comes Marching Home Again," among others.

When Wes and I were engaged to be married, with music a mutual love, we visited Danny's House of Music each week to purchase a favorite record for our collection. The store had booths where customers could listen to music selections prior to purchase. We soon had a collection of songs by Bing Crosby, Guy Lombardo, and Perry Como; we were the proud owners of such tunes as "I'll Be Seeing You," "Serenade of the Bells," and the immortal "White Christmas"; as well as some silly little tunes popular then like "Three Little Fishes in the Brook," "Doggie in the Window," and "Goofus."

At the altar, music would play an important part in our ceremony. Wes and I chose as our special songs "The Lord's Prayer" and "I Love You Truly." Another popular song of that time was "Lavender Blue, Lavender Green," which influenced the color for bridesmaids' dresses—my maid of honor wore lavender blue and my two bridesmaids dressed in lavender green. Our two-day honeymoon to Milwaukee found us dancing to Jan Garber's band at the Hotel Schrader.

Music continued as a part of our household with the purchase of a piano—the first being a secondhand, outdated, but beautiful school upright. Later, we invested in a lovely maple Storey and Clark console piano. When our children came along, there were piano lessons for daughters Janet and Jean. Son Rodney took lessons on the guitar. Youngest son Paul celebrated his love for music vocally, singing as an elementary school student and later as a member of the concert choir in high school. Jean also played the clarinet in the high school band.

I, too, satisfied my longing for piano lessons, and, thanks to Danny's House of Music, who awarded me two weeks of lessons for purchasing our new piano, I began taking instructions from a gentle and patient music genius and professor at La Crosse State University, Dr. Thomas Annett. Due to my father's ill health at the time, plus a full-time job, I was unable to put much practice time in during my schedule, and finally had to give up the sessions.

Music has comforted our family in times of sadness: "Rock of Ages," my mother's favorite hymn, honored her passing; religious music played a farewell message for my father and my dearest friend, Lillian. When we lost our beloved son Paul, whose beautiful voice gave us so much joy, the heavens opened up with the singing of "Morning Is Broken." He will always be remembered by the wonderful melodies he loved.

Now grandmother can rock the grandchildren, singing the lullabies known so well by their predecessors, along with the tune "You Are My Sunshine," another of our children's and grandchildren's favorites.

Our people continue to show their genuine spirit of loyalty by flying our country's flag and singing patriotic songs. "God Bless America" and the national anthem echo at our ballparks, on stages, at theatres, at the Olympics, etc., reinforcing faith and aspiration for all people in our great country. Through the ages, this public-spirited music has followed our courageous soldiers into unknown lands and affords comfort to the families they leave behind.

Music is our special gift throughout all lands, as the whole wide world continues to sing.

# The Story of Flax:
# An Excerpt from *Anna's Story*

### Anna Muktepavels-Motivans

The use of the flax plant is probably as old as history. Through the millennia, flax has been a source of fiber for clothing, and oil from the seed is still used in medicine and food. I grew up in Latvia—a Northern European country on the shores of the Baltic Sea, before coming to the United States. The soil in Latvia was very good for growing flax. On our farm, about seventy years ago, my father grew flax, and it was one of our main cash crops. I also have read since then that flax was introduced by European immigrants into this country, and was cultivated here in Wisconsin and Minnesota.

To produce and process flax into a spinnable fiber and linen cloth is backbreaking work. In our home, my mother and auntie spun the flax into fine, strong thread and wove it into linen tablecloths, towels, undergarments, bed sheets, and yardage material for blouses and dresses. Especially during the winter months in our warm kitchen, the spinning wheel was always whirling. Mom spun even at night by a dim light, as spinning does not require seeing so much as feeling with your fingers. While the spinning wheel gently purred, my mom, auntie, and neighbor women gathered in our kitchen, sang songs, and shared stories with us children. The time of my family together in that kitchen is still one of my fondest memories.

Mom wove during daylight hours, because weaving required a good light at her loom so she could set up the intricate designs and weave them into beautiful material to be sewn into garments and other items used on the farm. Mom taught me how to wind bobbins on the spinning wheel. She needed hundreds of bobbins in the shuttle for weaving. Thus, I learned early on how to pedal the spinning wheel evenly. This skill accounts for my joy in spinning when I grew up. I still spin and use my yarn to knit and weave.

On our farm, the production of flax fiber (linen) began in the fall with the fertilizing and plowing of fields for springtime seeding. Flaxseed prefers a rich, dark loam soil. In the spring, the seed was sown evenly by spreading it by hand in a sweeping motion. If the rains came at the right time, the seed germinated quickly, and the plants grew into slender, tall stalks with flower heads on top by the end of June or early July.

I have never seen anything else as blue as or more beautiful than a flax field in bloom! The whole field looks as blue as the bluest sky! One really has to see it in order to experience that beauty. By August, the seedpods had matured—I can still hear the sound of the seeds shaking when a pod was touched. My mother and my sister were the ones who usually pulled the flax stalks from the ground. The stalks were tied in bundles in a size that could be held in both hands and piled next to a seedpod-cutting device. My father combed the seedpods off, being careful not to damage the tall stalks. The seeds were dried and threshed to separate them from the chaff. Dad made sure that enough seed was saved for the next year's seeding.

Flaxseeds are small, brown, and shiny, and they flow through the fingers as smoothly as silk. Some of the seeds were used to make linseed oil, a very valuable preservative for wood, leather, and other household items. I remember well that whenever I came home from school with a sore throat, Mom filled a stocking with steamed, still-warm flaxseed, tied it around my neck, and put me to bed—it really did soothe my pain. Flaxseed also has laxative and emollient properties.

The combed, green bundles of flax were tied securely into larger bundles with a strong string and placed into a pond. These ponds were kept for soaking flax only. When the pectin layer started to disintegrate, the smell was very strong—like rotting vegetables, and the water became cloudy—even the cattle did not drink from these ponds. The bundles were weighted down with logs and large rocks, so that the entire bundle was underwater. The bundles were kept in the pond for five to seven days, depending on the sun and the temperature of water, until the fiber started to separate from the woody stalk. The timing was key—overdoing it would ruin a whole batch of fiber. If it was kept too long underwater, the fiber became discolored and weak. My father must have known the timing very well, because his flax was always graded as excellent by the cooperative that bought it. Of course, the price depended on the classification of the fiber, so the timing at any stage of preparation was crucial.

After soaking, the bundles were removed from the pond, untied, and spread out on the already harvested oat field. The stubble of the oats served as a drying rack for the wet flax stalks. The sun bleached the stalks, and the wind dried them thoroughly. Then they were tied in very large bundles and brought back into our barn. It was important to get the dried bundles into the barn before rain caused them to mildew and darken while in storage. The dried stalks were stored in the barn until January, when the weather was dry and cold. My father and mother then took the loads of flax to our neighbor's heated drying barn. This barn was called "Rija," and it was built from large round logs and had a very thick straw roof extending almost to the ground. Inside there were drying racks and a very large fireplace fired by wood. It could heat up a fully loaded barn until the right temperature was reached to dry flax or grain.

The flax was dried in the hot air until the wooden part became very dry and brittle. It was then ready for the mangle. Dad tested it by feeling and breaking the stalks. The bundles were run through a machine that consisted of several rollers that broke up the stems and separated the silky flax from the chaff. Horsepower operated this machine. Two horses were harnessed to a big boom connecting the mangle inside the barn to the large, geared wheel on the outside of the barn. The horses went around and around in a circle, which moved the boom and the large gear, which moved the smaller gears, and, finally, which moved the rollers inside the barn.

My job was to drive the horses around the circle and keep them in line and walking at an even pace. We got up at 1 A.M. and did this until daylight. During the day, Dad had to leave for his job in town, and Mom could not do this hard work by herself. Many a time I fell asleep atop the big boom behind the horses and rolled off. The horses usually stopped before stepping on me. Finally, my mother attached my sled to the big boom so I could sit in it and drive the horses. I must have had a special guardian angel who watched over me, for I'm here to tell this story.

We shook most of the wooden chaff out of the mangled fibers, tied the fibers in bundles again (being careful to keep the fibers even and straight), and brought them home to the loft of our cow barn. The next step was to comb the fibers until they became fine, silky, smooth, and shiny—and completely free of chaff. To do this, my father used a thin, wide, wooden paddle and worked every night for weeks by the light of a petroleum lantern until the flax lay in big, smooth bolts ready for the market.

It was a big day for our family when Dad took the load of flax to the Preili market. The money earned provided the income he needed to sustain the farm and all of us.

## The Month of June
### Anna Muktepavels-Motivans

It was June 1931,
when I was born,
in a little log cabin,
amongst the birches,
oaks, and meadows.
It was June 1941—
the night of the 13th to 14th . . .
The fields were luscious,
meadows fragrant with blossoms,
yet, the night was filled with
crying children and mothers,
and barking dogs—
I will never forget.
That happened in Latvia,
after Russian takeover:
The great deportations of
my people to Siberia—
fifteen thousand of them
in that one night!
I was just a child then,
and I asked my mother:
"How can people be so cruel?
So cruel at a time
when the clover smells so sweet,
the linden trees bloom,
the aroma of honey is in the air,
and the meadowlark sings
in the meadow by the river?"
It was June 1944—
when Mom and I left our home,
with the sounds of war and
a red glare in the sky
from the burning cities.
We left the clover fields,
in full bloom, and . . .
the sweet smell in the air
I cannot forget.
June—the month of blossoms!

*Author's Note: This poem was written in the summer of 1999 on my visit to Latvia, after it had become independent in 1991. As I walked the meadows of my homeland, I remembered other years and other months of June. My poem is a remembrance of Russian deportations of Latvian people to Siberia on the night of June 13th/14th, 1941, and of my family and I leaving our home in 1944.*

## Welcoming Strangers
### Robert Cook

Mother, Dad, and I were returning from visiting my two brothers and their wives, who, coincidentally, were stationed then in the Philippines. Gary worked in Manila for the State Department. Kevin was a Navy dentist in Subic Bay. The three of us were ready to board the flight for the long ride home. In the gate area with us were seventy-five or more Philippine citizens of all ages, preparing to emigrate to America.

Mother was in a reflective mood. Her heart went out to the people whose luggage consisted of black garbage bags and cardboard boxes. *Manila luggage,* it was called! "These people put me in mind of our ancestors fleeing the potato famine in Ireland," she said. "Except we had a longer ship ride on a stormy Atlantic. Otherwise, they're like us." She was right. I was inspired by her spirit of hospitality to those poor, yet hopeful émigrés. She could identify with them.

There's a famous political cartoon from the nineteenth century showing a group of affluent-looking types trying to prevent a downtrodden immigrant from getting off a gangplank. The shadows cast by the affluent men are drawn as caricatures of an Italian, an Irishman, and a Jewish peddler. The affluent men had the same backgrounds as the new immigrants, but they weren't ready to extend the same opportunities to others.

Someone once said that if you poll a thousand Americans about what makes America great, among the top ten factors is the immigration experience. Ask the same Americans to list the top threats to America in this century. They'll mention immigration, too. We seem somewhat two-faced about the question of immigration.

That's all the more reason for the National Conference of Catholic Bishops, in a recent publication, to give direction to this important reality. "The presence of so many people of so many different cultures and religions in so many different parts of the United States has challenged us as a Church to a profound conversion, so that we can become truly a sacrament of unity . . . . We Bishops commit ourselves and all the members of our Church communities to continue the work of advocacy for laws that respect the human rights of immigrants and preserve the unity of the immigrant family . . . . Simple, grace-filled kindness and concern on the part of all parishioners to newcomers are the first steps." (*Welcoming the Stranger Among Us*, NCCB.)

*Historic Manila Bay a day or two after a big typhoon, 1986, The Philippines, by David J. Marcou.*

# The Immigrant
## *Ursula Chiu*

I had been a visiting teacher two years ago and had now become an immigrant teacher. I had just landed in New York Harbor on the *S.S. Bremen* in April 1957. This was the month in which I celebrated my twenty-seventh birthday and I had been a teacher for four years. The eight-day passage across the Atlantic, through calm waters and one heavy storm, had daily found me with mixed feelings.

The lonely figures of my parents, waiting and waving from the pier when I'd left, were fixed in my mind as if on a super-screen, overpowering every other image. After a walk through the colossal hull of the ship, my father had embraced me and whispered with barely controlled feelings, "Go with God, Ursula." My mother, much more given to emotions, cried, as she had so often during the preceding weeks, and implored, "Be sure to write to us at least once a week. Otherwise, we cannot bear the worry."

Why had I undertaken this significant step? Was I really sure that I had made the right decision? Those whom I loved were hurting and knew so much better than I what it meant to leave the familiar and force the growth of new roots in a foreign land. My pain must have been very visible, because an elderly woman remarked to me, shortly before we entered New York harbor, "Your face has been lightening up as we get closer to the coast. The hope of meeting your friends is giving you new strength. Do not worry about your parents. They will come and visit, as I do my daughter, now for the sixth time."

The return of more lighthearted feelings was, indeed, brought about by the expectation of meeting familiar faces, but also through lively conversations with other immigrants on the boat. In exchanges with them, I found that all of us shared the same fragile foundation for our livelihood in this new country. We were not allowed to bring more than seventy dollars into the country. Seventy dollars! What does this sum mean, when thirty-five dollars had to be used to pay for the train to Chicago—and how much for meals on the way? If I missed my waiting friends, what would I have to spend for telephone, taxis, or hotels? Most of our little group of immigrants did not come from impoverished situations. We came to study or to teach, leaving secure and well-ordered lives behind. We now shared the same poverty and insecurity. As on my first trip to this country, two years before, the excitement among the passengers rose again to a high level when we saw the Statue of Liberty emerging out of the mist. What did her image promise to us, coming from Europe, India, Pakistan, and Egypt? Tolerance, acceptance, a chance to live with dignity, new friendships, and families?

Soon we were among those who poured down the gangplanks, hoping to find the luggage that contained all of our possessions. We did not notice the counters for the luggage or the well-organized customs controls. The luggage—in my case a big footlocker—had to be placed on the floor, and the customs officers strolled from one to the next. "Do you have anything to declare?" I was asked, while the official studied my passport. After my answer in the negative, he ventured further, "Are you bringing any gifts for friends?" I explained that I carried a silver-plated carving set (two pieces), which had been requested by a family friend. He asked to see the objects, which I pulled from my carefully packed footlocker.

"Unpack the set," I was told. While I nervously took off the gift wrapping, the officer busied himself searching through the rest of the footlocker. I waited along with hundreds of fellow passengers undergoing the same scrutiny. Finding that everything in my possession was legal, the official was ready to evaluate the gift objects in my hands. After one brief look, he directed me to pay twenty-eight dollars in customs fees, more than the objects were worth. The indifferent customs agent did not realize that I quickly calculated how much would be left of the seventy dollars I was allowed to carry in. In contrast, a professor from India standing next to me understood that the sum deducted would increase my financial insecurity and anxiety. He saw me hand the money to the officer, and he also heard the official tell me to pack up, ending his directions with "Heil Hitler" and a snide smile. I would have liked to reply, "We are done with him in Germany. Will I now meet him again in this country?" Yet my situation seemed precarious enough, so I kept quiet. I do not remember whether he handed me a receipt for the money I had given him; nor did I know that a request for one might be of any further advantage.

Close to tears, I was preparing to find a porter for the footlocker when the professor from India, with whom I had also conversed during the passage, approached me. "Please allow me. I can see that you are very worried now about the rest of your trip." His outstretched hand presented three ten-dollar bills to me, which he had gathered from his own seventy-dollar immigration fund. There was no way I could refuse him. He simply insisted and asked for the privilege of having me accept his money. "I have friends waiting for me at the exit of the customs area. From this point on, I do not need the money any longer," he explained. "But you still have a long trip ahead of you." He stuck the money into my pocket, and at the point of farewell stated, "In the future, you might want to do the same when you meet someone who is in similar difficulties."

The two personalities—the customs official and the scholar from India—became key parts of my first impressions of my new country, and remained firmly embedded in my memory: The offensive "Heil Hitler" greeting and the hand stretched out to help and heal were forerunners of attitudes I would encounter in the new country. I, as an immigrant, had to learn, again and again, to deal with hostility and exploitation; yet the outstretched hand was never far away, either.

# Visiting Grandma

### *Karmin Van Domelen*

As a child, going to Grandma and Grandpa's house meant embarking on a long weekend away. We always referred to it as "Going up North," but the fact was, we drove directly west and went from one side of Wisconsin to the other. We started out on flat land, but when that gave way to gently rolling hills and the road began to narrow and wind, all passengers knew we were close to our destination. I can still hear my mother say, "Only eighteen more miles," as we turned off the highway toward La Farge. Surely it was the longest eighteen miles on earth.

Anticipating our arrival, Grandma kept a watchful eye on the street in front of her house. As soon as we pulled up, the front door swung open and she stepped out onto the porch. You could hear the delight in her voice as she hollered, "Hi there, everybody!" There she stood, wearing a cotton, button-down-the-front dress and a full apron. The ensemble was complete with stockings and wide lace-up shoes that kept her short, sturdy body firmly planted. Her light reddish hair, freshly removed from pin curls or rollers, bounced gently as she motioned us toward the house. Hurriedly, we made our way down the walk, and one by one, she pulled us in for a hug and kiss. Sometimes she took a moment to hold my face in her hands—hands worn smooth from years of hard work and often stained with berry juice.

Inside, we could smell the pleasant aroma of freshly baked treats. A trail of woven rugs led to the kitchen, where an assortment of cookies, breads, and pies awaited us. The small house was tidy, but every spare drawer and hiding place was stuffed with balls of foil, paper bags, bread wrappers, plastic buckets—items Grandma could not bring herself to throw away—a lesson learned from living through the Great Depression and persevering in rural poverty.

Since keeping up on the local gossip was central to her life, a day never came and went without the telephone ringing. "Hello. Why, I never heard tell of sich a thing! I heard she was off her rocker." (A sign that senility had crept into some poor soul's life.) "You looky here, it's a-goin' all around the town." The chat was also sprinkled with words like us'ns, his'n's, jawin', and my favorite, the word "why" stretched out. The "I" sound sort of lingered in the back of her throat. This vernacular always struck me as funny, but it was common among those who had spent the better part of their lives in this region.

Without fail, when the visit came to a close her bright eyes would well up with tears. I can still see her waving good-bye until the car was out of sight. Over the last several years, dementia has sapped her fortitude, leaving her to exist in a place in time known only by those who share her plight. She no longer recognizes those who love her, but the memories of the woman she once was, drift through my mind like the breeze that whispers through the Kickapoo Valley.

# Integrity

## La Vonne Woodhouse Mainz

*Reprinted from* **The Other Side of Purple Mountain,** *Golden Apple Press, with the author's permission.*

She opened her purse and fumbled around.
A ten-dollar bill fluttered down to the ground.
From the depths of her bag, she found the car keys,
unlocked her Cadillac and slipped in with ease.
Sitting on a park bench, just a few feet away,
a shabby young man was resting that day.
He watched as that money was left on the ground,
and quickly took note, no one else was around.
He scooped up the bill and paused a bit.
Many thoughts crossed his mind as he gazed at it.
Supper for my kids, or maybe shoes for Ted,
or a gift for my wife, I could buy instead.
He looked at the lady in the sleek Cadillac,

and walked toward her car, he didn't step back.
"Hey, lady," he said. "This fell from your purse."
She rolled down the window and thanked him, of course.
The man turned around and walked down the street.
He smiled to himself, and felt strangely upbeat.
He kissed his children, and looked them straight in the eye.
His conscience was clear, his soul did not cry.
Let this be a lesson for you and for me:
Being honest is great, don't you agree?
It's the test of your values; you play by the books,
And do the right thing when only God looks.

# Jennifer's Story: Growing Up Hmong in America
### Jennifer (Choua Yang) Xiong

*Jennifer (Choua Yang) Xiong, wearing a traditional headpiece, circa 2000, courtesy of the Xiong family.*

**Editor's Note:** *See Jennifer's short biography at the close of the book for a thumbnail sketch of her accomplishments.*

The exact origin of the Hmong culture, the culture into which I was born, is unknown. Hundreds of years ago, Hmong ancestors originally came the Middle East and moved downward to China. After the nineteenth century, they again moved downward, to Laos, Burma, and Thailand. Because of the Vietnam War in Southeast Asia, the Hmong are spread throughout the world. French Catholic missionaries, who used the Latin alphabet, did not develop the Hmong language until the 1950s. Schools were few and far between in Southeast Asia. The majority of the Hmong population was illiterate. Today, although many people are able to read and write Hmong, the vast majority of the elders are illiterate.

Polygamy was often practiced

in Laos—men were permitted to have more than one wife. A large and extended family is important in the Hmong culture. Typically, grandparents, parents, children, and grandchildren, all lived in the same household. Having more family members meant having more workers in the fields, which resulted in a larger crop at the end of farming season.

The Hmong have a patrilineal society. In Laos, marriages were often arranged. Girls also married at a very young age. All that is changing now. The man and his family are responsible for paying the wedding costs. During the wedding, there is a feast that takes place for one day and one night. Friends and relatives attend the wedding ceremony with money and gifts for the bride and groom to start their new life.

I have no recollection of the time I lived in Laos. I wish I did, because that was an important part of my life. I can only reflect on stories told by my parents of what Laos was like and how hard life was then. Life included hard physical labor for my parents. Parents and their children farmed all day long. The more children there were, the more help they had. I would like to visit Laos someday to see what was once my homeland, my birthplace. My brothers, sisters, and I never had the opportunity for a formal education in Laos. Education was only available for the rich Hmong who could afford to send their children to school.

I have five sisters and three brothers. My older brother passed away when we were about to come to America. I believe, if we'd had the money to seek medical attention for him, he would still be alive today.

According to things my mother has told me over the years, I cried a lot when we lived in Laos. It was believed that children who cried a lot kept their families from being safe from their enemies. Many couples told my parents that they should poison me, because my crying was putting them all in danger. My parents loved me very much, and they did not want to end my life, so they risked their lives for me. They lied and said that they had poisoned me already, and that was why I was crying so much.

My family and I came to this country when I was only three and one-half years old. When we came to America, my father stayed behind in Laos. He had another wife there and he chose to stay with her. This made me very sad, because it made me feel like my father didn't love us anymore. To this day, I remain sad, because I feel that I am not like anyone else. I do not feel like my life is whole, because I don't have someone to call "father." While other kids' fathers took them places, gave them piggyback rides, and played with them, I didn't have the privilege or opportunity to know my father or even know what it was like to have a father. It still brings tears to my eyes when I think of all I've missed in life because of this. I always imagined how much better life might have been. I never had the support of a father and had to depend on my mother to be both parents to me. Still, I am very grateful to my mother. She had to go through so much and sacrificed so much to give her children the opportunity to learn, which she did by bringing us to America and giving us a better life.

My family arrived in Philadelphia, Pennsylvania, in 1980. I was young and didn't know what my family was going through. In the beginning, life in this country was very hard for all of us. No one in my family spoke English. We didn't understand what anyone was saying, and didn't know what was going on in the community we lived in then. We had no car, and my mom didn't know how to drive. She didn't know how to read and write in English, which prevented her from learning how to get a driver's license. We had to walk to get to places we wanted to go. I feel that my mother is the most courageous person in the world. Alone, she brought us to this country of opportunity—to the land of the free. If it wasn't for my mother, I don't think I would have survived. She brought us here so that my family could get an education and better our lives. Although she didn't know how to speak English and she couldn't help us in that way, she always gave us support and encouragement.

My mother encouraged me to get an education so I could be successful in life. She didn't want me to have the life she did in Laos. I started preschool when I was four years old. A few years after we arrived in the United States, my sisters married, so I was my mother's main support. I went everywhere with my mom and translated for her. In 1985, we moved to Eau Claire. When I started school, I had a hard time learning English, but with her there to encourage me, I soon caught on.

I am proud to be Hmong. The Hmong people are unique because of their language, customs, traditions, and way of life. We are different, and just by being Hmong, I faced a lot of discrimination in the past. I believe that this is because other people are not educated enough about the Hmong culture. I've been around people who have called me names, who have told me to go back to my country, or who have tried to make fun of the language I speak. I have learned to ignore them. If I try to say something to them to make them understand that I am just like them, only from a different culture, it just makes the situation worse. Just because we are different from them, people shouldn't treat us differently. They are different from us, too, but we try to get along with them and to be friends. It saddens me to try to live freely in the world and still experience discrimination in it. Even though we look different on the outside, we are all made up of the same stuff on the inside.

The Hmong are a unique people. We have what is called a New Year every November or December. In Laos, the New Year is usually seven days long, but in this country we have it for only two days. During this special occasion, people from all over come together to socialize. This is a time when men find their partners. Men and women engage in several activities, such as ball tossing. They toss a ball back and forth to each other, and sometimes they sing traditional songs while tossing the ball. This is a way of communicating with each other. Dances and traditional songs are also performed on this occasion. Elders come together then to converse or spend time together, because they've had a long, hard, and busy year and just don't usually have the time to sit and socialize.

When I graduated from high school in 1995, I went straight to college. I knew that if I didn't further my education, my chances for success wouldn't be good. I wanted my family to be proud of me, and I didn't want to let them down. Neither of my parents had the opportunity for any kind of formal education. Their dream was for their children to be successful in life.

I faced many difficulties while I attended college. I married at an early age and had a family to help support. I did not have the opportunity to get involved with extracurricular activities. Right after classes, I had to go home. I was a traditional Hmong wife. When I got home, I made dinner for my family and then cleaned up afterward. After dinner, I studied with my children, gave them baths, and put them to bed. After all those chores were done, it was usually very late. It didn't matter how tired I was, I knew I had to study. I had projects and papers that were due and tests coming up, so I had to work hard. I was trying to satisfy everyone else's needs, and then, of course, my own, too. Now when I look back on those days, I wonder to myself, *How did I ever do that?* That is a question I can't answer. I just did it! That was my regular routine and I got used to it. I believe that I made it through college because I had the most supportive husband in the world. He understood what I was going through and he supported my educational goals. He encouraged me to go on to college so our future would be brighter. I need to be a good role model and set a good example for my own children and others in my culture to follow. You can do anything as long as you put your mind to it and never give up on your hopes and dreams.

**Never Give Up Hope**
Life is dark like the night
No one can see their future as clear as in daylight
Never forget who you are and what you can be
Follow your dreams and someday you will see
What you plant today, you will harvest tomorrow
There will always be barriers and heartfelt sorrows
But for all the struggles and hardships that come your way
Success will awaken you from the darkness and let you see the light of day.

## America's Melting Pot
### *Doris Kirkeeng*

"Well, Martha! What a surprise! Please come in. I'm so glad to see you. I'm afraid things are in sort of an uproar right now. Today is Timothy's birthday and he's having a party."

"Oh, I don't want to interfere," said Martha.

"We've so much to talk about. Please, can you stay overnight? We have plenty of room."

"If I can be of help, I'll stay, Jane."

"Sure you can. How about pouring some lemonade?"

As Jane started serving the little fellows, Martha started to light the candles on the birthday cake. The familiar "Happy Birthday" song rang through the air, and Jane told Martha about the boys.

"That little boy's name is Flying Dove. He has told his pals that he was named that because he was a very quiet boy but was very swift on his feet. The kids nicknamed him Dovey. His father used to live on a reservation, left, married, and is now a schoolteacher.

"The smaller, dark-haired boy is Honshu. He does outstanding painting and writes excellent poetry. His folks moved from China because of his father's work with a restaurant chain.

"The other little boy sitting on the other side of him is Nakiro. The kids call him Naki for short. His mother was a Japanese war bride from the aftermath of World War II.

"Billy Townsend and Dickey Grant are a couple of other neighborhood kids. The two African American boys down at the end of the table are brothers Timmy met in Sunday school. Their names are Isaac and Little Willie. They say they had relatives that were slaves. Can you imagine?"

As Timmy started to open his gifts, Martha watched the little friends of different races and backgrounds.

"Jane, I have to hand it to you. What a wonderful lesson these little boys are learning about accepting each other as friends, regardless of differences. It's an excellent example for adults, too. Too bad we don't have more of them here to see this."

"Oh, well, at least the parents will be here to pick them up," Jane said. "They're nice people."

After the partygoers had gone home and Jane's husband had returned from work, the three friends relaxed before a crackling fire in the fireplace. They chatted into the wee hours, updating one another about their circle of friends.

The next morning, shortly after breakfast, Jane received a call from Pat O'Malley, who lived down the street. Her husband had been rushed to the hospital that morning and was going to have bypass surgery. Pat needed someone to baby-sit for her two little girls. After expressing her concern about Pat's husband, Jane told her to bring the children to stay at her house as long as need be.

"Oh, thank you so much. It's so hard when you don't have relatives nearby at a time like this. I hate to impose upon people," said Pat.

"Think nothing of it. I'm glad to do it. Timmy will enjoy having the girls to play with. Besides, what are friends for?"

Soon afterward, Martha finished packing her suitcase. Jane and Martha hugged each other while saying good-bye. They promised to see each other at their upcoming class reunion.

Friends, precious friends—of any creed, race, or background—are the sustenance of life.

# An Excerpt from "My First Long Train Ride Alone"

### *Sam McKay*

Union Station was much cleaner and looked newer than La Salle Street. It was built of granite, I guess, and the waiting room was a huge area surrounded by shops. Above the shops were what looked like offices going up several stories to the roof. The roof had a series of skylights in it. The light shone in and filtered down through the haze of cigarette and cigar smoke until it brightened the shiny marble floor below in big patches. The waiting room was fairly full, as this was the station that serviced the Milwaukee Road and the Burlington, which ran across the western part of the country. Everybody was seated on rows of long, wooden, two-sided benches with a backrest that ran down the middle.

As I had several hours to kill, I put my overnight bag in a locker and walked out onto West Jackson Boulevard. I didn't want to wander too far away from the station, this being my first time in Chicago. The river was just a short distance away, so I walked over to it. I stood at the foot of a bridge and looked down into the water. It was an awful dark green color and had lots of stuff floating in it. However, coming from Boston, I was used to dirty rivers. I watched several tugs go by and some big, expensive-looking pleasure craft. They were almost like ocean-going yachts. People were busy going back and forth across the bridge during the lunch hour. I could see across to Wacker Drive, and it was bumper-to-bumper traffic. The whole scene was bustling and very noisy.

After a half hour or so, I thought it was time to get back to Union Station and get some lunch before the train left. I didn't know if they would have a dining car or not. It would be cheaper eating in the coffee shop, or so I thought. Devouring two hamburgers, a container of milk, and a cup of coffee satisfied my hunger. Traveling always makes me hungry. I found my departure gate. The final destination was Madison, Wisconsin. Two semi-express trains ran from Chicago to Madison and Madison to Chicago in the morning and vice versa in the afternoon. One was called the *Badger* and the other was the *Varsity*. I can't remember which was mine. The trip was only a few hours, and it was much faster than driving. But Milton Junction was not listed as a stop on the billboard.

Being concerned, I began looking for the Milwaukee Road ticket window or someplace else to get information. I was experiencing a travel crisis. Finally, I found someone to talk to. He explained that Milton Junction was a flag stop. I had never heard of such a thing. "You mean if they wanted the train to stop, they would put out a flag?" I asked.

"Yep, that's the way it's done," he explained. "But in your case, they'll telegraph ahead to let them know you are coming."

I thought to myself, *Wow, I'm really going out to the sticks.* But I was relieved to know that everything was okay. I picked up my bag from the locker and returned to the gate that was now open and joined the passengers entering it and walking down the platform. It was an all-coach train, and you could get on anywhere. It was nowhere near as long as the *New England States* had been. The cars were modern, clean and pretty, with bright, shiny yellow-orange colors. At this time, they were still using steam engines on these short runs. I boarded a car, found an empty seat, put my bag in the overhead rack, and sat down by the window. I must confess that I don't remember who sat next to me—or even *if* anybody did. I was pretty tired at that point, and all the excitement of the previous day had dissipated.

The car was getting pretty full by the time the "all aboard" call was given. There were lots of passengers from Wisconsin who had been to the big city to go shopping during the day. The train lurched, and we started the last leg of my journey. I noted that the northwest side of Chicago had more residential suburbs with less industry than the Indiana side. We made pretty good time, stopping at Des Plaines, Crystal Lake, and then went on to Rockford. This was a longer stop, because more people got off and on than at the other stops. We had passed many other stations on the way, but this was not a commuter run, so we didn't stop at every station. Between Crystal Lake and Rockford, we had passed many farms with corn stretching as far as one could see, growing on the flat land that had once been the bottom of Lake Michigan. I had never seen this much corn growing in one place out in hilly, rocky New England.

From Rockford, it was a short time to Beloit, Wisconsin. We had crossed into the state where I would spend a great deal of time in the next five years. The land was still flat and covered with the ubiquitous corn. I knew there was a small college in Beloit that I had considered going to, but I couldn't see it from the train. On the way to the next stop, Janesville, the train passed a huge General Motors plant. I could not see the cars being assembled as I had been able to at a plant in Toledo. At Rockford, we encountered the Rock River and would cross it several times as it flowed through small cities and towns.

As we left Janesville, the conductor stopped at my seat, smiled, and said that Milton Junction was the next stop. I got my bag out of the rack, set it in the empty seat next to me, and peered out of the window with great anticipation. Soon we slowed down as we entered a small village, and then we came to a stop. All of the other passengers looked at one another as if to say, "What are we stopping here for?" I was a little red in the face when I walked down the aisle and disembarked from the car. Out on the platform, there was an attendant with an old wooden railroad cart that had big wheels with wooden spokes. My suitcase and a mail sack were the only articles on it. With a huff and puff, the pretty yellow-orange cars disappeared into the afternoon sun. It had been over twenty-four hours since I had climbed aboard the *New England States* at the South Station in Boston, and now my first long train ride alone had come to an end.

For many years to come, I was to travel that same route—I can't really say how many times. I never got used to the banging around all night without getting any sleep. In the early 1960s, I took my first jet airplane ride from Madison to Boston. It was a big thrill. It took forty minutes from Madison to Chicago with a one-hour layover at O'Hare Field in Chicago. We had lunch on the plane between Chicago and Boston. During the two hour-and-forty-five-minute flight, I peered out of the window as we flew over the same route I had rattled over for all those years. I vowed to myself that I would never take another long-distance train ride again.

# Stirring Up

### *Sharon Swenson Schmeling*

She says, "I bought some lard, Sharon. Let's stir up some good old-fashioned doughnuts." I look at the lard my mother is showing me. There are several purchased blocks of it and a plastic pail of the home-rendered kind. I think of the pounds that I need to lose, but my mother, petite and eager, wants to celebrate my being here. She is sixteen at heart, and I love her homemade doughnuts, so of course I say, "Let's!"

She stands beside her white stove, which is newer than her white refrigerator. Both are working just fine and both have a reason for being in this kitchen. Kind of like the two of us. My mother scoops out the stiff lard with a strong spoon, which she hits against the side of the cast-iron kettle in order to release the lard, and then we wait for it to melt and to heat to the right temperature for frying doughnuts.

My job is to stir up the batter. Which is how my mother always puts it: "Let's 'stir up' some cookies—or how about 'stirring up' a cake?" Do other people use that expression? I don't know of anyone, but of course there must be others. How else would she have learned it? I see that she has dusted the countertop with flour and has brought out her rolling pin and the round doughnut cutter with the hole in the center. My batter is now dough, and I hand her the bowl. She plops a big piece of dough onto the floured counter. Her narrow shoulders move forward and back again as she rolls and pats, then cuts the dough into rounds. The back of her neck is girlish. I think of how my mother has always made baking—indeed all kitchen work—look easy. It's in the way she uses her hands, the familiarity, the respect, and the relish of her movements.

"Will you see if that grease is hot enough?" she asks. I reach around her waist, pinch off a scrap of the floury dough, and drop it into the sizzling fat of the kettle. As it hits the hot grease, it plunges, lengthens itself, then bobs and twists into a final shape before rising to the top, where it turns belly up, a golden puff with a tail. I scoop it out with the old slotted spoon and drop the sputtering piece onto a flattened grocery bag. The hot grease quickly stains the brown paper. I think what a funny little pinch of a doughnut this is. My mother regards it and laughs gaily.

"We used to call these 'Curly Peters,'" she confides. She pops the Curly Peter into a small lunch bag of sugar and gives it a shake.

"Let me, I'll get it!" I say. The doughnut is warm and light to the touch, and the smell of it is pure heaven. Through the sugar, I can feel the crunch of it—the way the delicate center gives in to the pressure of my fingers.

"Open your mouth," I tell my mother. She closes her eyes so as to better taste it.

"Oohhhhhh" she breathes. "Is this GOOD." The doughnuts are launched!

My mother picks up a round of the dough and slides it into the kettle. She takes up yet another. The kettle holds six doughnuts at once, all nestled in the bubbling hot liquid, the white circles of their stomachs puffing upward. There is flour on my mother's face and arm, and I am stepping into some sugar that has fallen onto the vinyl floor. The sink is full of mixing bowls and measuring cups. A cold half-cup of coffee sits at my elbow. We are having a grand old time! She is sixteen, and I am my mother's daughter.

### Mom's Fluffy Potato Doughnuts (8-15-95)

| | | | |
|---|---|---|---|
| 3 | eggs | 2 | tablespoons oil or melted shortening |
| 1⅓ | cups sugar | 4 | cups flour |
| 1 | teaspoon vanilla | 1 | teaspoon salt |
| 1 | cup mashed potatoes, cooled (Use two medium potatoes. Pare and boil, drain, and mash with butter and milk to make light and fluffy.) | 6 | teaspoons baking powder |
| | | 2 | teaspoons nutmeg |
| | | ½ | cup milk |
| | | | fat for deep frying |

Beat eggs with sugar and vanilla until light. Add potatoes and oil or shortening. Sift together dry ingredients. Add them alternately with milk to potato mixture, beating well. Chill dough for three hours. Roll out and cut into rounds. Fry in deep hot fat (lard makes the tastiest doughnuts, but you can also use Crisco, at 360 to 375 degrees) about three minutes or until browned, turning once. Makes 2 to 2½ dozen. Sprinkle with sugar when warm, or ice with butter frosting when cool.

# Cookbook Memories

*Barbara A. Pauls*

My children are grown, and I've not needed to use the self-cleaning feature in my three-year-old stove yet. I use it only to broil sandwiches or bread. My stove and I live alone. It doesn't know the joy of baking cinnamon rolls, cream-filled coffee cakes, pies of all kinds, pot roasts, and all the other foods that feed the body with their content and the soul with their smells.

My daughter called from California for "Mom's Banana Cream Pie" with the graham cracker crust. I had to call my son, who had borrowed my cookbook, for the recipes I had published in it that we all loved. He returned it, and, as I looked for the pie recipe, I went down memory lane.

Lemon pie my dad loves. Lisa's coconut-topped sponge cake, Ted's calico beans, Todd's jelly roll, and Sheila's banana cream pie are important to them.

At Thanksgiving, they all like the turkey dressing made with real bread, not store-bought croutons, and with pork sausage. I get up early to stuff the turkey and make the pies. And I always had to have pumpkin, lemon, cranberry orange nut crunch, and banana cream in a cinnamon graham crust. That reminds me of the year we went out to eat for Thanksgiving. I secretly brought my homemade pies to the restaurant to surprise the kids, and it *was* a surprise. I think it fed our souls more than our stomachs.

My Betty Crocker cookbook I received as a wedding present. I set a goal of making every recipe in it. (I never did.) It bears splatters and has loose pages from all the kids learning to cook from it. The pages for chocolate chip, peanut butter, and all the other cookie recipes have bloops and smudges of ingredients on them. I complained when they messed up the pages, but those pages bring good memories now. Memories of how much they were used show the pride and accomplishment of the kids creating and sharing cookies with the family and at the same time filling the house with all kinds of good smells—smells that speak of family, brothers, and sisters; smells that were a comfort and made us feel good, bonding us together.

I only look at that cookbook to go down memory lane. I don't go through the recipe box. It makes me feel too lonely.

SECTION 2

# NATURAL AMERICA

*Wolf in the Brush Trophy Room Museum, circa 2000, rural Centerville, WI, by Jim Solberg.*

# Moon Dance: A Frog Surveyor's Rhapsody
### Jim Solberg

With notebook in hand and watch at the ready,
I stood by the roadside, in a wilderness setting.
The sun had receded, below the far hills,
and from many directions came the first whippoorwills.

Their repeated entreaties made sweet symphony,
while owl hoots had joined, in complete sympathy.
Together, the feathered ones hooted and crooned,
while over the swamp mists hovered the moon.

I listened intently, to hear what I came for—
The melodious chorus of amphibious amour.
The love sounds of frogs would soon come alive,
when the stillness of night completely arrived.

As the glimmer of dusk gave way to the moon,
and the owls and the whippoorwills continued to swoon,
the first of the peepers began their group trill,
and the earliest tree frogs chirped on the hill.

Soon, all the swamp was alive with the chorus
of amphibian lovers, in the break in the forest.
I noted the singers and tallied the crowd,
but as always the peepers were screaming too loud.

I clapped and I shouted, and slammed my car door;
and finally they stopped, so I could listen some more—
To the frogs, in the distance, whom I hardly could hear,
over peepers so close that they rang in my ear.

As I strained to record the songs from afar,
I suddenly heard a new sound in the air.
Then closer once more, I heard the refrain,
of a deep, throaty howl, repeated again.

I couldn't believe it—from out of the blue,
without any warning, not even a clue,
The sound that I heard could only be one:
The howl of the wolf—but soon it was done.

To listen to frogs was the goal of my scheme,
but to hear such a wonder, not even a dream . . .
That night, I had heard the first wolf of my life.
And I danced with my shadow in the misty moonlight.

The rest of the night was anticlimax,
and it was tempting to quit, and simply relax.
But I finished the counting of amphibious croaks,
and drove back toward home, past the pines and the oaks.

The counting of frogs, on a fresh night in spring,
is certainly enough of a challenge to bring
to a guy or a gal, any day of the week—
but to throw in the wolf was truly a peak.

For years, I have thought, what a joy it would be
to hear in Wisconsin, a wolf's rhapsody.
I gave thanks to the spirits that answered my prayer,
And returned to my home, a most happy surveyor.

# Trees: Nature's Wonder

## *Helen Bolterman*

One of my favorite phrases is "I think that I shall never see / A poem lovely as a tree . . ." from the poem "Trees," by Alfred Joyce Kilmer. What a true picture he paints of nature's gift of trees, which we often take for granted. If we humans could, for just a moment, observe the beauty of these giants of nature reaching upward into the heavens, we would remember what an important part they play in our environment and in the air we breathe.

At this time in the Midwest, when winter has us in its grip, and nature has given most trees and growing things a hiatus, I view through my window our barren maple tree. I note the many thrusting, twisting, and turning branches that form an artful display of fascinating designs. Each branch holds within it a promise of the new birth of green finery when the spring warmth encourages the developing buds to burst forth with new leaves.

My gaze follows the many wintering birds—cardinals, sparrows, woodpeckers, among others—that patronize our bird feeder as they congregate in a nearby pine tree, a protection from the cool breezes of winter. The recent snowfall covers the trees with its delicate white snowflakes, painting a pleasing picture of a winter wonderland.

I reflect that a few months hence, we will welcome the return of the robins and other migrating birds to our northern area. Again the trees will provide a place for the birds to build their nests and raise their young. Trees are also places for mischievous squirrels to caper and hide—among the brilliant leaves.

Afternoon tea has become a ritual for my husband and me in the heat of the summer months—a time when we can relish nature's beauty under the sheltering ash tree in our backyard.

When cooler autumn weather arrives, we feast our eyes on the beauty of the colorful maples and fall's spectacular views around us. How fortunate we are! May we always appreciate these gifts and protect our trees, for all of us and for future generations.

# On the Trail of the Trailing Arbutus

## *Jim Solberg*

The winter-browned hillside basked in pre-spring sunshine as my botanist friend pointed to an unremarkable-looking bare spot. I gave him a sort of "So what" look, and he responded, saying that the spot held a special memory for him. This little hill near North Bend in Jackson County was one of the locations where he had been lucky enough to find and photograph a beautiful patch of trailing arbutus. His wistful description of the popular little wildflower was infectious and even triggered a vague memory of a poem about those flowers.

The Mississippi River is as far west as the arbutus grows, and it has become scarce throughout its range. Soon after I visited this spot, I felt a yearning to return, to find the arbutus for my own photo files. To prepare myself for the project, I first did some research. I needed to learn what the plant looked like, when it blossomed, and what habitat it liked. I wanted to make sure that the hillside would still have the right conditions for those flowers when I returned. As I looked up information about the little ground-hugging plants, I grew nostalgic about similar research projects I'd done on other Wisconsin wildlife in the past.

Usually my research efforts paid off, helping me to find, sometimes for the first time in my life, a plant or animal I wanted to find. As often as not, though, I had to go off on a wild goose chase before I succeeded. But on a few joyous searches, I stumbled upon something I wanted to find in a somewhat more—well, how can I say it?—"lucky" vein. The advance research usually seemed normal enough, but the actual encounter on those blessed occasions was pure serendipity—I'd even call it magical.

Take my first wood frog, for instance. I was a typical kid, familiar with leopard frogs and green frogs. They hopped around the Mississippi marshes of my youth in the millions, but I had never run across the little wood frog. I learned later that they did live fairly near my home, but our habits and habitats did not cross. In the pictures of the wood frog I'd seen in my field guides, though, it looked like a pretty neat little critter, and I longed to see one. My opportunity came during a rare family vacation.

My brother actually saw the frog first, as it hopped through the grasses lining a northern lake we were exploring. I urged him to catch it, saying that I had always wanted to see a wood frog. After he grabbed the squirming amphibian, we both admired the attractive tawny body and racy brown stripe across each eye. It *was* a wood frog, and we both did a double take when we realized I had identified it before I had even seen it. There were, of course, other kinds of frogs in the area, so how I was so sure it was a wood frog remains a bit of a mystery.

Still in my youth, I had another amazing encounter. My friend Tom shared my enthusiasm for wild critters, especially snakes. We kept a crude cage in his backyard to temporarily house any snakes meriting our further observation. Unfortunately for us, they were all the same kind—garter snakes. Some had white stripes, some had yellow stripes, and some even had orangeish stripes. There was considerable variation in size and temperament, but frankly, we were getting tired of stripes.

One day, though, Tom's sister's boyfriend (our hero), who had rattlers and all kinds of other neat snakes, helped out. On this fateful day, he brought over a large, friendly fox snake. It was very tame and, unlike our garter snakes, would coil itself endearingly around our arms and hug snugly with his strong body. But best of all, it had a distinctive pattern of brownish blotches and *no stripes!* We simply had to find ourselves a fox snake.

I looked up fox snakes in as many books as I could and soon realized that a dead snake I'd seen earlier that month must have been a fox snake. I had no idea what it was at the time, but having now seen pictures and a live one, the ID seemed certain. I'd seen it in a sadly flattened condition along an intriguing little back road called Swamp Road. As soon as possible, Tom and I rode our bikes the ten miles to this great-sounding place in search of a live fox snake.

The road was encouraging: it had some houses at the start, farms at the other end, and a foreboding, wild "swamp" in between. It was in the swamp that I spotted a fallen tree about a hundred yards away in the middle of a marshy spot. I skidded to a stop and pointed to the decaying log. Silently but purposefully, we left our bikes in the dust and pushed our way through the thick brush. Once at our destination, we scoped out the log and moved to one end of it. I carefully pulled back some peeling bark and then stood transfixed as we both peered in awe at our first fox snake. Just like that! It was a long time before either of us found another fox snake. It turned out that they aren't all as easy to come by as that first one.

My interest in reptiles did not fade as time went by; if anything, it increased. I became a science teacher and thrilled my students by bringing in snakes and other critters I'd found. I was always on the lookout for anything scaly—dead or alive. I should have a bumper sticker that says, "I brake for snakes!" Once, though, I got a huge surprise. As I stopped for what seemed to be a routine snake DOR (Dead On Road), I noticed that the serpentine critter lying shattered into pieces before me was *not* a snake. It was a legless, snakelike creature called the slender glass lizard. I vaguely knew that they once lived somewhere in Wisconsin, but I'd no idea they actually lived near my county. This one was just over the county line; I decided then and there to find a live one in La Crosse County.

I did the usual research, even looking at aerial photos to locate the sandy areas the lizards seemed to prefer. I focused on one spot in particular, where an old farm road led back to a sandy region that looked promising. I wasted little time and set off as soon as possible to explore it. My wife protested, as usual, but I told her that I would be back soon. "I'm just going to get a glass lizard—I'll be right back!" I shouted as I jumped into the car. She had long been used to my bizarre missions and strange critters showing up from anywhere I went, but I still wonder what she thought I was after that day. A lizard made sense in my case—but a glass lizard?

I drove straight to the sandy back road I'd seen on the aerial photo. I had been working for a surveyor and could accurately interpret distances and features on maps and photos. It was almost as if I'd already been there—I knew right where I wanted to go. The habitat looked perfect. The only thing I didn't get right was the depth of the sand, and after a few hundred yards I had to abandon any plans to go farther by car. I started to turn round and clipped a log lying alongside the path. I got out and went to the log. My wheel had knocked a piece of bark loose, and I pulled the piece off. There, of course, was a beautiful, shiny, full-grown glass lizard.

I nervously grabbed the frightened creature, trying to be careful not to let it thrash too violently. They are named for their ability to break apart at the tail, which is over half of the body length. A predator is likely to be left holding the twisting tail while the main part of the lizard scoots away. Eventually, it grows back a new tail.

Somehow, I got it safely home, where I was able to photograph it and establish it as a new location record for La Crosse County. I more or less forgot about glass lizards until 1989, when Mike Mossman, a DNR researcher, asked me if I'd ever seen any more of them in the area. I had to tell him I hadn't, but out of rekindled curiosity, I drove back to the site of my previous discovery. The old road was paved, and some homes were now built in the area, but overall, the habitat still looked pretty much the same. I searched up and down the road, turning over logs and bark, but found no lizards. Eventually, I gave up and started to head home. As I left the side road and started to cruise down the county highway, I almost ran over a small snake—or at least it looked like a snake. From habit, I stopped the car and backed up to check on it. My jaw dropped—here again was a perfectly healthy glass lizard.

By this time, the glass lizard had been placed on the protected list. I photographed the little fellow and sent in a report on it. I learned, as time went on, that there is a healthy breeding population of glass lizards in La Crosse County, but their further development here is cause for concern. I continue to monitor their progress and that of other critters throughout southwestern Wisconsin.

On one such trip in the early 1990s, I was exploring the shore of Big Bear Flowage, near Black River Falls. As I walked along the dike, I remembered that spring day earlier in the year when my botanist friend had talked about the trailing arbutus. I realized that now was the period when this intriguing plant would be blooming. Since I could pass by the same hillside when I headed back toward La Crosse, I decided to try to add another first to my list.

As I walked along the dike, accompanied by the melodic trilling of frogs and the distant honking of geese, I tried to recall the kind of habitat I'd need to look for when I got to the spot. Reminiscing upon many other first-time "miracles" I'd experienced, I grinned to myself as I imagined jumping out of the car and walking up the hill straight to my first patch of trailing arbutus. That's ridiculous, I mused—surely I must have used up all those "luck" cards by now. Suddenly, my foot froze in midstride. In my reflective state, I'd almost stepped on a beautiful patch of pink and white—the delicate blossoms of the trailing arbutus!

# When the Waters Rise
## *La Vonne Woodhouse Mainz*

"The water edged up on the doghouse. Rowdy paced nervously on the one remaining patch of dry ground. His rope was pulled taut. He threw back his head and bellowed. He had no coon treed; rather, he was the victim of a fast-rising river.

"He bellowed again, ending with a sharp series of yips. His owners did not hear. They were gone, having fled from the water that now threatened the life of their pet.

"Luke opened his jackknife and leaned over the side of the flat-bottomed boat toward the muddy brown hound. The blade jerked through the rope, and the dog swam free—with a foot and a half of leash dangling from his neck."[1]

The year was 1905, and the mighty and untamed Mississippi River had once again wreaked havoc on the city of La Crosse. Living in the great river valley is, for the most part, a scenic and pleasant experience. There are times, though, that it is not a river of pleasure but a wild and destructive enemy.

In 1927, nine years before the Corps of Engineers completed the lock and dam system in this area, the Mississippi River tore out of her banks, leaving 250 people dead and 700,000 homeless. It destroyed 4.5 million acres of crops, 250,000 head of livestock, and 1.5 million head of poultry along its path.[2] Other destructive floods were also endured in 1880, 1899, 1918, 1922, 1952, 1965, 1997, and 2001.

On April 18, 2001, the Mississippi River reached its crest at La Crosse, Wisconsin, at 16.41 feet. That was the third highest level since records started being kept in 1872.

In 1880, the river crested at 16.5 feet. On April 20, 1965, it crested at 17.9 feet, the highest ever recorded. In 1965, the La Crosse and Black Rivers performed an unusual feat

—they flowed backward! Railroad cars were parked on the La Crosse River Bridge to hold it down and keep it from washing away. At the five-story W. A. Roosevelt building on Front and Vine Streets, the basement floor exploded from outside water pressure. The basement filled with water and a corner of the building sagged.

In the 1965 flood, Causeway Boulevard, Lang Drive, and portions of Gillette Street went underwater on April 15. On April 17, the Old Clinton Street Bridge, a bascule-type (counterbalanced) drawbridge, was opened and remained open, stopping traffic to a flooded French Island. The only route from the south side of La Crosse to the north side and on to Onalaska was Highway 16, County Road SS (later renamed PH), and Highway 157.

Our home is on County Road PH, and the traffic then was horrendous—continuous bumper-to-bumper cars. At that time, our mailbox was located across the road, and trying to cross it to pick up the newspapers and mail was an almost-life-threatening process. We had to wait and wait until some kind drivers slowed down and allowed us to run across the road to the mailbox. The same scene played out on the return trip. Our dangerous mail run went on for two weeks, until Lang Drive was finally reopened, ending the eleven-mile detour between the north and south sides.

Attempting to make a left turn from our driveway during that time was impossible. We shared a driveway then with the Leonard Pralle farm, which is now the site of Cub Food Store and Crosseroads Center shopping mall. Fortunately, we could drive through the farm and exit onto Highway 16 by the Pralle vegetable stand via one of their farm roads.

Access to Brice Prairie was also threatened when roads were washed out in 1965. On the only remaining route, ZN, people worked and trucks traveled endlessly as the flood crested. To keep ZN above water, they raised the roadbed an average of two feet over much of its length.

On April 19, 1965, a northside dike broke, quickly flooding twenty-five homes on the south end of the north side. Water caused a washout beneath a 250,000-gallon-capacity Texaco Oil Co. gasoline storage tank on the Causeway. The tank contained 107,000 gallons of gasoline. People feared that the tank would tip over, rupture, and spill gasoline over the water, but that did not happen.

The Burlington and Milwaukee Railroads halted service to La Crosse when water covered the railroad tracks. Two runways of the municipal airport on French Island were closed when a dike broke and they were covered with water. That same day, water seepage caused damage to telephone cables under the Causeway, cutting off service to some 4,900 customers on the north side of La Crosse and French Island and in Onalaska and Holmen. Telephone linemen, using high-wheeled National Guard trucks, strung temporary lines above the water along the Causeway to provide emergency service. Ham radio operators kept the lines of communication open with shortwave radios.

The city constructed 4.8 miles of dikes during the 1965 flood. Many were not dismantled after the flood and became a permanent part of the city's flood preparedness plan. They were put to the test by the flood of 2001.[3]

In June 1965, the Eagle's Club presented a monument with the Ten Commandments inscribed, dedicated to the volunteers who fought to hold back the flooding waters of the Mississippi River. It was placed in Cameron Park in downtown La Crosse.

*Eastern U.S. coastline, 1990s, by Barbara A. Pauls.*

The water level in the thousand-acre La Crosse River Marsh increases significantly during a flood. "As the Mississippi River rises, so does the marsh," said David Vetrano, a DNR fisheries biologist regarding the crest of the 2001 flood. "I think this will be a real learning experience for people about what we would do without the marsh," he added.

"If development in the flood plain continues, the water from bursting rivers and tributaries would have no place to be stored and would instead fill city streets. With the marsh taking in some of the overflow, the rise is slower elsewhere."[4]

Mr. Vetrano is right. The marsh acts like a sponge, absorbing excess river water. Already half of the original La Crosse River Marsh has been filled in for commercial development.

In April of 2001, Wisconsin Governor Scott McCallum introduced a wetlands protection bill to both the State Assembly and the State Senate. The bill was passed. It restores protection of isolated wetlands to the state Department of Natural Resources.[5]

What is really important is that the wetlands and marshes, nature's sponges along our main waterways, need to be preserved. They absorb some of the brunt of the destruction to cities along the mighty Mississippi River when the waters rise.

**References**
1. From *The Way It Was*, published by First Bank of La Crosse, 1984.
2. Kemper, J.P., C.E., *Floods in the Valley of the Mississippi*, distributed by the National Flood Commission, New Orleans, Louisiana, 1928, p.10.
3. *The La Crosse Tribune*, "Special Flood Section," May 7, 1965.
4. *The La Crosse Tribune*, "Hometown Section," April 16, 2001.
5. Dave Pericak, *DNR Water Regulations & Zoning*.

# A Simple Affair
## *Mark D. Smith*

Lynn was the first of the special girls in my life, and I will never forget her. She holds a place in my heart that even my wife or family could never understand. I don't believe I'm the only guy who could admit this about someone in his life, if he dared tell the truth. Worse yet would be to tell your wife a story about an indiscretion with another gal that happened on a trip home from Iowa. That is the story I intend to tell here.

This gal came into my life at a time when I had just moved my family to a new home. I was also busy sorting through the learning phase of a new job. There had most definitely been major changes in my life. My relationship with the gal in this story was somewhat different from that with Lynn. Lynn was with me in my youth; I'm now older and have a family. Even though Lynn and the gal on that fling in Iowa shared many physical similarities, their personalities were quite different. This little gal wasn't quite as outgoing as Lynn. Even my wife thought she was pushy, too work-oriented, and definitely too affectionate toward me.

Of course, I disagreed with my wife about our relationship and assured her that she was just overreacting. It was, I told her, totally work-related. Even so, my being with this young lady all day didn't help, and it was not something my wife really cared for. My wife had, however, come to accept that I was going to go do my business, with or without my helper along. Besides, this time we were going to Iowa, just an hour away, and we weren't staying overnight. How much trouble could we get in?

The day together in the Hawkeye State was spent working hard, and we were both exhausted at day's end. When we reached the car, I opened the door for her, and she got in. This was a routine we had been through many times at day's end. In fact, my opening the car door for her had become quite natural. She often would just stand there patiently, waiting for me to do so. Then I closed her door and walked around to my side of the car.

That day, I noticed that her eyes followed me. I got in and sat down, closing the door behind me. The seat felt welcome after a long day on my feet, and I settled in. That's when it happened. Without hesitation, she slid over on the seat and leaned gently up against me, resting her head on my shoulder. My immediate thought was to push her away. Just say no! We had been down this road before, and I had made it quite clear flirting was unacceptable. Ours was a working relationship, and if I were to remain boss, this just could not happen. But that day, I just sat there. Maybe it was the fatigue in my body. Maybe the gaze from her soft brown eyes. What could I say? I mean, I did consider her quite a babe. Long, slender, muscular legs—those of a real, honest-to-goodness runner. Raven black hair that shone as we worked together in the Iowa sun.

Then again, there were those eyes—soft and brown and seeming to see right through me. I was, at the moment, quite smitten. She just sat there silently, head on my shoulder, looking up at me sideways. On my side, I could feel the beating of her heart in her chest. I'm sure she was waiting for rejection, but when it did not come, she relaxed and let more weight lean against me. It was nice to feel her warmth against my tired body. All I could think to do at that time was start the car and head home. But secretly inside, I was smiling. The trip home was uneventful, and our positions in the car changed little. I will admit, though, that several times I caressed her face gently. I felt a little guilty when we finally reached home. I had to wake her up, as she was now sleeping peacefully. It seemed a shame that we had to end our little fling.

For the first time since I'd been married, I felt like kissing someone besides my wife or kids. She sat there not knowing what to expect as I got out of the car and went around to open the passenger-side door. There would be other days together, but this one had come to an end. I closed the gate to the yard and walked her to the door. There I said goodnight, without a hug or a kiss. I did watch as she disappeared inside her house. Then I turned around and walked back into my house, without even looking back.

Hunting dogs have a strange effect on men. I knew Babe wasn't allowed on the car seat; she had been trained to stay on the floor. But how could I tell her no? She had worked harder than I had for the pheasants we collected that day. Both of us were tired, and how could I not take note of her affection? And why should I reject it? Maybe my wife was right: Babe was pushy. She didn't show much affection for most people, but then she was my dog. She's gone now, like my Lynn, who was also a black Lab.

Gun dogs are often held in highest esteem by their owners. They can soften the hardest heart at the end of a long, tiring day. I know for me there will never be another Lynn or Babe, with their moments of indiscretion. But then, I do have my eye on this little blonde-haired girl.

# Life, Like Nature

### Barbara A. Pauls

Life, like nature, is not always calm.
This, God's way, preparing us to
    appreciate
when life and weather are sunshine and
    breeze.
Would man be fickle if all was well—
be bored and discontent?

If there were not some strife in life for us
we wouldn't appreciate the calm.
Life, like nature, changes, always
    changes,
As humans, most accept weather
    changes easier
than life changes.

# A Gentle Giant*

### Ursula Chiu

**Editor's Note:** *This is a story Ursula wrote for her granddaughter, Ellie, who loves the character of Marika, as well as the giant.*

Rays of the sinking sun slanted through the mixture of thin aspen, birches and pines, throwing long tree shadows toward the house and the patch of grassy land, now covered with fallen leaves. Dappled sunglow lit up the bronze and gold leaves on the ground, making them appear like pieces of a vast treasure. Little Marika stomped through the leaf heaps and gathered them up to be dumped on leaf mountains.

"I make a big castle of leaves," she said to her dad, who was stacking wood nearby.

"I'll help you, Marika, when I am done with the wood," he replied, and carried another armful to the pile on the other side of the house.

"Whoo, swish, swish." He soon heard her voice as she flung herself into the biggest leaf pile, wiping out the castle and covering herself with the scrambled, dry leaves. A brittle blanket they were, with a slight acid smell of fall decay.

The game entertained her for a while, until she decided to search for the biggest oak leaves that she could find. Her grandmother had shown her how to join them into a crown or a necklace. Each step led deeper into the woods and promised bigger and better leaves than those she already clutched to her coat. This new idea kept her spellbound until her focus on the ground was distracted by a strange, dark shape among the trees, some distance from her house.

*What is this?* she said to herself. *I never saw this thing before. If I go a little closer to check what it is, Daddy will still be able to see me from the house.*

With determined steps, Marika stamped across the soft forest ground, sinking into layers of leaves up to her knees. Nobody had walked that way in many years, so the leaves had piled up high at the feet of the bare trees.

There she stood now, in front of the mysterious shape, which was covered with mud and measured more than five times her height, reaching far beyond her outstretched arms. Could this be a body with open arms and kneeling legs, all covered with thin, hairy roots growing out of the mud caked into the crannies? She talked to it as if it were human, using her most cautious, gentlest voice: "Who are you? Can you see me? Can you hear my voice? Will you be nice to me when you wake up?"

*Ellie Chiu, the author's granddaughter, playing in leaves, 2002, New Hampshire, by Monica Chiu, Ellie's mom.*

There were no answers except for a few anxious bird voices coming from the tree crowns. Marika did not give up.

"You are so big. I am little. You need not be scared of me. Maybe you can try a few steps and show me that you can walk. I need somebody to play with me, and you look like a lot of fun . . . . If you can move, I will let you help me find more oak leaves."

The anxious call that came forth—"Marika, Marika, MARIKA, where are you?"—did not come from her mysterious discovery, but from her dad, who worried when he did not find her submerged in the leaves anymore. She ran, stumbling and tripping, back to the lawn toward her dad, excited with the news of her discovery. In his relief at having found her, Marika's dad did not listen to her question about her discovery. Mom was waiting with dinner inside, followed by the usual playtime, bath, and bed she disliked so much.

That night, she fell asleep sooner than usual, and dreamt about the figure in the forest. He appeared taller than she remembered, and the thin branches sticking out from his body looked like hair that covered his eyes and ears. Even a mouth seemed hidden underneath.

After school the next afternoon, she asked her mom about the strange shape in the forest.

"Oh," Mom said, "it is just a giant tree-root pulled up by a falling tree during last year's winter storm. Do not go there—the branches are dirty, and many insects live in the the roots."

With her thoughtful face expressing disbelief, Marika went out to play, holding a stack of cookies in her hand. She now knew where to step without falling into leaf holes. In front of the mass of roots, she stopped.

"I have seen your hair, your eyes, and maybe your mouth," she said. "You are not a bundle of roots. I know you are alive. You really could be my playmate if you'd speak to me, or at least walk around."

Then she heard it—the voice—whispering like leaves in the wind: "I thank you for believing that I am alive. You deserve to know my story. Do not be afraid when you hear that I am a giant who long ago came from a country called Ireland. Many other

Giant tree stump, circa 2001, New Hampshire, by Monica Chiu, Ursula's daughter.

giants came with me from that country, but they were untamed and silly. They threw stones at one other for fun and in competition, never thinking that they were hurting animals and people who lived here. Look around you. All the heavy rocks lying in fields and forests have been scattered by giants who once lived in these woods and then disappeared. They used to holler to me, 'Bran, come play with us,' but I did not like their wild, hurtful ways, so I hid in a cave until my body changed to look like a tree root, although I am still the gentle giant, Bran, underneath. You have looked beyond my disguise. This makes me your friend forever. Come and talk to me whenever you want. I am lonely. Call me when you are in danger. I can be helpful, but do not tell anybody who I really am. I fear heartless people."

From then on, Marika was proud and happy to have this unusual friend. Although he did not romp in the forest with her, he named the trees for her, and told her about birds that lived in their branches. All the plants around his rooty body became familiar to Marika, and she learned about those that were poisonous and others that could heal.

In her eagerness to bring more unusual plants for Giant Bran, Marika remembered the pond along the road, where she had seen rare water plants. For quite some time, she had wanted to walk on the spiky, fallen tree that lay across the dark waters like a bridge.

With excitement, she mumbled to herself, *The pond is not too far from home. I can hear Mom calling me if she comes out of the house. From the tree bridge, I can reach for the flowers floating on the water.*

Carefully she stepped on the thick trunk of the fallen tree. There was no way to lose her balance with so many branches she could clasp for support. With cautious, little steps, she moved toward the middle of this magic bridge, where she crouched down to reach for a water plant. Holding onto a flexible branch, she bent forward and reached as far as she could. She did not know that the fragile branch would not support her weight. With a scream, she slid off the bridge into the black water, never releasing the branch. Her feet did not touch ground, nor did her fearful cries reach her mother's ears.

With her other hand, she clutched another branch and let go of the first one. Cars driving by did not see the little girl struggling against the depth of the water.

Crying and calling, she suddenly remembered the gentle voice: "Call me when you are in danger. I will come and help you."

Holding onto her support with waning strength, Marika called out loud and clear, "Bran, I need your help. I am by the Dragon Bridge. Bran, I am afraid of the water."

She waited anxiously, her arms numb and her legs frozen in the icy water. Her face lit up when she heard the rustling of leaves and saw Bran's heavy body moving stealthily through the trees, making sure that no other human would see him. He bent down over the water, disentangled Marika from the branches, and gently pulled her into his arms. He folded his wide smock, woven from roots, around her, and she soon felt warm and safe against his body.

The sun was near setting when in the twilight of the vanishing day Bran laid her down at the door of her parents' house and gave a gentle knock at the window, then strode away with long steps.

Marika's parents, who had just returned from an anxious search, took her to her bed, while she kept mumbling sleepily about Bran. "He came when I called him. He was so strong. He helped me out of the water. He is my friend forever."

Marika's parents thought she was talking in fever, but were relieved when she was healthy and happy again the next day. She kept her secret, as promised to Bran, but she visited him often and laid unusual pebbles, feathers, and flowers at his feet. In spring, she planted a flower garden around him and invited birds, with breadcrumbs from home, to keep him company. They were both delighted when an owl settled among the roots of Bran's head. Day after day, when Marika visited him, he seemed happier and more human. From under the long, thin roots, she saw soft eyes in a kindly face and gnarled hands with a powerful grip. Last of all, feet and legs emerged from the shapeless bundle of roots.

"I am turning back to being the giant I once was," he said to Marika, "but I am useless here. People are afraid of me, and I cannot hide forever in this place. I will return to the north woods, where no people live. There I might protect the forest creatures and even encounter some good giants of long ago. It is your efforts and your faith in me that have made me human again, Marika. I will never forget you, and I promise to help you every time you are in danger. Just call me, and I will come as I did before."

Marika cried and held his rough hand, not wanting to let him go.

"Let me give you a gift that will remind you of me. The owl who has her nest in my hair will stay here and become your friend and helper. She will live in a tree near your house and watch over you and your family. Her voice is loud enough to reach me, if needed. Remember, owls are very smart birds, and this one has also learned human ways from me."

As he had once before, he lifted her into his arms and held her close, then released her and strode deeper into the forest, while the owl settled on a branch and watched Marika with her unmoving eyes.

* Katharine Briggs, *An Encyclopedia of Fairies*, Pantheon Books, New York, 1976, p. 186. This source refers to him as "Bran the Blessed," who obviously once had been a god. His strength was tremendous, but he was essentially benevolent.

## Let It Snow, Let It Snow
### *Aggie Tippery*

**Editor's Note:** *This is one of Aggie's columns from the* **Houston County (Minnesota) News.** *The winter of 2001-2002 was evocative (and provocative) for many reasons. But it was short on snow in our area. Aggie reminisces about why she doesn't, yet does, like snow.*

November this year was perfect. I love a brown and green Thanksgiving. December comes along, and the fields and hills will soon be white. I have mixed feelings about winter and the inevitable snow and ice that come with it. If I had my way, there would be no icy, snowy roads or walkways this winter. I fear them and feel like a handicapped person when it comes to walking on snow or ice. I have the spiky things that I can put on my shoes. They help me stay upright, but they do not allay my fears.

Despite hating snow and ice, I still look forward to the beauty of a fresh snowfall. In winter, as soon as I awake in the morning, I go to the window to see if it has snowed overnight. I delight in watching the snowflakes swirling and falling and finding their resting places among the other flakes. The last snowstorm north of us produced as much as two feet of snow. Just imagine for a minute how many flakes there are falling to pile up that much snow. It has to be trillions and trillions of those tiny white fragments, each one resting on top of others. Even flurries must amount to millions of flakes.

Catching one flake and looking at its fragile beauty makes one wonder how it can cause so much trouble, so much fun, so much talk, so much work, so much joy and sadness. Snow is useful for protecting the farmland in winter and providing moisture in the spring. It is useful for businesses—the factories that make snowmobiles, skis, skates, snowboards, snow-blowers, snow shovels, snow suits, road salt, snow plows, snow tires, boots, mittens, and caps. Each little flake will be shoveled, tramped on, plowed, blown about; the flakes will be squashed by tires, snowboards, skis, sleds, and snowmobile tracks. They will turn black along the roadsides. They will be rolled into snowmen and snowballs. They will be formed into snow angels. They will fall on the tongues of boys and girls, for a taste of winter.

Most important of all to me, they form snow diamonds in my yard. As the sun peeks over the hill, I stand at my window and take in the beautiful sight of brightly colored diamonds all over the lawn. For five minutes or so, I am the richest person in Butterfield Valley, if not the whole county! As the diamonds disappear, my memory sees tracks back and forth on the lawn. A circle for the Fox and Goose game comes to mind. Five little boys made short work of a smooth, diamond-encrusted snow-lawn. As soon as they could get into their winter gear, they went outside to play. I often joined them in Fox and Goose.

Their next venture would be to build snow forts or tunnels, if the snow was deep enough. With the protection of a fort, the snowballs piled up. When sides were chosen,

Jerry, being the smallest, was picked last. Time to start the war, and Tom was cold and ready to come in. They pelted him for quitting as he ran across the lawn. He never liked the cold for long. Jim was the next to come in. Lee, Bob, and Jerry stayed out, playing snow games all day, finally coming in wet, cold, and hungry. Hot chocolate time! I walk away from the window, wishing the boys were here for the hot chocolate ritual again.

Although I hate the thought of snow, I vow to look at the positive side of those tiny white flakes and enjoy their beauty. Happy Snow Time! . . . when and if it comes . . .

## To the Rescue?
### *Mark D. Smith*

I sat there and watched it all happen. Thirteen years old, fish pole in hand, my bobber dancing on ripples in the water. The mid-morning sun on my back promised another beautiful summer day. The roar of the water through the spillway filled my ears. The aroma of the river was like that of a good friend sitting next to me.

Distractions are many on the riverbank, so I didn't see them at first. Giggles and laughter brought my attention to two little girls. I thought them little, because they were younger than I was. Shoes in hand, they walked in the shallow water that flowed over the top of the dam. Crossing through the water was necessary if a person wished to get to the other side of the river. This is where everyone went if they were looking for others. Swimming was the big attraction in the slough, on the far end of the dam.

Shoes held waist-high, giggling and laughing, they did a kind of dance as they walked. Their bare feet walked on rocks and concrete worn by years of water flowing over them and covered with green slime. It was enough to make your feet wish you had chosen to get your shoes wet, and the girls wobbled and jerked as they searched for a place to put their feet. I watched them until they were about three-quarters of the way across.

That is when the laughter stopped. With a bob and a weave, the girl walking in front slipped and fell. It seemed funny at first, as she landed flat on her bottom, shoes flying in the air. Then, as quickly as she had fallen down, she slipped sideways and dropped four or five feet into the spillway below. I think everyone who saw her stood in disbelief, slack-jawed, motionless, for a second or two. The girl left standing alone on top of the dam began to scream as her friend thrashed in the water below, trying to stay afloat.

Another girl, sitting on a wall nearby, also began to scream. I found out later that the girl in the water was her younger sister. I ran closer now, right up to the edge of the spillway.

The water pouring through, with a steady roar, seemed to muffle the screaming and yelling.

Standing there, I was helpless, knowing that my limited swimming skills were no match for the spillway's rush, which was now slamming the girl up and down, back and forth, against the face of the dam. The whole time, her hands scratched at the air and water, as if she was trying to climb some invisible ladder. I could only stand and watch.

On the other side of the spillway, closer to where the girl was, some older boys were fishing. While everyone who had heard the commotion watched, one boy threw down

*Eddy in stream, 1990s, while visiting the Stange family, Chile, by Barbara A. Pauls.*

his fishing pole and dove into the water. Swimming several strong, quick strokes, he reached and held onto the girl. Help seemed to have arrived! Together now, they both were bounced and slammed against the face of the dam. The thrashing white roils refused to let them swim clear.

From downriver, a boat was coming. Alerted by the yelling and screaming, those onboard had pulled up their anchor and were now motoring quickly upstream. People were shouting and pointing at the two heads bobbing and swirling at the face of the dam. It was hard to tell who was holding whom as the two disappeared and reappeared, trying to stay on the surface.

As the boat neared the spillway, the younger man sitting in front already had his arm outstretched. The waves splashed on the bow of the boat, as it too bounced up and down. The two people in the water disappeared as the dam belched again. I saw the girl for a second as they both reappeared.

Then she was gone . . .

**Editor's Note:** *This is a semi-fictionalized account of a girl's near-drowning. Her rescue, in fact, took place on a Wisconsin waterway when Mark Smith was a youth. He has long remembered her rescue, and it inspired him to become a water rescue-and-recovery expert for the La Crosse Fire Department and to write this story, perhaps for all those who haven't been rescued in time from those waterways.*

# SECTION 3
# GROWING UP IN AMERICA

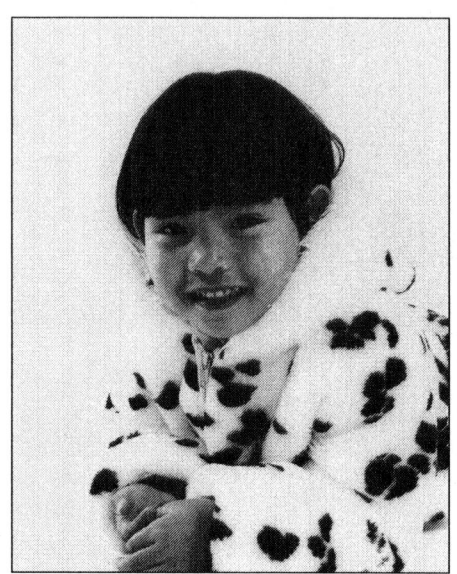

*Anna Li, the author's granddaughter, 2001-02, courtesy of Elizabeth (Betty) Holey.*

## Anna Li
### *Betty Holey*

She is just three and one-half years old, thirty-eight inches tall, and slender as a young bamboo stalk. She comes to see us once in a while. When I see the black, black hair and the dancing black eyes, my heart melts, and I think of what life might have been like for her if Karin and Eric had not traveled all the way to Nanning, China, to bring her back to our family.

She comes to where I am sitting and asks, "Do you want me to tell you a story?"

"I would love to hear your story," I tell her.

So she takes a pencil, flips over a page on a small notepad, and begins.

"One up-ponce a time, there was a woman who was going to," and she flips over a page—blank, of course—and continues. "And there was a wolf running after her, and she wanted all the porridge." Next page, and then several more pages, going too rapidly for me to keep it all in my head, she concludes, "and they lived happily after, after."

We admire her storytelling ability, but immediately, she shifts gears. She sidles up to me, holding the notepad and pencil expectantly, and says, "Oh, there you are. What can I do for you today?"

Now she is a waitress, awaiting my order.

"What do you have that is good?" I ask.

"Carrots and macaroni, and ice cream," she tells me.

"Well, waitress, I'd like to have some raspberry ice cream."

"We only have chocolate," she tells me. So I order that, and she whirls over to a chair, waves her hands wildly, and returns with my imaginary dessert.

That game was so successful, she repeats it, and then repeats it about ten more times. I tire of it before she does, but we play it out to the end.

I find my energy going before hers begins to flag, so we put on a video—*Mulan*. She cuddles up against me to watch. I have seen it five times. No telling how many times she has, but getting her to cuddle is a gift I cannot ignore. She hides her eyes at the scary parts, and we think *Mulan* is pretty great.

She is learning to ride her bicycle—with training wheels, of course. And she can turn somersaults and walk like a wheelbarrow, a new trick since we last saw her. She is still parking her potty-chair in front of the fireplace for use, but is having no more accidents. When she's tired or when she watches the television, she holds "Nana," a short, white face-towel like the one she needed when they left China. She pats it against her mouth and makes soft, clicking, comforting sounds. We wonder how and why this was a part of her life before we knew her.

She is probably an ordinary little girl. But—not to us!

# Birthing Creates
### Barbara A. Pauls

Birthing creates
what created birthing.
A spirit, a being
we call Creator.
What do we create?
Physical monuments.

Where is the spiritual
happiness and joy,
not anger or strife,
worry, not peace.
Choices are ours
to create,
from our Creator.

# Sister Janet (a.k.a. Elaine McNally) and the 50-Year-Old Secret
### Mary Lou Ryan

I don't remember exactly when Elaine McNally and I became friends. I know she wasn't attending Columbus Grade School from the first grade on, as she doesn't appear in our class's First Communion picture. But somewhere along the line, I recall walking to school with Elaine, who had moved into a house on Winona Street, along with her big, noisy, Irish-American family. It was a two-story frame house—a duplex—and their grandmother occupied the second floor.

My first memory of Elaine is of a very short, blond girl, with long braids and a big smile that featured a top row of teeth with a decided gap between the front two. She had a blue bike, and we did a lot of riding to school together, until adolescent self-consciousness caught up with us: In ninth grade, we stopped riding bikes and walked, which was much more dignified.

We were in several school activities together, also. One day after school, she invited me into her home, so she could show off her new baby sister, the ninth addition to their family. After that, she invited me into the kitchen for a Coke, and we visited while she attacked a huge pile of dirty dishes. My offer to help was declined. Apparently, this was her assigned chore each day when she returned from school. Because I was the younger of a family of two children who lived in a home scoured daily by my compulsively clean Norwegian mom, I was a bit appalled at the messy state of that kitchen and the house in general.

A couple of years later, our friendship dimmed a bit. Elaine was becoming scrupulously religious, spending more and more time in church, and a lot of time with the nuns. It seemed she was trying to be a perfect person. Walking to school one day, she informed me that she didn't want to walk to school with me anymore, because I talked about my relatives too much! I was stunned. I didn't think my chatter was in the least malicious, but to Elaine it must have seemed like gossip. Of course, that puts the best face upon the rift from the perspective of time. Back then, I was sure it was just a case of jealousy, as those relatives I talked about were quite prosperous people, and in my teenage mind, I thought she was envious.

At any rate, another friend had recently moved from the north side to the south side, and I simply chose a different route to school and walked with Robella. And after a time, Elaine seemed to forget she'd banished me and tried to be friends again. Among the many high school activities, an important one in a Catholic high school was the Sodality of Our Lady. I believe membership in that organization was compulsory, and we had general meetings once a month. They were student-led, and the organization was dedicated to increasing devotion to the Blessed Mother—our motto was "Ad Jesum, Per Mariam"—and to increasing devotion to Jesus through the Eucharist. To achieve these spiritual ends, there were five committees, which met in small groups, also once a month. Besides the spiritual aspects, the "advising" sisters used the committee meetings to teach the democratic election process. Chairmen of the committees were elected by the members. The officers of the general organization were nominated by the membership from the floor and then voted on by ballot.

When I was a junior, both Elaine and I were nominated to be prefect of the sodality the following year. The voting was school-wide and held in the spring. I was pronounced the winner. I was surprised, as by our junior year, everyone knew that Elaine was headed for the convent after graduation. I voted for her and thought everyone else would, too. It was an honor, however, to be elected, and I couldn't help but be pleased.

I attended the summer school of Catholic Action in St. Paul, which helped the elected students of several dioceses learn leadership skills needed for running the sodality—courses like parliamentary law and how to publish a sodality newsletter as well as workshops on social justice, sodality social events, etc. You can imagine my surprise, then, when in the fall, Father McGinnis, the young assistant who advised the sodality, informed me quietly that I "shouldn't get too conceited about the election," as he had counted the ballots, and though it was close, Elaine had really won. Too conceited! I was aghast. "Then why did you say I won?" I asked. Because, he answered, he was afraid that since this was an organization dedicated to increasing spirituality among the student body, they would be less inclined to follow a leader in these activities who everyone knew was destined for the convent. He felt it took someone who had a "mission in society" to do the job. I was admonished not to tell anyone, and he said he was sure I would do well.

Why in the world didn't he just keep his "secret" to himself? We hadn't heard of the term self-esteem in those days, but if I had any, finding this out knocked the wind out of my sails. But good little obedient girl that I had been trained to be, both at home and at school, I continued to do the job, and it never once occurred to me 1) that Father McGinnis had lied, not only to Elaine, but to the whole student body, 2) that I could have resigned so that Elaine would have the honor, and 3) that I bought the "ends justified the means" argument without one second thought. I should have done more thinking. Weren't we being taught a course in logic by that very bearer of those strange tidings?

Why am I telling this story? Because I got word on a Christmas card that Sister Janet (Elaine McNally) died a few months ago. I started thinking of our history and remembered how rarely I had seen her since she entered the novitiate. She attended class reunions held in the summer months when she was at the Rochester Motherhouse. I did have an opportunity to visit with her in March of 1970. My mother and I were in the intensive care waiting room of St. Mary's Hospital's neurosurgery unit, where my father was being treated. Elaine saw my dad's name on the patient list and came to inquire about his progress. She was being retrained as a nurse, as her ambition was to live at the motherhouse and take care of the aging, retired nuns who lived there.

She had been a schoolteacher for the order for the past twenty years and was quite honest about her dislike for teaching. "I told Mother Superior that I felt that I had done a job willingly that had not been my first choice, and I felt that if I retrained now, I would do a good job at something I really want to do." Her petition was granted, and she was in training now. After a short visit, she invited us to be her guests at lunch in the sisters' cafeteria the next day.

On that following day, she escorted us down to the lunchroom, opened an unmarked oaken double door, and ushered us into the hall. Everything was made of beautiful, highly polished wood. The room smelled like butcher's wax. We filled our plates at a small cafeteria counter. At that time, nuns in her order were just getting around to discarding their habits; they could choose to wear the traditional habit or retain just the veil. Sister Janet was still wearing the habit, and although she was a short person, she had learned to stand very straight, and she looked taller as she gracefully swept ahead of us in the halls that day.

When lunch was over, she showed us to a small window at the side of the room, where we were to deposit our trays. "There," she said, with rather a proud smile. "Isn't that a lovely way to do the dishes?" At that moment, I couldn't help but remember Elaine struggling—albeit cheerfully—with that sink full of dishes when she was so short that she had to pull an old egg crate over to the sink to reach the water faucets.

The next time I saw Sister Janet was at a class reunion. She had discarded the habit, but still wore the small, black veil with skirts and jackets. This time her father was ill, and she couldn't spend much time with the old classmates. The fiftieth reunion for the class of 1948 from St. Augustine High School met in Austin in the fall of 1998. It was the last time I saw Sister Janet. We had a "girls only" luncheon that day, as the guys had scheduled a "guys only" golf game. As we talked, she remarked, "You and I were pretty good buddies way back when." Of course my "banishment" during our teen years crossed my mind, but I wasn't about to mention something she had apparently forgotten.

It occurred to me that it was time to let her in on that darn secret. I turned to her and said, "I want you to know that you really were the one who won that sodality election. Father McGinnis stuffed the ballot box." She looked pensive and said, "I always wondered about that. Did he tell you why?" There was no gracious way to answer that, so I simply told her the truth. She just raised her eyebrows and said, "I'm really glad you told me," and reached over and patted my arm. And since there were six other classmates at that round table, the talk went on to other things. So that is the story of Sister Janet and the fifty-year-old secret. Farewell, Sister Janet. May you rest in peace.

# Born a Girl

## *Mary Claire Fehring*

"This is Mary Claire. She was supposed to have been a boy." My mother was talking to a man and woman I didn't know. All I could think about was having done something I wasn't supposed to—again. Whatever it was, I guessed Mama didn't like it.

I must have been four or five years old, and I don't remember that I had ever done anything that my mother liked. I tried extra hard to please her, but my toys were always in the wrong place, I pestered my younger brothers instead of playing with them, I stepped in all the wrong places in the garden, and when other little girls came to play, I didn't make them behave. I wondered if not being a boy had anything to do with not doing things right, so one day I asked Mother how come I was supposed to have been a boy. Her answer was merely that my daddy wanted his first child to be a boy—the same as all daddies did.

I knew there wasn't anything I could do about changing myself into a boy, and besides, Daddy had two boys by then.

It wasn't until I had *my* first baby—a boy—that I realized my mother thought she was responsible for the gender of her babies. Her first letter to me after Jim's birth said, "You certainly believe in giving your husband what he wants." The odd part was that my husband didn't care whether we had a boy or a girl. By this time, I knew that the male determines the sex of the baby, but I decided that it wasn't up to me to enlighten Mother.

By the time Tim, our third baby, was six months old, I knew I was pregnant again. As soon as I wrote Mother, she called me to ask what I meant by having another baby when I couldn't take care of the ones I already had. My mother sounded very displeased with me. She also was not very happy about my having a miscarriage a few years later, because I hadn't even told her I was pregnant.

There were only two times in my life that I remember my mother congratulating me for doing something right. Once was when I suggested having someone else disc her garden, after the person who had plowed it left it in unsatisfactory condition. The other time was when I wrote her about being so grateful for her making it possible for me to get an education and being able to help support our family. She called as soon as she received the letter to tell me it was the nicest letter she ever got.

Dad died when I was thirteen. I really don't recall that my brothers got more special treatment from him than I did. I was in my thirties when Aunt Clare (Mother's sister) and I were having a talk about Mother's attitude, and I mentioned Mother's telling me that I was a disappointment to Dad because I wasn't a boy. Aunt Clare told me that simply was not true, that my dad couldn't have been more pleased than he was with me.

To compensate for not pleasing my mother, I remember trying to do things to please everyone else. I tried to do things to make people like me and approve of me.

To this day, I try to do things my family and others will like. I try to do what is expected of me. A few times I have put pleasing myself first, and usually I have had such repercussions that I have had guilty feelings. Could this be a holdover from my mother's expressed displeasure in me?

Too, I have often wondered if Mother really thought she had let Dad down. I know she didn't like his family. This leads to a lot of speculation about his and her family relationships, which I don't feel like trying to sort out now.

One thing I will probably never forget is the time a very dear friend told me he was glad I was born a girl and not a boy.

# The Significance of the Year 1914
## *Mary Claire Fehring*

"In the early 1900s, all women's bathing apparel included stockings, but by the year 1915, stockings were no longer available." This information came from the expert on textiles and fashions at the La Crosse Public Library. Using this and some fancy figuring, I decided the year my mother and her friend could no longer get stockings when they rented bathing suits in Clear Lake, Iowa, was 1914.

Even though that's more than eighty-five years ago, there was concern then about many of the same topics that are of interest today. Look at such things as birth control, women's rights, movies, jobs and wages, the president's family, transportation, tax dollars being spent on apparently meaningless surveys and research, and unrest around the world.

June 28, 1914, will be remembered in history for the assassination of Archduke Francis Ferdinand and his wife. He was heir to the throne of Austria. His death was the start of a war that by August had stormed across the European continent. Then, as now, the president walked a tightrope in regard to international affairs.

It was on that same day, June 28, 1914, that women marched on our nation's capitol, demanding voting rights. Their counterpart suffragettes in Britain, though saying they were committed to nonviolence, threw rocks at and broke public buildings' windows and set fire to a park. It was not until the passage of the Nineteenth Amendment, in August of 1920, that the suffragettes realized their goal in our country.

In 1914, Margaret Sanger, then thirty-one, introduced the term "birth control" in her publication, *The Woman Rebel*. She fled to England to escape prosecution for publishing and mailing brochures on contraception. These brochures were titled "Family Limitation."

That was the year there were great contributions to the field of literature. Joyce

Kilmer's "Trees" was published. So was E. R. Burroughs's *Tarzan of the Apes*, Booth Tarkington's *Penrod*, Henry James's *The Golden Bowl*, and James Joyce's *Dubliners*.

That was the year Hollywood became the world's film center. Cecil B. DeMille's decision to film there was influenced by the variety of locations in the area for shooting his movies. Mary Pickford, in *Tess of the Storm Country*, became everybody's favorite. The first full-length comedy was filmed with Charlie Chaplin, Marie Dressler, and Mabel Normand. In Britain, *The World, The Flesh, and The Devil* was the first full-length color film made, but it took many years for the process to become a popular one.

That was the year Mother's Day got nationwide recognition. It was in the preceding year that President Wilson proclaimed the second Sunday in May to be designated as such. In August of that year, President Wilson's wife died.

That was the year doctors held a national conference in Michigan on "Race Betterment" and declared thin women "imperfect." They expressed their inability to understand why thinness was favored by fashion.

That also was the year Dr. C. T. Ewart, a distinguished brain specialist, published papers concerning types of women. He concluded that there are types who experience an emotional accompaniment of elation following the putting on of attractive garments. He was said to have analyzed scientifically the motives that made women adore clothes. "Type I" women love clothes for self-display but are careless about unseen garments. "Type II" women have aesthetic sense for the beautiful and delicate. These women are particular about the intimate relationship of clothing to their bodies. My sources did not elaborate on the usefulness of this study.

That was the year the first cargo vessel traveled through the Panama Canal and President Wilson asserted the Canal Zone's neutrality.

It also was the first year there was a telephone line connecting New York with San Francisco.

Ford was paying a minimum wage of five dollars a day. Dodge manufactured a car with an all-steel body, which was an immediate success. On October 4, the first German zeppelin raided London.

There is always the world of sports, and that year a horse named "Old Rosebud" won the Kentucky Derby for a purse of $9,125. Compare this to recent purses of one million dollars!

The World Series was a quick one, as Boston beat Philadelphia, four games to none.

And finally, that was the year a Norwegian man in Hibbing, Minnesota, started a transportation system that was later purchased by Greyhound. He transported iron mine workers from Hibbing to Alice for fifteen cents. Maps of today are no help in trying to determine the distance—Alice is no longer there.

# Inner Child

### Barbara A. Pauls

I didn't think this would be hard, but the tears are
running down my face as I look at your picture and think
of communicating with you, my little lost girl, me, for

*The author as a little girl, at a wedding, courtesy of Barbara A. Pauls.*

the first time in my life. You were born with so much innocence, and at five years old you already have a sadness and maturity in your eyes far beyond your age. I remember that coat and hat you're wearing. I hated that hat. It was all wool and scratched and hurt my sensitive skin. My mother didn't care, because she made it from an old coat, and was proud of it, no matter that it hurt my neck.

You didn't have much time to be a little girl, as can be seen by another picture, of four children born in four years, you being the oldest. Mom and Dad, so steeped in doing the religious right, count days, count kids. Both innocents, with their own horrors passed on to them, and now on to you. Did God think you could handle it, the load you carried? And it was big, the whole family you tried to provide for. With your dad gone for weeks at a time, working away from home, you tried to run the farm. With your mom always pregnant, you tried to help her, too.

Thinking back, I cannot remember being held or hugged. God, it hurts! I never thought of it before, but it may have been because of all the kids at one time and you being the oldest.

The only approval you heard was when you worked hard and did things to make people happy. But for yourself, you were lost. Lost in an atmosphere of violent arguments, hair-trigger anger, and abuse, beatings you didn't deserve.

No one deserves to be violated so badly and made to feel
so worthless and so wrong. What could you have done so
wrong to be hit so hard and so often? Nothing, my darling
little girl.

I look at your pictures again, and you look so shy, and you
are. Your hands are held closed; were you already
withdrawing and losing yourself and becoming somebody you
weren't, just to not get hurt?

At your discovery, I want to treat you as softly and
gently as a down feather or dandelion fluff, with the most
gentle and loving touch and tenderness that I can, to make
up for all you have endured. You need not feel ashamed
because of your past or even your present, because you're not
perfect, and you can make mistakes, and that's all right.
As a child, you were not at fault when people older than
you abused you. They should have been your protectors, not
allowing you to be violated.

I love you so much. I hope God can help me make good on
my promise to you, to love and protect you the rest of my
life. I thank him for finally letting me find you, as you
have been so brave, more than I can tell you. The
feelings I feel for you are so intertwined with emotions,
I cannot express them in human words. They are beyond my
mental capacity to comprehend properly or understand.
Just know you are loved, always.

# Growing Up in Mississippi
## *Anene Ristow*

It was State Line, Mississippi, where I was born, a small town of about 300. I was number five of six children; there were three older sisters and two brothers, one older and one younger than I.

The house we lived in was called the "Westerfield House." A family by that name owned the house and land. It was an old, wood-frame, unpainted house that sat up off the ground several feet and was not enclosed underneath. The windows had no screens. Two black walnut trees grew in the backyard, and the house and yard were surrounded by a pecan orchard. Walnuts and pecans were ripe and fell in the late fall, along with the leaves. The yards then were a carpet of leaves and required many brush-broom sweepings. The brush-brooms were made of small, low-growing bushes tied together with twine. Yard rakes were unknown, at least to us.

Our front porch was high off the ground. I was told later that once Mama was practicing driving when Daddy wasn't around, and she ran the front of the car up under the front porch, knocking the corner foundation-post loose. She never tried driving again!

We often played underneath the back porch, sometimes having to shoo the chickens that had sought a cool spot away from the hot sun. My sister Glendean remembers that it was also a good place to get away from Mama when she came after us with a switch.

The floors of the house were rough, unpainted wood. Linoleum was not affordable, so all the floors, except for the living room, were bare. I remember getting splinters in my behind many times from scooting around playing on the floor. In the living room, Mama had a large oriental-type rug that covered most of the floor. The pump organ was in there, with a wicker settee and chair. This room was seldom used then, except for company.

Every week when Saturday rolled around, Mama had the kids help her scrub the kitchen floor. The "scrub head" mop was about eighteen inches wide, with corn shucks clamped together to do the scrubbing. The floor was bare and had cracks between some of the boards. Glendean said, "We never had to worry about wiping the scrub and rinse water up—it ran right through the cracks to the ground." Even though there was no linoleum, those floors were always clean.

After the kitchen scrubbing and yard sweeping were done on Saturday, the kids could go to town. I tagged along with the older ones, to Daddy's watch repair shop first, where he gave each of us a nickel. Off we traipsed to Miss Sally Kate and Miss Gertie's drugstore (they were sisters) for a double-dip ice cream cone piled high, or a large rectangular banana Popsicle. Then we headed for the stairs on the side of the drugstore building to eat our special weekly treat. Those stairs were a fun place to play. We also played on the several steps leading up to Burney's Store (later Kennedy's) and plundered in trash piles behind the stores, amazed at finding so many thrown-out treasures.

My brother Paul was just four years younger than I. I have just a faint recollection of when he was born. It was unusual that all of us were sent over to our neighbor Mrs. Hartley's house for several hours. It was not a custom for us. When Daddy came to get us later that day, he was beaming as he told us we had a new baby brother, Paul Daniel! We couldn't wait to get home to see him.

When I was five, we moved closer to town, to a newer house. The house had been dismantled in another town, Piave, Mississippi, then moved and rebuilt in State Line, one block from the town's main street. It was a white-painted frame house with a front porch. There was something very special about having a white house. There were screens on the windows. The front porch had solid, enclosed banisters about four feet high all around, and the top ledge was wide enough for Mama to set pots of blooming flowers on. She had small-leaf begonias, a beefsteak begonia with wide leaves, geraniums, sultanas (impatiens), her Christmas cactus, and others, which made a variety of blooming colors.

Aside from the pots of blooming flowers, large, overflowing ferns were placed in the corners of the porch, growing in galvanized peck buckets. There was a Boston fern that took a big part of a corner, asparagus ferns with green berries, and lace ferns. Repotting seemed to me a big chore, but not to Mama. She hummed continuously as she pulled the ferns from the pot, shook the old dirt off, removed some matted roots, and then placed them back in the pot with fresh soil, watered them well, and, after draining them, set them back in their place of prominence on the front porch. In the wintertime, all flowers were brought into our living room. If flowers could speak, I'm sure they would tell of the cozy warmth from the fireplace, the busy-ness of kids and parents popping in to warm their hands, schoolwork and conversations of the day, and the almost nightly gathering of the family around the organ, playing and singing hymns.

Besides the potted flowers, there were also flowers in the yard. Some old faithfuls were the marigolds, zinnias, petunias, and periwinkles. A hedge separated the yard into two parts. There was also a sweet-smelling Cape jasmine (gardenia), a large shrub with white, waxy blooms and shiny leaves; a red japonica (camellia) bush, with its dark, glossy leaves; and a purple crape myrtle bush. On the side of the house facing town was a huge wisteria vine on a heavy trellis, proudly showing off its beautiful upside-down blossoms of lavender-purple that resemble the upright lilac blossoms.

Daddy built a sidewalk to the gate entrance, and the edges were lined with blooming periwinkles or verbena. At this new home, there was a grass lawn. There was no push mower until later years, and Daddy cut the grass with a sling-blade. I remember trying to imitate him one day—I came close to cutting my big toe off.

A pitcher pump was a few feet from the back door for our water supply, and beyond the large vegetable garden was a huge scuppernong arbor. A pecan tree shaded the back yard and supplied pecans for eating and baking. Near the back corner of the house was a fig tree.

To complement the white house, Daddy built a picket fence in front of the yard. I remember helping him by holding a picket tightly in place next to the one just nailed, while he placed another beside the one I was holding, and nailed it. This made the spacing between all the pickets exactly the same. I thought my daddy was pretty smart. He built a gate to match the fence and put a weight on it, so it would swing shut in case we forgot to close it. Every year the fence and the gate got a new coat of white paint to match our white house.

Our house was one block from Main Street, which was "downtown," one block from State Line Baptist Church, which we attended, and two blocks from school. We had neighbors who lived in a house just like ours that had been moved at the same time. Our yards and gardens adjoined. The family had one child, Jimmy, who was my age. How nice it was to have close neighbors and someone close to play with. On the other side of us, across the ditch at the far edge of our garden, lived another family, with four children still at home. Eloise was my age and we became friends.

My oldest sister, I.V., later bought this house. She was our half-sister, and had saved money received because her daddy had died in the first World War. We all grew up in this house, and Daddy and Mama both died while living there.

The house has now been sold, moved, and renovated, and is hardly recognizable as we remember it. But if it had feelings, it must be proud to have sheltered the Irby family children as they were taught, disciplined, and molded to venture out into their various professions.

# Mercy from the Bride of God
## *Sue Silvermarie*

Susie gobbled up her treat with no thought of resisting its compelling sweetness. That spring day at St. Bernadette School, each third grader had received a piece of yellow candy right before morning recess, courtesy of a classmate's birthday. It was Susie's favorite—a soft candy that dissolved on her tongue like a Communion wafer. As she and the other children filed in from recess, she could still taste the candy in her mouth.

The girls' line was first. They walked to their alphabetically assigned seats, past Sister Pascalita's huge, wooden desk, and down the connected rows of their own little desks. Susie's eyes were pulled to a piece of the yellow candy sitting right on the edge of Sister Pascalita's desk. Without thinking, she picked it up smoothly in her eight-year-old hand.

It grew hot in her clenched fist while she walked all the way to the back of the classroom. At her desk, she flipped the top up just enough to drop the sticky sweet into a corner. Then she shut the desk quickly and sat still. She pretended she was the statue of St. Bernadette in church.

Sister Pascalita always seemed tall and beautiful in her flowing black habit. She stood gracefully at the green chalkboard, revealing how to form the magic cursive letters, but Susie heard none of the lesson. She only appeared to be paying attention to this majestic person. Inside, she felt like a different girl—blank and strange and floating.

All of a sudden she noticed that Sister Pascalita was now seated, gazing at the class from her polished blonde desk. Out of the unusual silence, Susie's beloved teacher spoke quietly: "I want whoever has taken the treat from my desk to walk up here and put it back." To Susie, her voice boomed like the priest's when he turned around for the sermon at mass.

Susie's eyes got wide and her ears buzzed with Sister's swirling words. A long tunnel seemed to stretch between her and Sister Pascalita.

Fear and shame and confusion spread through her body. She rose as in a dream—as if underwater. Traveling the long corridor didn't seem possible, but something pulled her forward. Twenty-five classmates and their open mouths of astonishment vanished. While her feet moved up the narrow aisle, her face flamed in torture, like St. Tarcisius in the *Lives of the Saints* stories that Sister read out loud every afternoon.

When Susie reached the enormous desk, Sister Pascalita motioned her to come all the way around. Now the whole room was pulsing with light and heat. When Susie finally stood still at her side, Sister Pascalita reached out and wrapped both arms around her. Susie buried her burning face in the clean, cool, black serge bosom. She heard Sister Pascalita tell her softly, "The treat is yours to keep."

*© Sue Silvermarie 2002.*

# Michael's Story Quilt

### Nelda Johnson Liebig

I sat at my desk in the empty classroom and opened the note. It read: "Dear Miss Johnson, Michael is home from the hospital and has been asking to see you. Could you come for dinner Thursday?"

With my hands over my face, I pleaded with God: "I can't! He's so sick. What would I say?"

It was 1950, my first year of teaching. Back then, little could be done for leukemia victims.

"Lord, I won't know what to do if I visit him," I continued. But even as I argued, a strong desire to see Michael overcame me. God's still, small voice was persistent: "Go to him!"

As I walked to his home that Thursday, I thought of the past seven months. Michael, so caring, was a special friend to his kindergarten classmates. On his last day of school, despite dark circles under his eyes and exhaustion in his voice, he offered assistance to a child next to him. Afterward, I put my hands on his shoulders and asked, "Would you like to rest awhile?"

He nodded, and with a weary sigh rested his head on my arm.

"You don't have to finish your work now," I said. "There is always tomorrow." Instantly, I regretted my words. Michael's tomorrows were uncertain. That night his mother called to say he was in the hospital.

• • •

As I stepped onto the porch of Michael's home, the door opened. His parents were waiting for me.

"How is Michael?" I asked, hoping they wouldn't sense my uneasiness.

"We live one day at a time," his father replied gently, as he ushered me into the house. His kind, blue eyes reminded me of Michael's.

We walked through the small, attractive living room into Michael's bedroom. I had envisioned drawn drapes and low voices. Instead, bright yellow curtains filtered the late afternoon sunshine, a bouquet of spring flowers overflowed a vase by his bed, and one wall of the room was covered with drawings and paintings from Michael's classmates. But it was the bright, handcrafted quilt that caught my eye.

When Michael saw me, he sat up, welcoming me with open arms.

As I sat on the edge of the bed, I prayed silently, *Lord, give me the right words to say.*

"Oh, Michael, what a unique quilt—a very special one!" I ran my hand over the crayon-colored squares. Each block had a small boy and a symbol that portrayed some activity, such as biking, swimming, or playing ball.

"Mom and I made it together," Michael said. I had to lean forward to hear him. "It's my story quilt."

His mother, who was standing quietly nearby, stepped close to the bed. "Michael gave me ideas for the blocks when we worked on them together," she said. She pointed to one with a boy carrying a fishing pole. "This one represents fishing trips with his grandfather."

I realized Michael had lived a full life in his five short years.

His mother explained each block, sharing much about their family life. I noticed she was thinner than the last time I had seen her, but her voice conveyed only joy. *Where are her tears and anguish?* I wondered.

Then Michael pulled the folded edge of the quilt from under his thin arms. He held it up for me to see the embroidered words: "Jesus loves me."

"We placed that at the top," his mother explained, "because Jesus watches over all we do."

Michael nodded, then said, "Mommy, show her the last block."

His mother pulled the quilt from the foot of the bed. There on a long, narrow block, spanning the width of the quilt, were a dozen or more stick figures of people with their arms uplifted toward a cross. The brightly colored block was outlined with flowers and birds.

A smile spread across Michael's face, revealing space where he had recently lost two front teeth. "That's the heaven block! The cross is for Jesus. And that's Mom, Dad, and Grandpa." He pointed to the figures as he named them. "And this one is you!" (The red dress represented my favorite corduroy I wore so often.)

Then Michael sank back in bed, exhausted from his efforts. Although I blinked back tears, a quiet peace filled my heart. I hugged him good-bye and thanked his parents for a special evening—more special than they would ever know.

As I walked home, I realized my fears were gone and the heavy feeling of loss had been lifted. Now, when I think of Michael and his family, I remember how they helped me look beyond the fear of dying toward eternal life. I remember a gentle family drawn close to God as I think of Revelation 21:4: "And God shall wipe away all tears from their eyes; and there shall be no more death, neither sorrow, nor crying, neither shall there be any more pain; for the former things are passed away."

## Baby Boomer Bandit
### *Terry Smith*

With the rigorous days of the 1958 grade school year finally over, the warm summer wind of a Wisconsin vacation blew freely through my short, blond hair. I slammed my cowboy hat onto my head and gave my Roy Rogers six-shooters one more spin; it was obvious that many days of youthful mischief were about to begin.

Leaping onto my bicycle, I raced down my aunt and uncle's driveway, trying to catch up with my cousin Tom and a group of his friends. Everyone wanted to be first to arrive at Skogen's grocery store on old Highway 53 in Onalaska, Wisconsin. With change burning holes in our pockets, candy and comics were the only produce on our minds. For a normal pack of seven- and eight-year-olds, that, and using up every minute of summer daylight, were all we lived for.

Gliding down the side streets and zigzagging around each other, we zipped across South Third and then flew down Hickory Street hill, using our brakes and our heels to screech to a stop. Quickly, everybody dropped their kickstands or leaned their bikes up against the side of the building, and we practically ran over each other trying to be the first inside. Being the youngest of our group and having to rearrange my western duds, I was the last kid to enter the store. Luckily for me, my mother had hidden my spurs while we were packing for the trip. Though they might have helped with my braking on the hill, I probably would have gotten them hung up and wiped out long before that.

With the western breeze to my back, I swaggered on in. All the other boys were either at the comics rack or the main candy aisle. After wandering around for a while, I had all the candy and fresh caps for my guns that I could carry. Standing at the checkout area and waiting for the rest of my gang, my eyes suddenly popped open wide, as I spotted a large basket of Bazooka bubble gum, my favorite. Looking at the gum and then back to my hands, full of goodies, I just knew I didn't have enough money with me for goodies *and* gum. All of a sudden, I had the perfect answer. Collecting all my goods in one hand, I reached down and grabbed one comic-wrapped square of gum, then slowly stood back up. While looking around, I quickly slipped the gum into my pocket.

Moving up to the counter, I rolled out all my candy and caps. Glancing back to my left, I saw my cousin Tom staring right at me, jerking his head toward the far aisle and making some sort of grunting sound. As I reached up and placed all my money in the clerk's hand, my body went numb as I saw Mr. Skogen at the far wall, looking straight at me. My trance was broken as the clerk leaned over and gave me my purchases, and no change. *What do I do?* I thought to myself. As a chill raced through my body and my stomach began to knot up, I put my purchases in my pocket and headed for the door. *Too late*, I thought. *I'm an outlaw now!*

Out the door I ran, with my cowboy hat flying back and hanging by its cord. With my little feet in high gear, I headed for my trusty bike, Trigger. Reaching into my pocket, I pulled out the gum and started unwrapping it as fast as I could. Soon, the other boys ran out of the store, yelling and running for their bikes and their lives. Tom yelled at me that I shouldn't have stolen the gum and said, "Now we'll all get in trouble!" I just gave him an innocent look, socked my comic gum wrapper away in my pocket, and climbed on Trigger. Suddenly, everyone went silent as Mr. Skogen barreled out the door. With eyes of fire and the looks of a giant pro wrestler from my uncle's TV, he moseyed toward us.

His big hand rose up as he pointed at me and said, "You hold it, right there. You either give me that gum or pay for it, *right now!*" As I looked up to where the demanding voice was bellowing from, all I could see was his hulk of an outline, silhouetted by the sun. I instantly swallowed the gum in one large gulp as someone yelled, "Let's get outta here!" and everyone, including me, pedaled away as fast as we could. Never looking back, we all scattered in different directions. I could see Tom, way out in front of me, and suddenly I realized that he would tell the folks.

Slowly, I glided my bike up the driveway and came to a stop by the back door. Leaning old Trigger up against the house, I tried to find enough courage to face what lay ahead. With my hand on the door handle, I pressed my face up against the screen, watching and listening for the signs of my imminent doom! I was jolted out of my semi-sad reverie when my mother appeared in the kitchen and called me inside. I stepped in and acted totally innocent, and my mother looked down at me with her hands on her hips. I gave her my best dumfounded look and asked, "What?" Out of the corner of my eye, I could see my cousin's face poking around the doorway from the living room. *Boy, am I going to get him later*, I thought.

My mother, Marcilee, was a very beautiful and intelligent southern woman from Alabama. She had followed her sister, Lucille, north into the land of four seasons—Wisconsin. It was here, in the coulee region of La Crosse and Onalaska that she met and married my father. Always warm and forgiving, she could also be a versatile opponent when defending her children.

Kneeling down and looking into my eyes, she asked, "Bobby, did you steal some gum at the grocery store?" Broken down in one quick swipe, I dropped my head and slowly nodded yes.

Without saying a word, out the door we went, into our car and straight to Skogen's. She was about to put an end to this type of behavior, right now. Though we made it in record

*Young author in cowboy gear, 1950s, courtesy of Robert (Terry) Smith.*

time, it was my longest trip. As if in a dream—or a nightmare—we were suddenly standing inside the store. "Let's hope he hasn't called the police, yet," my mother said in a low voice. A new level of fear was beginning to take over my body. As if that weren't enough, a southbound train roared through town and crossed the highway right in front of the grocery store. With the visual blur of the train passing by, whistle blowing, ground vibrating, I thought for sure that this was God, coming to take me away. It may have been a warm June day, but at that moment I was standing in the middle of a January blizzard.

That's when my mother jerked my arm as she pointed to Mr. Skogen, who was standing at the back of the store talking on the phone. "Well, let's hope he's not talking to the police right now," she stated while looking down at me. At this point I was literally shaking out from under my cowboy hat. Tears ran down my cheeks, and I came very close to peeing in my pants.

Mother then told me to stay right where I was and she would go and try to talk to Mr. Skogen. Well, I wasn't going anywhere. My legs were like lead, and somehow my shoes had become glued to the floor. I thought to myself, *I'm going to jail for the rest of my life.* I watched them intently as they talked and glanced back at me. Then my mother called for me to come back by them. At first I couldn't move. Then, slowly, I began my walk of shame, as if in a trance, but still with dry pants.

Reaching the two of them, at the end of my death march, I gradually raised my head, ready to receive my punishment. Mr. Skogen had to be the biggest person I'd ever seen in my whole, long, seven years of life.

"So this is the little bandit," remarked Mr. Skogen. "Is that a Roy Rogers outfit you got on there, fella?" I nodded my head yes.

"Would Roy steal anything, from anyone?" he asked.

"No sir," I said quietly, lowering my head again.

"So what did you do with Mr. Skogen's gum?" my mother asked.

"I swallowed it."

"He sure did!" laughed Mr. Skogen. "His eyes almost popped out, too."

"Tell you what," he said. "If you apologize and promise not to steal again, I won't call the sheriff. Okay?"

I looked over to my mother as I wiped the tears off my cheeks, nodded yes to Mr. Skogen, and said, "I won't ever do it again. I'm sorry."

"OK," he said, looking over to my mother as he turned to go back behind the meat counter. "Get that little bandito out of my store before he finds something else that he wants."

# Life in a Small Country School
## *William Kulas*

The small parochial school I attended was near the end of its life. Though indoor plumbing had been added onto the building, we had to go outside to get to it. Using the outhouses was the norm in the warmer months. Despite its age, the old school still retained its character. Old, creaky steps announced the comings and goings of the students; they betrayed latecomers every time—until we learned where to step to avoid the telltale sound.

Because of a limited budget and a strong work ethic, students were delegated to experience the practical lesson of cleaning the buildings. Narrow boards held the iron desks in their places. The smaller children were relegated to cleaning under the desks with a hand broom. We looked forward to growing up so we could use the big broom—then we would not have to crawl around and under those awkwardly shaped desks

We all accepted this cleaning task—some less so than others —as part of our academic routine. Chauvinism still ruled in our school. The girls got the job of cleaning the erasers. They clapped them together to pound out the built-up chalk residue. Though the work was light—"woman's work"—it was not without problems. On windy days, positioning became important. Standing downwind on a breezy day resulted in a gust of chalk in the face. Reprisals often followed, and then sharp words. The dear sisters had to break up more than one hair-pulling contest.

My most vivid memories of grade school are of recess. Bad weather meant classroom fun; colds and missed homework also meant staying in the room, but with far less enjoyment. Winter brought out games like King of the Mountain and a tag game called Fox and Goose. In the warmer months, we enjoyed the usual playground items. Going up the slide the wrong way always presented a challenge. The merry-go-round tilted on the side hill, offering an easy run downhill and more strain on the return trip. The teeter-totter provided great enjoyment—until one's partner made a quick exit. The ensuing encounter with the earth resulted in a sore rear and some newly learned language relating to one's partner.

Games such as Annie-Annie-Over and Rover Red Rover were the most favored options for play. Little kids used the outhouses and the big kids the storage barn for Annie-Annie-Over. Rookies to the big league usually had a hard time getting the ball over the roof of the barn. After tiring of "pigtails"—a ball not able to clear the roof—and "sideball"—one that veered off the side—complaints started resounding over the roof. In the end, rookies had to give up the ball, but not without a few tears. The old elm tree acted as a sympathetic mother for weeping children.

Because football had yet not reached national prominence, we played it just as a game. The real game was baseball. With the hopes of following in the footsteps of one of our baseball idols, we played with the enthusiasm of rookies. Each age group had its own field. Unlike today's fields, made to exact specifications, each of our fields had its own obstacles. To accommodate conditions, we bent the rules to our needs. The garage by the little field caught all foul balls hit to the right. A big tree turned potential home runs into singles or outs—the forerunner of playing in a dome. As always, right field went to the youngest and poorest of players. The overhanging branches deflected balls in any direction, making a catch all the more difficult. Of course, few could hit the ball that high, so the branches served more as observers than obstacles. Three hits into the branches promoted a player to the next level.

The field for the middle grades bordered the orchard, but was not mowed. Thus, no matter the force, all ground balls came to a sudden halt in the tall grass. No one knew why the field was not mowed, and no one asked. We just accepted it as part of the game.

We all dreamed of playing on the big kids' field, though it offered its own set of perils. Any ball hit over the center field fence resulted in one or more of three problems: avoiding the rather docile bull in the pasture, not disturbing its crabby owner, or the center fielder delaying the game until he completed his quick dash to the local store for candy. At first, we objected to this delay, but the hope of treats for all led us to hide the this player from the watchful eyes of the sisters. However, their street smarts often resulted in the seizure of the contraband *and* the culprit.

Left field provided few obstacles except for the two outhouses. A sharply hit ball into the open doors and holes could result in postponing the season—at least until we could get a new ball. The cemetery intruded into right field, leaving little room for a hit. Any ball hit over the cemetery fence led to a forfeit of the game. No one was allowed in the cemetery, and Big Brother—or here Big Sister—was always watching. Our only left-handed hitter was restricted to ground balls to right or hits elsewhere in the field. More than once, he received the wrath of the teams when he broke the right field rule.

Since the field was on a hill, baserunning provided an adventure. The uphill run to first base required extra effort, while the downhill dash to second proved easier. Speed picked up a bit on the level ground to third, with added effort needed to get home.

One boy stood out over the others in ability. He was always the first chosen when we picked sides. Having him on one's team was a sure bet for a victory. Barely above rookie status, my hitting extended mainly to occasional singles; my lack of speed limited me from getting much past first. One day proved to be my day of glory. We were behind by two runs, with two runners on base and the bell ready to ring. With a mighty swing, I made a solid connection and sent a sharp grounder by the shortstop and past the left fielder whom a pretty eighth-grader was bedazzling. Once the embarrassed young man realized his miscue, he dashed for the ball that had bounced into the girls' Half-Moon Hilton. It had cleared the open door, but had managed to avoid the holes. Stunned at the prospects of breaking the rigid gender barrier, the young man paused for a few seconds before favoring the hope of victory over the rules of chivalry. This pause, along with the pushes of several teammates, got me home just in time to beat the throw. We had our victory over the superstar's team.

I received a triumphant hoist on the shoulders of my teammates and many pats on the back and lower areas. In the midst of it all, the bell ringing did not stop our enthusiasm. As a result, we were late returning to class and had to stay after school to write a hundred times: "I should be on time for class when the recess bell rings for the closing of recess," or some similar sentence of extraordinary length. Such is the fleeting nature of glory!

## Fatherless
### Barbara A. Pauls

Even as a little boy,
with great big eyes of blue.
He always tried so hard to do,
what his mommy wanted him to.

He very rarely ever smiled—
the burden that he carried—
without a daddy in the home,
the load was very heavy.

## Challenge Academy Deserves to Be Saved
### Doris Kirkeeng

*First published in the* **La Crosse Tribune**, *as a letter to the editor.*

Doesn't our governor, Mr. Scott McCallum, believe in giving our youth a second chance? They are the citizens of tomorrow. Like everyone, they learn by life's experiences, bad or good, and try to be acceptable, wholesome representatives of our future America.

Challenge Academy, which is located at Fort McCoy, between Sparta and Tomah, is an organization that gives an opportunity to young people approaching seventeen or more years old. Perhaps they were individuals following their peers down the wrong road, coming from bad home situations or discouraged after a difficult beginning. Consequently, they didn't complete their high school education.

In the Challenge Academy, they are strictly disciplined, eating all meals together and being supervised twenty-four hours a day, leaving no time to get into trouble. This program has been in effect in Wisconsin for four years; former participants have praised its results.

After graduating and receiving their diplomas, they meet with a mentor twice a month for one year for support and encouragement to stay on the right track, which helps give them a chance for a future they can be proud of—when they can become

*A concept conceives the birth of an idea.*

George W. Bush,
2000 Presidential campaign,
La Crosse, WI, by
Matthew A. and
David J. Marcou.

acceptable, productive citizens. Graduates seek higher education or join the work force or the military service. The federal government pays 60 percent of the cost of the Academy, and the state pays 40 percent. There are twenty-six Challenge Academies in the United States, with Wisconsin rated among the best, with a 90 percent success rate.

Why would our governor choose to eliminate from his budget this great, effective way of promoting education ? When President Bush refers to education, doesn't he say every child should be given a chance? These young people deserve a second chance to receive their high school diploma.

**First Congressional Response—Ron Kind**
Dear Doris:
I saw your letter to the editor in the March 1, 2002, *La Crosse Tribune*, and I wanted to update you on action I have taken regarding the Challenge Academy.

As you know, the Challenge Academy program is funded at the state and federal level. Sixty percent of the funding comes from federal defense appropriations, while 40 percent of the funding comes from the state government. For FY2002, Congress has authorized $63 million for Challenge Programs nationwide, $1.6 million of which is earmarked for Wisconsin. Currently, there are fifteen states on the waiting list for participation in this program. If the state of Wisconsin does not fund its portion of the program for the upcoming year, it may forfeit its opportunity to participate in this program in the future.

I believe we cannot afford to lose this successful program. I have visited the Challenge Academy numerous times, and have seen firsthand the difference it makes in young peoples' lives. You will be pleased to know that I have written to Governor McCallum, urging him to reinstate funding for the Academy. Furthermore, I have written to the House Appropriations Committee, asking that the federal government continue to fully fund this exceptional program. I have enclosed a copy of my letter to the Governor. Please be assured that I will continue to monitor this situation closely.

I hope you find this information useful. If you should have further comments or questions, please do not hesitate to contact my office.

**Second Congressional Response, Ron Kind**
Dear Governor McCallum:
I am writing today to strongly encourage you to reevaluate your Budget Reform Act, and reinstate full funding for the Youth ChalleNGe Program at Ft. McCoy.

As you know, Congress first authorized funding for the Youth ChalleNGe Program in 1993. The mission of the program is to intervene in the life of an at-risk youth and produce a student with values, skills, education, and self-discipline necessary to succeed as an adult. The National Guard Bureau enters into agreements with state governors and conducts the program.

Since 1998, Wisconsin has operated its WING ChalleNGe Academy, based at Ft. McCoy, under the direction of Colonel M. G. MacLaren. This program has brought students in Wisconsin brilliant success. In fact, since the program's inception, over 84% of the 530 graduates have earned their GED or HSED, and, nationwide, over 90% of former dropouts are free of law violations.

While I understand that Wisconsin faces a budget crisis, this is one program that we cannot afford to cut. Spending a small amount of money now to help our at-risk youth saves money in the long run. The cost of the ChalleNGe Academy is significantly less than the societal costs the state will face in the future if we neglect these children. The majority of students who participate in this program go on to be productive members of society who give back to the community that supported them.

Therefore, I once again urge you to fully fund this exceptional program. For FY2002, Congress has authorized $63 million for Challenge Programs nationwide, $1.6 million of which is earmarked for Wisconsin. Currently, there are fifteen states on the waiting list for participation in this program. If the state of Wisconsin does not fund its portion of the program for the upcoming year, it may forfeit its opportunity to participate in this program in the future. We cannot afford to lose this successful program.

Thank you in advance for your prompt consideration of this matter. I hope I can count on you to do what is right for the youth of Wisconsin.

# A Child's Soul
### Barbara A. Pauls

A child is very precious,
or that is what is told us.
But does anyone ever say
the real reason why?
What is applied to us as children,
we apply to our own children.
Kind and gentle, harsh or cruel,
are lessons of living
we learned and felt.
Only when they're gone,
or grown and self-owned
are we haunted or blessed
by the lessons we taught,
by the image we left.
Left in the beginning
of a brand new life
entrusted to us.
A mind as pure as newfallen snow,
untouched by us.
Untouched by beauty, or by beast—
beast of cruelty, beauty of kindness.
Blemished by turbulence,
anger, and strife
instead of kindness,
gentleness, and grace.
Why does harshness linger more
than softness, sweetness,
beauty and grace?
Softness touches, caresses, and cares.
Harshness bruises, dents, and breaks.
Verbal or physical, it doesn't matter—
the precious innocence, forever
changed.
Remember new birth in all God
made—
purity, fresh and clean.
Newfallen snow, crisp, clear moonlight,
northern lights throughout the night.
Birth of new spring, all newly formed
and free,
not yet shaped or twisted
by lifetime's weathers.
Remember the lesson life's hand has
written
on the pages of your life
for you to write, or not to write,
on the blank pages of an emotional,
innocent soul—
entrusted to you, your babies, your
children.

# Emily
*Evelyn Wilhelm*

My granddaughter Emily is in kindergarten. I saw her teacher after the school Mass one day, and she told me how much she enjoys having Emily in her class. She then proceeded to tell me that a few weeks earlier, she had sent a note home to the parents, asking for donations of things like tablets, pencils, pens, fabrics, etc., that she could use for art projects or as rewards for the children when they did well in their work.

Emily took the note home. The next morning when she got to school, she gave her teacher a shoebox filled with a hundred pens and pencils. The teacher was quite surprised to get the almost full box and thanked Emily for bringing them in.

At the end of the week, when the teacher was giving out rewards, she gave Emily a pencil. Emily looked at the pencil, then at the teacher, and said, "Thank you. I really need this. We don't have any at home."

# Brick by Brick
*Nelda Johnson Liebig*

I anticipated a good year as I taped name cards to desks and decorated my classroom with autumn-colored posters. I loved teaching third grade. Eight-year-olds are openly frank and eager to learn.

My new charges trooped in, dressed in new trousers and cotton dresses, and with freshly combed hair. It was 1957, and our school in Madison, Wisconsin, had a dress code. No long-haired boys or jeans-clad girls.

Then I saw her. Her red plaid skirt swished as she flipped her tight, black braids over her shoulder and tossed me a quick smile. "Good morning, Teacher," she said.

A black child! I had taught Eskimos in Alaska and Chippewa-Crees in Montana, but never blacks. In my native Oklahoma, we had segregated schools and churches. We had our place, and "they" had theirs. My thoughts startled me. I was an open-minded Christian, free of prejudice—wasn't I?

The class, too, was curious about her. "My name is Margaret Camellia Winters," she announced, as the children gave their names. "I'm called Peggy." She handed me her enrollment card from the office. Pert little Margaret Camellia Winters was very self-assured—or she was putting up a good bluff.

In true third-grade form, everyone quickly received a nickname. Margaret Camellia became Marvelous Chameleon, so named by Tim, who was proud of his knowledge of reptiles.

"Chameleon?" demanded Peggy. "Chameleons change colors." She laughed. "I don't. I stay black and I like it." There was an air of challenge in her voice as she gave me a long, steady look through her wire-framed glasses. I felt mildly irritated. I had never known a spunky black child.

I grew more uncomfortable with my thoughts about her and began to include her in my prayers. *Bless Peggy and change my attitude toward her, Lord. Help me love her.* But I sensed resentment welling up within me.

Jerry, a shock of red hair in his eyes, had chosen the seat farthest from my desk. I knew he was one to be watched. He eyed Peggy, eager to make trouble. Outwardly, she ignored him, but I wondered what was going on behind those owl-eyed glasses.

"Where did you live before you came here, Peggy?" I asked one morning, determined to create a more compatible atmosphere between us.

"Detroit. We will be here two years. My father is a student at the university. Someday we are going to have a home and stay in one place." Her voice dropped, as she added, "I hope."

Peggy was not only an excellent student, but also talented in art, as I learned when I asked the children to draw pictures for our transportation mural. Most of the class produced the average third-grade drawings of cars, ships, and planes. Peggy drew a large, impressive truck, complete with diesel exhaust and chrome grill. It was a handsome eighteen-wheeler with attractive lettering—M.C. Winters Transport Company—on the side.

"That's very good!" I exclaimed, and pinned it in the center of our mural.

As I brought the class in from recess, several children pointed to the mural. Someone had scrawled "Nigger" in red ink across Peggy's artwork. Without comment I removed the drawing and put it on my desk. Peggy did not look up, but concentrated on a little book she took from her desk.

After school, I searched desks to learn who had defaced Peggy's work. In Jerry's desk, I found a sketch of an African hut with stick figures around it. One figure, a girl in large glasses with a bone in her nose, had "Peggy the cannibal" printed under it. The drawing was made with the same type of red marker used to write across the truck. I folded the drawing and put it in my pocket. I would confront Jerry with the evidence.

I was not surprised to find Peggy's desk neat and orderly. The little book lay on top. It was a New Testament. On the inside cover, I read, "Remember Matthew 5:44. Love, Dad." I turned to Matthew: "Love your enemies, bless them that curse you, do good to them that hate you, and pray for them which despitefully use you, and persecute you." I replaced the Testament and closed her desk. I was beginning to understand Peggy.

The next morning, she came in with her usual Pollyanna smile, carrying a box of writing pens. Each had a bubble of liquid in the top with a tiny plastic boat floating in it. "Dad gave these out at Sunday School and had some left over," she told me. "He said I could give them to the class."

I watched her move up and down the aisles, giving out the pens, waiting for unkind comments or for someone to put his foot out and trip her.

"Hey! Pretty good!" Jerry called, trying his pen on his arm.

We began the day with book reports. As usual, Peggy was prepared and wanted to be first. She held up her book, *Heidi*, and gave an interesting summary of it.

"What did you like best?" I asked.

She hugged the book to her and studied her classmates. "I liked the part where Heidi goes to live with her grandfather, but he doesn't want her. She keeps being nice to him until he decides he wants her to stay, after all."

The class was silent. Did they understand the message in it for them?

A few days later, Peggy approached me after school as I sat at my desk grading workbooks. "May I talk to you?" she asked.

I put my work aside and noticed that she twisted her braid, the first sign of insecurity I had seen. "You can't make them like me, you know," she said, peering at me over her glasses.

"They shouldn't be unkind to you," I replied.

"I know, but I'm using the P.P.T. plan."

"What is that?"

"Prayer, patience, and time. Dad says nothing really worth having will happen without time, patience and prayers." She paused. "You try to help, but it just makes everything worse." She looked down. "I want them to like me."

"Maybe we are both trying too hard," I said, taking her hands in mine.

"You mean I should stop trying to be best in everything?"

"No, you should always strive to do your best, but . . ."

"But I don't have to be first in everything," she interjected, as she straightened her thin shoulders. "Some of them like me."

"Of course they do. Even Jerry is changing."

She smiled. "When we love our enemies like the Bible says, then sometimes they aren't enemies anymore."

I marveled at the insight of this very special child of God.

After she left, I studied the empty desks and thought of the children who had sat in them. Peggy was right. Some were changing.

I went to the window and watched her join two other girls. They walked down the sidewalk together. I knew God had a special purpose for Peggy, his unique ambassador with remarkable racial esteem. It was going to be interesting to watch her daily endeavor to tear down racial walls, brick by brick.

Suddenly I realized I could feel mortar and brick crumbling in me, too. I wiped a tear. "Thank you, God, for changing me through Peggy."

Through the years, I have wondered how many other lives Christ has changed through Peggy.

## We Wrap the Arms
### Barbara A. Pauls

We wrap the arms
of the world around us,
instead of arms of permanency.
Notice, whatever is permanent
gives off peace. Peace,
based on continuity,
is comforting.

## Building a Cathedral
### Robert Cook

I had enjoyed the pleasure of working at Boy Scout Camp Decorah for five consecutive summers. It was productive work that taught me something about youths and about responsibility. It was also fun. I'll forever be indebted to scouting for the contributions it made to my life and to the lives of my four brothers.

But after those five years, when I was well into my college years at Holy Cross Seminary, I decided it was time to become a laborer. Monsignor James Finucan was the Chancellor of the Diocese at the time. He offered to secure jobs for several seminarians on the construction of the new Cathedral of Saint Joseph the Workman. So, Charlie and I joined the union. I paid dues for three years so that a job would be waiting the next two summers, too. With other laborers, I built parking lots, loading docks, and a bridge over the Milwaukee Road railroad tracks. The memories of work on the Cathedral, however, surface most often.

When walking through the Cathedral's boiler room today, I still have flashbacks about struggling with concrete frames. I still have memories of the wheelbarrow full of concrete that spilled out of my hands onto the dirt floor of the undercroft. I still recall the misstep that almost sent me hurtling to the floor of the narthex from a third of the way up the tower. Now and then (this will surprise no one), I think of how lucky I was that I wore a hard hat on the day the hammer fell on my head from two stories up! I remember fondly some of the people with whom I worked, too. They worked hard, told good jokes, and, begrudgingly, gave their respect to two young college students.

Now, as the addition to the Cathedral rises, I look back on my involvement with this church with greater pride than ever. My role has changed, of course. Then, I had more dirt under my nails, more sweat on my back, more aches in the evening. It is exciting now, more comfortable now—my work with engineers, architects, designers, the parish committee. Still, on the not-too-hot days of summer, I envied the physical satisfaction of seeing a wall rise and being part of it.

Father Peter Kaberenge told me this summer he was impressed by my statement in some publicity material: "Not every generation has the chance to build or to enhance a Cathedral." Especially fortunate, I think, are those who have the chance twice in one lifetime to do so. To do so with you, the dear Faithful of the Cathedral parish, is especially a treasure.

"Common Cloth," 2002, Cathedral of St. Joseph the Workman, La Crosse, WI, by Gerald A. Bonsack.

SECTION 4

# HUMAN INTEREST STORIES

*Malamute puppy, 2002, Onalaska, WI, courtesy of Joyce Crothers.*

## Finding the Right Puppy: An Alaskan Malamute
### Joyce Crothers

I hadn't planned to write about this, but I've been intensely preoccupied with it for the past few weeks, so I thought I'd better get it off my chest.

I have been looking for an Alaska malamute puppy, but there just aren't any around. It's not as easy as looking in the paper for a Lab or golden retriever; there are lots of those, but there aren't any malamutes.

People think I'm nuts. I already have two seven-year-old golden retrievers; why on earth would I want a third dog? In fact, I have to go before the Onalaska Town Board tonight to ask permission to have a third dog. My husband, Bill, isn't real excited about a third dog, but, nevertheless, he is being very supportive and helpful with my quest.

I want a sled dog, not to race with, but just to do recreational sledding. I have been interested in dogsledding for a very long time. I even went on a lodge-to-lodge dogsled adventure at Wintergreen Lodge in Ely, Minnesota, in 1996, and came home with a dogsled. Bill and I have had three Alaskan malamutes in the last twenty-one years, but never got into sledding because we were raising children.

Malamutes are what they call a freighting dog. They are the oldest of the arctic breeds and are related to the Siberian husky, the Samoyed, and the Eskimo dogs of Labrador, Siberia, and Greenland. They were developed on Kotzebue Sound in northwestern Alaska by the Mahlemuts, an Inuit Eskimo tribe. Not only did they haul their Eskimo owners' possessions from one hunting location to another, they could find the hidden air holes in the ice where seals would come up to breathe and kept these open with their claws so the Eskimos could hunt them.

Life continued for the Mahlemuts and their dogs for hundreds of years, until the discovery of gold in Alaska in 1896. The gold rush caused the population of Alaska to soar, and the demand for freighting dogs soared as well. The need for these dogs became so great that the Eskimo breeders could not keep up with the demand. This, combined with the popularity of the All-Alaska Sweepstakes Sleddog Race, led to the importation of many smaller breeds, with which the malamute was bred. The crossbreeding caused a decline in the purebred Alaskan malamute. The trend was reversed, finally, after the sleddog fervor spread to the lower forty-eight states. The breed was declining, but it was preserved by Eva and Milton Seeley of Wonalancet, New Hampshire, and, thanks to them, the first purebred malamute was registered with the American Kennel Club in 1935.

It is my goal to get a puppy and train it to pull my sled and obey voice commands: "Gee" to the right, "Haw" to the left, "Hike" let's go, and "Whoa" stop. People who run sled dogs are often referred to as mushers, but the word "mush" is not used to get the dogs to go, as most people believe. I don't want to race—otherwise I might get a Siberian husky; they are smaller and not as heavily boned as malamutes. Mals are not barkers and are not as excitable as huskies, which is an asset when living in a neighborhood, and one mal could pull me on a sled. Eventually, I would like two such dogs.

Our Alaskan malamutes have been wonderful dogs. They do shed, or "blow their coats," as it is called, twice a year, so there is some coat care involved with them. For me, their coats consist of fiber that can be spun and knitted into hats and mittens. I'm not talking about a brushful here and there, I'm talking grocery bags full! They are also prone to some diseases, such as chondrodysplasia (dwarfism), usually in the front legs; hip dysplasia; and juvenile cataracts; and one has to check for these diseases before buying a puppy.

I will continue my search and hopefully will be able to find a puppy before too long, although it may not be until summer.

**Editor's Note:** *Joyce found her malamute puppy, Trapper, before the onset of spring, 2002, as her photo shows.*

> *Use what you have learned in life*
> *to your advantage for good.*
> *If you don't, twice you have wasted your time.*
> *And time is life.*

## If It Is Truly Love
*Barbara A. Pauls*

If it is truly love,
it is magical.
And frees our spirit
to fly with eagles.
To spread our arms out to the world
and feel all of our "self"
is a joy that could only
have come from God.
No one, No one,
should be denied this right.
No love is real love
when spirit and self
must hide, and, sometimes, die.

## Surviving on the Power of Prayer
*Steve Kiedrowski*

*Reprinted from the **Winona (Minnesota) Post**, with the paper's and author's permission.*

In April of 2000, two days after returning from a Florida vacation with her family, Dianne Nelson, of Winona, Minnesota, went to the doctor for a routine physical, including a mammogram. Later, Dianne was called back to get a magnified view of her left breast.

The magnified view indicated she needed to have a core needle biopsy. This biopsy was scheduled for nine days later, a very long nine days for Dianne and her daughter, Amanda Sokolosky. "Real fright and fear came over me about halfway through the procedure" says Dianne. "It all came crashing down on me, and I cried from the depth of my soul. I was so scared. The thought of the possibility of breast cancer was frightening." After the biopsy came the excruciating waiting and praying until results were in. "As the sole support of my only child, my child whom I love above all else in this world, there isn't room for cancer," thought Dianne.

On May 4, forty-eight hours after the biopsy, says Dianne, "I got the call at work that my biopsy was positive . . . indicating that I had cancer. There are no words to adequately describe the feeling of being told . . . *You have cancer.* The doctor said I needed to make an appointment with a surgeon. The floodgate let go and I cried hysterically. I am very thankful for the incredibly supportive staff members who helped me make it through the day." Dianne scheduled an appointment with a surgeon for the next morning and began to prepare to tell her daughter.

"When I walked out of the doors of my workplace, I was startled by the totally different appearance the outside had. Everything was so vivid, it looked surreal. The colors were more vibrant, the trees were greener, and the sky was bluer. I looked back on that first trip outside after getting the diagnosis, and I realized that my world would never be the same," Dianne says.

Reflecting on that day, Dianne feels that the medical professionals should find a more humane way than a phone call at work to deliver the diagnosis of cancer.

The next morning, Dianne and Amanda met with a surgeon and a breast cancer nurse at Gundersen Lutheran Medical Center. "Reality still hadn't set in," says Dianne. "I thought maybe I could take a pill . . . I had heard about for breast cancer, or at worst,

I might need a lumpectomy. I was not prepared for the word *mastectomy* . . . which was the surgeon's recommendation." Dianne also was provided information from the pathology report of her biopsy, the *Breast Cancer Treatment Handbook*, and information about breast reconstruction.

"By the time we left the clinic that day, a surgery date of May 15 was set for a mastectomy and the beginning of breast reconstruction. It was so overwhelming, and everything moved so fast. The decision to move forward with surgery was hard, yet easy . . . I wanted the cancer cells out of me as fast as possible."

With that decision made, Dianne took a leap of faith and turned the worrying over to God. Faith, family, and friends made the waiting until surgery manageable. Dianne is a member of the Mt. Calvary Lutheran Church in Trempealeau, Wisconsin, and says she is grateful for that connection.

"I went to church on the Sunday after I was diagnosed, and taking communion was difficult. I fought tears and prayed hard. Several days later, I let my pastor, Rev. Jerry Hanson, know my situation. I knew that with his prayers and those of the congregation, I would be in good hands. I firmly believe that the hundreds of people who have prayed for me individually and in prayer chains have made a major difference in my physical and emotional recovery. I have prayers from people involved with many different religious beliefs—including Christian, Jew, and Muslim—and from people in Alaska, California, Texas, Winona, and Trempealeau. There *is* power in prayer!

"All I knew heading into surgery was that I was having my left breast removed as well as some lymph nodes. I had learned that there are many different terms describing cancer cells, tumor size, prognostic indicators; but I was still in a state of shock on that first visit."

A few days before her surgery, Dianne called her breast cancer nurse and asked what exactly the biopsy pathology report said. It was in that phone call that Dianne learned the clinical terms of her cancer—ductal carcinoma in situ, invasive cancer cells, well-differentiated cells, and lymphatic duct invasion.

"As I was talking with the nurse, I was circling and underlining these terms in my handbook. And then I read the details of what these terms meant," says Dianne. The most worrisome was that there were cancer cells in her lymph ducts, which meant they could have made it to her lymph nodes, one of the pathways to the rest of the body.

The surgery took two hours and required an overnight hospital stay. Again, the incredible support of family and friends made the process manageable. Then the wait began for the results of the surgical pathology report. The unanswered questions of whether she would need radiation, chemotherapy, or more tests to find out if the cancer had spread to other parts of her body plagued Dianne. Four days later, Dianne, Amanda, and Dianne's mother met with a medical oncologist. He explained the results of the report. The critical answer to Dianne's main concern—whether cancer cells had reached the lymph nodes—was answered. That pathology report stated that no cancer cells were found in the eighteen lymph nodes removed. "I cried tears of joy and thanked God for answering my prayers," says Dianne. The oncologist recommended no radiation or chemotherapy. She would have to take Tamoxifen for five years, with follow-up by an oncologist.

When they arrived home in Winona, there was a message on her voice mail from the oncologist, asking that Dianne return his call as soon as possible and have him paged. Dianne phoned the oncologist, who told her that he had taken her case to a breast cancer tumor review group that afternoon and asked the pathologist positively if there were no cancer cells in the lymph nodes. The pathologist felt confident his findings were correct, but others in this group had questions, so another pathologist was asked to look at the surgically removed tissue. That pathologist found cancer cells in a lymph node, and the first pathologist admitted that he had missed seeing them.

Five hours after Dianne had been told that her prognosis was very good and no radiation or chemotherapy were recommended, she was told that she needed chemotherapy, after all.

Dianne says that her tears of joy became tears of disbelief and fear, and another lesson learned from her journey with cancer. "Read about your medical condition, ask questions, learn all you can about what is happening to you, and advocate for yourself. Had I not asked questions and read the information I was given, I would have been off on a potentially ineffective treatment for the stage of my cancer, and I would never have known the difference."

Chemotherapy was started in early June. Chemotherapy kills all fast-growing cells, including cancer cells, bone marrow cells, and hair follicle cells. Dianne experienced the usual side effects of fatigue, some nausea, and the loss of her hair. But bald can be beautiful, even for women. Dianne decided not to wear a wig or cover her head with scarves and caps.

Dianne grins. "I've been told I have a nicely shaped head for a bald person. A friend said I have just the right size ears to go with my bald head." When friends ask her if she is bald by choice, she has a three-word answer: "Hairdo by chemo."

Dianne hopes to be finished with chemotherapy by December. After a month or more of recuperation, she will have another surgery to complete the reconstruction of her breast. Then she hopes life can return to somewhat normal, with fewer trips to the clinic for tests.

However, life will never be as it was before this journey. Both Dianne and Amanda have been challenged to think differently about the meaning of life, their relationship with each other, and their relationships with family and friends. Amanda, a junior at Winona Senior High School, was faced with a situation most teenagers don't experience. Being the only child of a single mom increased the fear and uncertainty of what was going to happen once she was told that the biopsy showed cancer. Amanda says that when her mom told her the news, all that ran through her head was that this couldn't possibly be happening. "I had a bad feeling when she had the needle biopsy—that the results were not going to be good. When I found out, I collapsed to the floor and felt like I couldn't breathe. My worst nightmare had come true. But since then, my mom and I have learned a lot about breast cancer, and now it doesn't seem so scary."

Day by day is how Amanda manages life now. The support of friends, family, and the staff and teachers at Winona Senior High School have helped her through this trying time. Amanda's message to all others who are experiencing a similar challenge is to keep your head up, look to the rise of a new day, have faith, and believe that you can make it through anything. "Life's challenges help to make us stronger. Everything happens for a reason; it is all part of God's master plan for us."

Over the past seven months, Dianne and Amanda have been a team with one thing in mind—winning the battle with cancer. Amanda has been to most of her mom's doctor appointments and chemotherapy sessions. Dianne says, "More than one set of ears needs to listen to all of the information that is provided. Sometimes I would forget parts of what was said to us, and Amanda would know the information."

Dianne has learned a lot and is eager to share what she has learned with others. "Educate yourself about your medical condition, ask questions, advocate for yourself, be responsible for your health, reach out to family, friends, and strangers, accept offers to help, work on developing a positive attitude, be a role model for others, rid your life of unhealthy stress, take one day at a time, and, if a day is too long to manage, take it one minute at a time. Be open to talking about what's happening to you, realize that you're on a roller coaster ride with emotional highs and lows, be thankful for the wonderful medical care we have in this country, and thank God for mammograms!"

Dianne has been fortunate to have managed the chemotherapy with few bothersome side effects. Within a few weeks of recovery after surgery, she was working full-time in her position as Executive Director of Coulee Children's Center, a nonprofit agency in the La Crosse, Wisconsin, area that provides services for children with developmental delays, child care, and a preschool program.

Dianne's fortitude was forged in her early years. She grew up on a dairy farm near Melrose, Wisconsin. "We worked hard and together as a family. It helped to develop my mental, emotional, and physical strength and endurance." She graduated from Melrose High School, earned a bachelor's degree from the University of Wisconsin-LaCrosse, then completed her master's degree in Education from the University of Illinois. She now lives in Winona.

There is no history of breast cancer in her family, and she had previously been a very healthy person. Dianne says, "Sometimes, I have what I call my pity parties, when I'm feeling sorry for myself, but then I look around and see someone who is facing challenges far more serious than mine, and it puts everything into perspective. Going through this cancer journey, I have gained far more than I have lost. Amanda and I have a much stronger bond, and I've reconnected with people I haven't seen or heard from in years, including my first grade teacher and a college roommate from thirty-five years ago. I realize that I have a vast network of family and friends who love and care for me . . . I continue to receive emotional bouquets in the form of calls, cards, letters, visits, and invitations to dinner and special events."

At her last chemo appointment, Dianne asked her doctor when she can say, "I *had* breast cancer instead of I *have* breast cancer." He said, "Anytime you're ready!" Dianne now points out she is confident in saying, "I had breast cancer, and I am a survivor!"

# To Live for Those Who Love Me

*Barbara A. Pauls*

To live for those who love me,
and the good that I can do
is remembered by the heart,
after the physical is gone.

# Some More Equal Than Others
## Robert Cook

Do you remember the dictum from George Orwell's *Animal Farm*? He created a world of talking animals struggling to establish a just society; in their foolishness, they developed a dictatorship. The leaders eventually came to this conclusion: "All animals are equal, but some animals are more equal than others."

That thought came to mind in a silly sort of way when I reflected on priests of the Diocese of La Crosse. I must change the dictum somewhat to read, "All priests I've known are memorable, but some priests are more memorable than others."

One of the most memorable priests in my life was Monsignor J. Francis Brady, Pastor of Saint Patrick's Church in Eau Claire; he was my first pastor as a young priest. How fortunate I was. He was the first pastor also for Bishop Paul and Father Dwyer and a host of others starting out eager, yet scared.

Three weeks before I arrived, Monsignor Brady had a heart attack. I have been assured by many people, the monsignor himself among them, that his ailment was not due to the news of my imminent arrival. That reassurance saved my fragile self-identity. The senior associate and I went to visit him in the hospital on the day of my arrival. In those days, a long hospital stay was not unusual. He was welcoming. When we left his room, I showed him my shaking hand. "What's that about?" he asked. "My first time in the confessional later this afternoon," I replied. He laughed.

Each Sunday, one of the three associates that lived at Saint Patrick's took a turn at being on call for emergencies at the local hospital. One evening, the cook had the night off. It was then that Monsignor Brady took the on-call priest to Austin's White House for a steak sandwich. A waitress named Alice always attended to us. Monsignor was known as an outstanding orator, a much-sought-after emcee, a preacher with punch and humor; but he was also taciturn—not a stimulating conversationalist. So those Sunday night dinners were rather quiet—until I learned a secret. During the 1920s and early '30s,

"Some bishops and parishioners, too . . ." Donald La Fleur and Bishop Raymond L. Burke at the Bishop's installation reception, February 22, 1995, La Crosse, WI, by David J. Marcou.

Monsignor Brady had been a pastor at Saint Charles's in Genoa. All I had to do was to ask him about those days, and he would wax eloquent about Sal Anny, about the Pedrettis, about the Berras and the Malins. He loved his people and had stories so rich in texture that I felt I was an associate at two parishes.

Monsignor Brady has been gone many years now. I remember still his kindnesses, his scholarship, his love for life, his humor. Come to think of it, in his case it might be true that "Some priests are more equal than others."

# The Family of Humanity
## Robert Cook

The D. B. Reinhart Institute for Ethics in Leadership of Viterbo University had produced another outstanding lecture in its series. I left the Recital Hall with a renewed dedication to idealism and decided to muse a little bit in my car before returning to the rectory. My ambling drive took me down Jackson Street to the flats behind Gundersen Lutheran Medical Center. Then, for some reason, my direction started to take focus. Deliberately, I drove past the building that my father had built in the early 1960s. "His building" was then the home office of Spence-McCord Drug Company, located at 1502 Miller Street. Today, the structure with the red brick façade is owned by the Gundersen Clinic.

I was in a reverie of memories. Shortly after it was built, the floods of 1965 struck. Home from the seminary at Easter time, I saw the efforts he had joined to sandbag the river to protect the building. It was a close call. Earlier, I remembered, he had served on the La Crosse Board of Education, which erected the new La Crosse Central High School. I have gained a new appreciation in recent years for his contributions to his beloved La Crosse. Dad was a neighborhood commissioner for the Boy Scouts, too, during that adventurous period of our young lives; he knew he needed all the help he could get!

Dad was exempt from service in World War II, but I think he was a member, anyway, of "The Greatest Generation." He graduated from Central High School in 1928. A year later, the market crashed and the Great Depression settled into the corners of every home and blanketed the hopes of every young man. Even in his earlier years of marriage, he thought it worthwhile to change jobs upward, to $25 per week. In the late forties, with four hungry sons at his dinner table, he announced proudly that he was making $100 per week. A fifth son came later, and by this time the oldest was already in college. Every one of the sons of this Presbyterian father attended Catholic schools from grade school through college. That, in itself, removed all doubt that anything could be more important to Dad than his family.

As I drove home, I reflected again about the lecture that evening, on ethics in business. Many institutions support us in the choices we make. Many bodies of values and cultural standards inspire us to do what is right. Still, the family remains, in my view, the primary source of whatever good we might do, and the best influence for right behavior. Thanks, Dad.

# Bobby L. Lyons
## Sam McKay

**Author's Note:** *In an earlier story, I wrote: "During the summer of 1956, I was assigned to the 205th Signal Company APR&D at Fort Bragg, North Carolina. The initials stood for 'Aerial Photograph Reproduction and Delivery.' Our mission was to pick up negatives from the Air Force of photos of the enemy's front lines, reproduce prints, and fly them to our frontline commanders. The company had several vans with photographic processing facilities. They were experimental machines, and every time one was moved, it would be thrown out of kilter. Civilian engineers would have to come from Fort Monmouth, New Jersey, to get them working again." This is the story's sequel.*

Due to the mission of the company I belonged to, the 205th Signal Company APR&D, we had been assigned about ten small aircraft and one medium-sized plane. The smaller planes were L-19s and were actually Piper Cubs painted olive green. They'd been used as observation planes for the artillery in World War II and Korea and had been quite effective. One didn't dare refer to them as Piper Cubs. The medium-sized aircraft we were authorized was another civilian model, a De Haviland Beaver, which the Army called the L-50. Of course, this being peacetime, and the company being experimental, we had only about a half dozen L-19s and no Beaver then.

However, we had a full complement of officers. The company commander and executive officer were pilots, and the other pilots there were assigned non-meaningful jobs such as mess officer, supply officer, education officer, recreation officer, and so on. The only officer who wasn't a pilot was the reproduction officer, who had the meaningful job of being in charge of our main reason for existence—reproducing aerial photographs. The company commander was a captain on active duty from the National Guard, the exec was a first lieutenant, and the rest were a mixture of first and second lieutenants. A couple of them thought they were real officers and were very gung-ho. The rest of them were pilots first and army guys second. My supply officer was a nice guy, and we always called each other by our first names when no one else was around.

One of the most popular officers in the outfit was First Lieutenant Bobby L. Lyons. I learned very quickly that his first name was Bobby, not a nickname for Robert, and his middle initial was just that—an initial. That was common in the South. He was the recreational officer. He organized volleyball tournaments, horseshoe tournaments, a softball team, and many other activities. He was an enlisted man who had received a battlefield commission in Korea and had gone to pilot school when he returned. He was very friendly toward the enlisted men, and we all really liked him. He had a wife and several kids, and they lived off-post in Fayetteville.

During the winter of 1956-57, the company moved to Fort Polk, Louisiana, which was going from bad to worse. It was said that if you wanted to give the world an enema, you would stick the hose in at Fort Polk. We were to locate at North Fort Polk, which was just like it had been when it was built during World War II. It was primarily kept up as a summer training post for the Louisiana National Guard. The main post was at South Fort, about eight miles away, and it was more permanent. We had the run of the North Fort airstrip, which was not paved as the South Fort's was.

We were assigned to the 3rd Armored Division, whose home was Fort Polk. The most irritating change we had to make was to wear helmet-liners instead of fatigue caps. This was out of respect for General George S. Patton. At this time, the Cold War was heating up as China threatened Taiwan, and the Middle East was also in turmoil. It was now easier to get authorized equipment and personnel. I was kept busy checking in and issuing bedding and field equipment to new grads of the Signal Corps photo school.

Then one day, a rumor buzzed around that we were going to get a Beaver. Everybody was excited. Finally, Captain Sawls, the company commander, called a meeting of all personnel and announced that indeed, we were about to obtain an L-50—a Beaver. It had just been flown in from Canada and was at the Air Force base in Alexandria, about forty miles away. He was going to pick it up the next day. When it arrived, everybody that could get away went up to the airstrip to see it. After I closed the supply room, I had to take my jeep back to the motor pool and just happened to stop at the airstrip, which was not on the way.

By the time I arrived, a small crowd had gathered. The Beaver really looked impressive parked next to the L-19s. It had a big, enclosed radial engine and a much larger cabin than the smaller planes. It could seat four, in two rows side by side, with cargo space behind. The L-19 only seated two, one behind the other, with little cargo space to spare. That night a special guard was posted at the airstrip.

Soon the excitement settled down and the company got back to its usual dull routine, all except for the pilots, who were like a bunch of kids fighting over who would get to fly the Beaver next. I guess they ended up Army-fashion, taking turns by rank, and then by date of rank within the rank. The only enlisted men who got to ride on it were the airplane mechanics. The favorite trip was to fly up to the base at Alexandria, visit in the coffee shop, and then fly back.

One summer day was brutally hot, even by Louisiana standards. This had brought sudden and extremely violent thunderstorms in the afternoon—and this was the day that Lieutenant Lyons's turn came to fly the Beaver. That evening during mess, it was announced that the Beaver and Lieutenant Lyons were missing. Everyone was shocked. Immediately, the whole post was organized in an all-out search. This was not an unusual event at Fort Polk. While I was stationed there, several small aircraft had disappeared, but this was a first for the 205th.

Early the next day, I was opening the supply room, which was located right behind the orderly room and the CO's office. A shiny jeep pulled up in front, and an officer jumped out and strode toward the orderly room, right past me. When I saw the two stars on his shoulder, my jaw dropped and I froze. He saluted me and said, "Good morning, Corporal," before I could even get my arm to move. It was General Shaywee, the post commander. I guess he was just checking on how the search was going. I learned later that this was not uncommon. The general often popped up unexpectedly. He was known for crawling under a truck where a mechanic was working and asking how it was going.

When the search entered its fifth day, I asked my supply sergeant if I could volunteer to be an observer. He said okay, and I went to the South Fort Airport with two other guys from the company. We waited out on the tarmac for about thirty minutes. Soon an officer came by and told us we could go back to the company, as the plane had been located. It was about halfway between North Fort and Alexandria, in a sparsely populated area in scrub pine and swampy terrain.

One of the men who went up to the location to get Lieutenant Lyons's body said that the pilot had hit the ground with such a force he had to be pried off the control panel. The rudder pedals had sliced through his shoes, cutting his feet almost in half. The plane had crashed near a cabin where an old man lived with his four daughters. According to my friend, they were really beautiful, dressed in "Daisy Mae" outfits, with bare feet. The old man said that he had heard the crash and, after the storm, had gone out to see what happened. He said that he saw the man in there and decided he didn't want anything to do with it. He had no phone and went to town only once a month. He figured someone would come after the body and plane.

At a company meeting later, it was explained that the plane had hit the ground going full-throttle. This was because, in the thick of the storm, Lieutenant Lyons had become confused. It's difficult, when one can't see anything, to distinguish up from down. Apparently, he'd been flying upside down and thought he was climbing at full speed, but instead was heading straight toward the ground.

After the investigation, a detail went up to retrieve the wreckage. As I was closing the supply room one night, two 2½-ton trucks went by on their way to the airstrip, full of twisted olive-green metal entwined with wiring. That was all that was left of our L-50 Beaver. I was with the company another year, and they never got another Beaver in that time. Captain Sawls issued an order that no pilot was ever to fly in shoes again. Combat boots must be worn. I don't think that would have made a whole lot of difference to Lieutenant Bobby L. Lyons!

## The Polish Prince
### *Steve Kiedrowski*

**Editor's Note:** *Vince Pinorsky has died since this story appeared in the* **Winona (Minnesota) Post.** *His spirit lives on, though, as does his fame. The paper and author have given their permission for reprinting Vince's story here.*

There is a prince living in Trempealeau these days—"Vince The Polish Prince." Vince Pinorsky has worn the Polish Prince crown well. His Polish pride runs deep.

Vince and his wife, Ginny, live along the Lake Road in Trempealeau, Wisconsin. Their house is located on the banks of the Mississippi River. They've always flown the Polish flag in front of their home, facing the river. In 1972, a bartender from Wason's Supper Club in Galesville, Wisconsin, Tom Twesme, was out boating and saw the bright red flag. After that, every time Vince came into Wason's, Tom would announce, "Here comes Vince, the Polish Prince." His monarchical title has endured ever since. Now, everybody knows Vince by that name.

"My father was Polish. I'm half-Polish and half-German," he'd always say.

Vince Pinorsky was born in 1921, at his parents' home behind the post office in Trempealeau.

His life in Trempealeau was pretty typical until he joined the Army in 1939. That's when Vince had a date with destiny. Before his stint in the service was over, he would become one of the most honored soldiers in Trempealeau County.

Vince was stationed in Detroit, New York, Georgia, Iceland, Scotland, England, and Ireland. He trained in Ireland for the D-Day landing at Normandy, the bloody battle that was depicted in the movie *Saving Private Ryan*, with Tom Hanks.

Vince was in the famous 5th Division Infantry and was on one of the first invasion crafts that hit Normandy Beach in June 1944. "We were to spearhead our drive to make way for General Patton," said the seventy-eight-year-old Vince.

With shells and bullets flying all around, he somehow made it safely to shore. A short time later, they were crossing the Seine River, in France, when his buddy was struck by a bullet in the arm. Vince pulled him out of the water and onto the riverbank. There, he and another friend, Bob Baker, stopped the bleeding with a tourniquet. A week

Vince "The Prince" Pinorsky, in his World War II uniform, 1945, courtesy of the Pinorsky family.

later, Vince was assigned to pick up dead bodies along the roadside. It was there that he came across the body of Bob Baker.

"There was a lot of crying by the recruits. Guts and body parts were laying all over. But somehow, you get used to the killing," he said softly. "We were told to kill the Germans before they killed you first."

His day of destiny soon arrived. Vince was out on patrol, guarding the streets of Frankfurt, Germany, when it happened. He was walking around the corner of a burned-out building just as a German major stepped out of a doorway. Only thirty feet apart, they stared at each other, both packing pistols at their sides. They drew on each other, with Vince having the faster hand. One clean shot to the chest of the German major and it was over. Vince stood there, motionless—it all had happened so fast. Combat and killing were all a part of living.

Vince was also a witness to the dreaded concentration camps in Germany. "We saw human skulls hanging up along the fences. It was terrible," he said.

Several months later, Vince took a bullet in the leg and shrapnel in the back. He recovered in a hospital in Paris. While there, the troops were to be entertained by the Glenn Miller Band, but Miller's plane was reported lost at sea.

When Vince was shipped back to the States in 1945, he returned to Trempealeau a hero. His medals include the Combat Infantryman's Badge, Purple Heart, Bronze Star Medal with oak leaf cluster, five campaign stars, the Good Conduct Ribbon, Silver Star, European-African-Middle-Eastern Ribbon, and the World War II Victory Medal. Points are given to service personnel for each encounter they experience, such as combat and river crossings. Vince was the highest point-man in Trempealeau County.

He was discharged from the Army on August 25, 1945. His is a soldier's story of survival, sorrow, and self-reliance. In 1946, the "Polish Prince" married Ginny Solberg, of Galesville. They have two daughters, Cindy and Linda.

Vince worked in the La Crosse area at Northern Engraving, Gateway Plastics, and Outers Laboratory. He retired from Outers after twenty-eight years, in 1983. He also worked part-time in maintenance at the U.S. Lock and Dam #6 in Trempealeau for a time. Ginny operated a beauty parlor in Onalaska for twenty-five years before she retired, too. Now they like to travel, visit old friends, and tend to their fourteen bird feeders. But they still recall 1944, when life and death met face-to-face.

Vince's commitment to his community and his country is commendable. Vince "The Polish Prince" Pinorsky—long may he reign!

# Variations in the Key of English
## *William Kulas*

In our great country, English is the common language. Some are even trying to make it the official one. After all, the vast majority of people here do speak English, but the question is, which English? In my travels, I have found that people use different words for the same thing. Shakespeare is right—"that which we call a rose / By any other name would smell as sweet." When he said that, he was predicting the sense or lack of same in American dialects. Some examples make my point.

Popular carbonated beverages, like Pepsi Cola, Coca Cola, and Seven-Up, go by different names in different parts of the country. In Wisconsin, these beverages are called soda; in Minnesota, pop. In some parts of the South, all carbonated beverages—whether referring to one or many brands—are called a Coke. Thus a host will ask guests, "Do you want a Coke?"—then ask what kind, meaning not just the different varieties of Coca Cola. To make matters worse, another part of the South refers to all beverages—hot or cold—as a cold drink. Someone asking for coffee there will receive a warm cup of coffee, though he asked for a cold drink. In our part of the country, he could end up getting a cup of cold coffee.

In some parts of the western United States, carbonated beverages bear the name "soft drink," while in New England they often are call "tonic." Midwesterners may think of a tonic as a remedy for an ailment. New Englanders should beware, lest the relief they seek on a hot day in the Midwest comes to them in the form of castor oil.

In our part of the country, customers can ask for a milk shake and get what they want—a whipped ice cream drink. In New England, the same order would result in a glass of milk, shaken. To get what Midwesterners call a milk shake (or malted milk) there, the customer should ask for a "froth." A large milk shake might mean the waitress would have to shake the cow before milking it. Pity the frail waitress and the cow!

While in Washington D.C., I pulled into a gas station. In bigger cities, stations often require prepayment, either with cash or by credit card. I left my card with the cashier and proceeded to fill my tank with gas. When I returned to complete the transaction, the attendant asked me for my tag numbers. Looking at him in amazement, I wondered what he meant. Certainly he did not think of me as an escaped convict or a soldier with a dog tag; dressed as a tourist, I hardly looked the part of either. He kept repeating his request with increasing frustration at my stupidity, and I kept wondering what he meant. Finally, he pointed to my "tags." Ah, license plate number! In my frustration, I responded that those are license plate *numbers* and showed him the license plate *tags* in the corners of the plates. He said: "You crazy! Learn how to speak, man!" I did not think of asking what they called the little tags in the corners of the plates. Maybe remaining ignorant was better than fostering another round of frustration.

Our differences in language are not limited to synonyms. Pronunciation can vary as well. As much as I respect African Americans, some I find difficult to understand. And communications between high school students resemble gibberish. Or so it seems.

Once, in a taxi, I asked the driver to take me to a meeting. I knew the location of the meeting, but not the address. The driver got to the general area and then was lost. So he called the dispatcher for further directions. The dispatcher kept saying the center was on Hair Rah Row, and the driver kept looking on the map. In the meantime, I could only watch the meter click away. Each moment of ignorance was costing me dearly. Finally, the driver heeded my calls to shut off the meter after the bill had gone past twenty dollars for what should have been a seven-dollar cab fare. He continued to study the map, and then concluded the road was by a garbage dump across town. I refuted his belief with an emphatic No. After repeated attempts at the correct pronunciation, the dispatcher got the words right—Howard Road.

We do not think of ourselves here in the Midwest as having accents, yet we do. After giving a sermon in Florida, a parishioner pointed out to me my Upper Midwest accent. He knew I was from either Wisconsin or Minnesota. I did not pursue his accurate assessment, but I started to guess at what the giveaway was. Only then did I start to see that our Upper Midwest word usage and pronunciation bear the same peculiarities as do features from other parts of the country.

When we pray the "Our Father," we give away our origins with the first word. Instead of correctly pronouncing it to rhyme with "hour," we pronounce it like the letter R. Thus, it comes out R Father. Bostonians, as a rule, do not pronounce the letter R as part of their dialect, but it comes out "Ah"—like someone about to sneeze. Is saying the Lord's Prayer, for a New Englander, a sign that he is coming down with a cold?

So even though national newscasters tend to come from the Midwest, we have no hold on perfect English. Of course, the very term Midwest is another story. People along the East Coast think of Pittsburgh as part of the Midwest. So when we are not understood in another part of the country, we can only say, "Ya, you betcha."

## Too Often, Reality
*Barbara A. Pauls*

Careening and reeling,
twirling and shielding.
My mother, my comfort,
whom I should not fear.
Ducking, dodging,
shouts and anger,
quivering and crying,
choking and sobbing.
Mother, my comfort,
whom I should not fear,
I fear thee,
with all my being.
Where is comfort, peace, and
    calm,
oh little girl in me.
When will I know the hold and
    hug
of softness and of peace?

## The Mysterious Boat
*Doris Kirkeeng*

Mary Donita, a recently widowed mother, decided that regardless of her heartache, she had to move on with her life. She decided to get away and see different things and meet new people. Something to help her forget. She needed a change.

Standing by an open window, she was enjoying the warm, fragrant Florida breeze gently blowing her soft, brown, wavy hair across her peaches-and-cream skin and melancholy brown eyes.

Her six-year-old son, Bobby, caused her to turn as he jumped off the bed, pulling up his bright red swimming trunks. He loved the water, but like his mom, he was not a swimmer. The two of them, wrapped in towels and shuffling in thongs, scurried down the hall to the elevator. They reached the pool and lowered themselves down the ladder into the water. They jumped, splashed, and kicked to their hearts' content.

Back in their room, they showered and watched *Barney* on TV until Bobby fell asleep. They both slept well following their long drive and the workout in the pool. Daylight arrived, with Bobby jumping up and down pulling on his mom's covers.

"Come on, come on, Mom. Let's go see the 'gators."

"Breakfast first," said his caring mother. She ruffled his brown curls and drew him close to her as they walked the hall.

Bobby licked cinnamon roll frosting from his fingers and ran his tongue across his milky upper lip. For a snack, he grabbed an apple and put it in his pocket.

"C'mon, Mom. Let's go."

Soon they were on their way, riding along in Mom's red Chevrolet. Bobby bubbled over with questions. "Will we see sharks? Why do some trees look like they have fans? Will we see pelicans?"

Trying to answer and explain as fast as she could, Mary pulled over behind a parked truck, where people were leaning over a railing and looking down into the water. There must be something here, she thought.

"Oh, look! Down there! Lying there like a big log. See it, Bobby? There's an alligator."

Overwhelmed and wide-eyed, Bobby squeezed against the railing and jumped with excitement, causing his foot to hit the decayed wood on the edge of the old bridge, which partly gave away. He slid under the lower rail. Mary screeched and reached for him, shouting, "Hang on, hang on!" as she clung to his arm. She called for help. He kicked with all his might. His mom's grip was weakening, and slowly, it slipped up his arm to his small hand.

"Oh, God, help me save my little boy," she prayed. She firmly grasped his hand, finding it more difficult to hold him as he kicked and cried. He was gradually twisting out of his mom's grasp. He flew through the air and landed in the turbid water with a loud splash.

"Oh, God, please," Mary shouted, running to the shore.

"Bobby. Bobby!" She couldn't see him anywhere. She screamed for help. People were coming.

Crawling onto a log on her hands and knees, she searched and searched for her little one. For a minute, she saw his little arms flailing in the water.

"Bobby, Bobby! Help! Call 911!" Mary cried. She was starting to slip off the wet log, partly stripped of its bark, and she desperately tried to cling to it. The log hit a rock, jerking her loose. Instantly, muddy, smelly water rushed over her head. She kicked and swung her arms mightily to keep from drowning. As she sank into the acrid liquid, she felt a firm, painful grasp on her leg. Aware, but helpless and pain-ridden, she struggled. Fighting for her life, there was another grab, around her waist. Her body went limp. Still another grab under her chin brought her head above the water.

The rescue squad that had been summoned carried her weak, barely responsive, water-soaked body to the shore. She slowly opened her eyes and faintly uttered, "Bobby."

"We got him. He's en route to Memorial Hospital right now." No one knew his condition. *Did he make it? How could he have?*

"You've had quite a battle yourself and need attention," she was told by the EMT as she was placed in the ambulance.

As her cart was rolled into the emergency room, the sad, serious eyes of medical personnel greeted her as they checked her vital signs. She pleaded, in her thoughts, *Oh Lord, please, my little boy.*

Mary awakened in a hospital room the next morning, looked around, and saw a doctor standing beside her bed.

"We decided to keep you overnight for observation," he said. "You were exhausted and there was a potential for pneumonia. Your lung sounds are close to normal now. I would advise you to use the remainder of the day to rest."

"My little boy? Bobby?" she questioned.

"He's doing okay," replied the doctor. "You can go and see him after the evening meal." The doctor opened the door to leave. Looking over his shoulder as he went through the doorway, he added, "Lucky he was in that boat." And he continued on his rounds.

Mary pondered his remark while she rested. *Boat, what boat? I don't recall seeing a boat.* She puzzled over the thought frequently throughout the day.

After eating her evening meal of baked potato, fish, and broccoli, she brushed her hair one more time and slipped her blue-and-white-striped cotton robe over her unglamorous hospital gown. She anxiously anticipated visiting the pediatric department, putting aside the thought of meeting someone dressed in her hospital garb.

Bobby was sitting up in bed, eating his favorite red Jell-O.

"Hi, Sweetheart." Mary hugged and kissed her little boy, while a tear of joy trickled down her cheek. "I'm so glad you're okay. God sure answered my prayers."

"Yeah, Mom," he replied boyishly, brushing her arm with his little fist and offering a high-five with the other hand.

"Maybe your rescuer was a fisherman," guessed his mother.

"Mom, he had all white clothes on. Really bright, and made me feel warm when he held me." Bobby thought about this stranger and what happened to him. He turned and looked in his mother's face. She smiled and patted his cheek.

"Mom," the small boy said, "Do you believe in angels?"

"Yes, my dear, I certainly do."

# The Mall is Always Greener on the Other Side of the State
*Aggie Tippery*

*Reprinted from the* **Houston County (Minnesota) News**, *with permission.*

Maybe it's because of the flour-sack dresses we wore, or because my sister Marian and I had a total of thirteen kids between us to spend our money on, but for whatever reason, we both love to shop. Be it a grand boutique or the Goodwill store, it is hard to pass by without shopping. When we left for South Dakota, it was no surprise to either of us that my '99 Buick LeShopper turned off I-90 at Austin and took us to the mall. But, alas! We were too early to go into Penney's or Younkers. We took a walk and found the Shopko store open. We each purchased a sweatshirt, reasoning that the weather is so unpredictable in September that we would need them on our trip. It sort of slipped my mind that I had packed four of them already! Soon we were on our way again. After lunching in Sioux Falls, we cruised along at seventy-five miles per hour (now legal in South Dakota). We did not stop again until we arrived at Murdo. We spent the night there, eating our evening meal at the Buffalo Bar, where we were warmly greeted by the waitress: "It's so good to see you two back again tonight," she said as she led us to our table. We must have doubles, because we had not been there before . . .

The next day, the car rolled along toward Wall Drug, which has a great deal of *stuff* to sell to the tourist. We played our roles well and shopped thoroughly. As we carried our purchases back to the car, I remarked that I should buy a pair of pantyhose for warmth in case we were outdoors a lot. As we approached Rapid City, the car turned off toward a mall. We drove along and perused the stores from the car window, finally stopping at the main entrance. I bought some things at a kitchen store, and almost forgot the pantyhose! We were getting close to our destination, and we had already had three good shopping sprees under our belts.

At Spearfish, we looked up my cousin at her daughter's surgery clinic. She had some work to finish, so Marian and I took off in search of a six-pack to take with us. We passed a resale clothing shop, and the car did a U-turn on the street and went back to the shop, where Marian purchased a jacket for five bucks.

We spent Friday, Saturday, and Sunday with relatives, sight-seeing in the Black Hills. Our cousin, Ardis, and her husband, Glenn Riley, have a large ranch outside of Belle Foursche, South Dakota. Glenn took Marian and me for a tour of the ranch (after much grunting, groaning, and straining on our parts to get into that pickup with no running boards). We examined teepee rings from another civilization; we saw a herd of elk and lots of antelope, some mule deer, and a few white-tailed deer.

Monday morning, we had breakfast in Belle Foursche and were on our way. We stopped at Al's Oasis in Chamberlain and found another place to shop. When we took our purchases to the car, we debated whether we should think about a U-Haul, but decided we still had the back seat to fill. At Mitchell, there was a Goodwill store open till 9 P.M. This provided us with entertainment for the evening. Good thing we had room in the back seat! Tuesday we got as far as Austin, and that darned car turned in to the mall again. Younkers was open, and they had a clearance rack! Life can't get any better than this. After leaving there, the car was full . . . so it did not stop again until we reached Judy's in Hokah, just in time to eat her Tuesday Special hamburgers. With a sigh and a hug, I dropped Marian and half a carload at her house and went home to carry in my gifts, souvenirs, and new clothes.

## "Too Old" to Learn

*Anene Ristow*

"No, Neil, I think I don't need one of those. I don't know the first thing about them, and I'm sixty-four years old—too old to learn!"

That's what I told my son when he suggested I get a computer. Why I could hardly handle the little Brother word processor I had bought three or four years ago for any typing I needed! And even the settings for that were hard to remember from one use to the next. In high school, my typing speed was sixty words per minute, but as I'd typed very little since then, I was back to the hunt-and-peck system.

After my husband, Glen, died, I'd started putting together stories from the beginning of his illness with non-Hodgkin's lymphoma through his death. The stories were written both from memories and from excerpts from the log I kept for our children. As I began this project, I was just blundering away at a typewriter. My skills did improve, but not without having to retype numerous pages, often several times. This made for some very frustrating days, but I was determined.

Then a retired friend about my age told me about getting a word processor, and I was interested. It seemed that one could type and make corrections before it printed, and it would do a lot of useful things.

Well, maybe I could handle that, I thought. So I took off to Best Buy and began looking over the word processors. I didn't even know at first what they looked like. I asked a million questions of the salesman, found one that he assured me I could learn, and came home with a new toy! I was told I could keep it for thirty days and then return it "if I wasn't satisfied." I was sure they meant "if I was too dumb to learn." But the deal did seem fair enough.

Frustrations followed, but I was determined not to let them get the best of me. It was supposed to be easy. I don't know if it's the age that makes it difficult to catch on or because our minds are not used to such technology. I prefer thinking the latter. But I felt so good when I learned so little.

When Neil heard about my purchase, he said, "Mom, I think you would enjoy a computer." Just the word "computer" scared me—let alone the thought of trying to operate one. No, the word processor was bad enough, I reasoned.

I was planning a visit to my son's home in Springfield, Illinois, for a few days to see his family, but he purposefully called a couple of times beforehand to encourage me and to see if I had given the computer any thought.

"There are so many more things you can do with them, Mom, and I think you would like one," he opined. He even offered me his 386 Packard Bell monitor, keyboard, mouse, and an Epson 4000 printer that had been used only about two years. He had been thinking of upgrading his anyway, he said. Well, I'm always game for challenges, so after much thought I packed the word processor back up and returned it to Best Buy before the thirty days were out.

By the time I arrived at Neil's, he had purchased an upgraded computer and had both the old and new set up in his office ready for me to learn. "How in the world do you click that mouse so quickly and in the right place?" I asked. I just wasn't coordinated. Learning how to turn it on was an accomplishment. I wrote down all the code words for getting into the programs. I had taken my floppy disc with writing from the word processor, but there were so many squiggles that had to be edited out when it was pulled up on the computer. That gave me more practice and helped me to get more comfortable with it. We loaded WordPerfect, so I could choose between that and the Microsoft Works word processor that was also on it. Neil had me install other things, to become familiar with the procedure of installing when I needed it in the future. We loaded a variety of card games, and playing them helped me learn to use the mouse. How much fun it was to play cards and not have to shuffle and deal them by hand. Just a single click of the mouse, and in a second they're all reshuffled and dealt!

After my week's visit, Neil packed the computer tower, the monitor, the mouse, the keyboard, and the printer all in their original boxes, after coding all the connections for me to put together when I got home. I wondered if I would ever get them connected in the right places—and would it really work after it was together?

The four-hundred-mile trip home passed quickly, and I set about unboxing my new toy. *Imagine, me with a computer,* I thought! Ah, Neil had done a good job. All the cords and connections fit together as he had marked them—and when I turned the computer on, it worked!

I took some computer classes at Western Wisconsin Technical College (WWTC) and learned to be more comfortable using it. I continued my story about Glen and his lymphoma journey, learning to make corrections, cut and paste, save and delete. It was fun. My kids said, "Mom, why don't you write some stories about when we were little, and about your childhood?" So that gave me another adventure.

I enrolled in a writing class at WWTC, and got ideas, suggestions, and encouragement from the class. I was reluctant to write, though, because punctuation, proper word usage, and sentence structure had left me years ago.

Later, I wanted to add a modem to my computer so I could be on the Internet and e-mail my family, and I wanted a CD drive for programs not loaded on my computer. Neil suggested I might want to upgrade to a computer that had all of this built in rather than having more attachments. Since I visited him, he had moved to the Minneapolis/St. Paul area, and one day he called and said, "Mom, I was just at Best Buy, and they have a really good deal up here. Maybe they have it in La Crosse, too. Check it out. We could always get it up here, if they don't have it in La Crosse."

I took off to Best Buy with the information Neil had given me, and sure enough, they had it as advertised. I ended up buying a 486 Packard Bell and a new monitor. Since then, I've learned much, with persistence and by trial and error.

Our writing class at WWTC began publishing preparations in 1997, and published a book, *Celebrate I*. I did over half the typing for that. A second book, *Celebrate II*, was published in 1999, for which I did all the typing and setup.

At the same time, I continued working on my book, *Cancer: A Different Trip*, with plans to self-publish. I learned to do the setup and layout and have everything camera-ready for the printers. It was published in January 2000. It's been a challenge, but it has also been rewarding.

Neil knew his mom better than I knew myself. I don't know if he was thinking it would be therapy for me after his dad died and I was left alone, but it was the best thing I could do for healing. It's been fun. It's a good pastime. And it's a challenge. It's amazing that I can feel so good and be so up, learning something new—and by just a single click of the mouse.

## Spirit of Ettrick Boy Lives On
### Steve Kiedrowski

*Reprinted from the* **Winona (Minnesota)Post***, with the paper's and author's permission.*

The *death of a child.* Those five words should be stricken forever from the English language. It's something that shouldn't happen—couldn't happen—but it does.

Ernie Jr. and Renee Komperud, of rural Ettrick, Wisconsin, are living proof of how deadly those words can be for parents. March 26 will be the fourth anniversary of the death of their son, Stevie. The eleven-year-old drowned while swimming in a hotel pool in Eau Claire, Wisconsin, in 1995.

Stevie was born with multiple medical problems. The first of his many operations came when he was only five hours old. Ernie Jr., forty-one, said, "Stevie went through a lot. He made the best of what he had. He never let his health stop him."

Stevie's short life was filled with adversity and suffering. At birth, his stomach and esophagus were not connected, and he also had intestinal blockage. Surgery was required immediately. He stopped breathing several times those first few days. Renee, thirty-five, said, "We thought we'd lost him."

Stevie was fitted with a tube in his stomach and needed five liquid feedings a day. Very little solid food was allowed. "In school, he would throw up almost every day," she said.

Stevie had trouble breathing because of long-term lung damage. At one point, his lung capacity was only 40 percent, but rose up to 80 percent. From age four through

*Stevie Komperud, circa 1995, courtesy of the Komperud family.*

seven, he was on antibiotics for pneumonia, and he had esophageal surgery again at age eight. Stevie had a total of eight operations, including eye, ear, and hernia surgeries. The heat was hard on him, so the Komperuds installed central air conditioning to help him breathe more easily.

Stevie had a passion for the Green Bay Packers, monster trucks, car racing and driver Dale Earnhart Sr., snowmobiling, basketball, and swimming. Swimming is where he felt free of all his health problems—where he could leave behind all those cruel injustices.

The Komperud family was in Eau Claire for the weekend on March 26, 1995, to attend a ninth-grade basketball tournament. Their oldest son, Ernie III, played on the Gale-Ettrick-Trempealeau tournament team. The basketball team was a separate entity from the high school team and was coached by several fathers, including this writer. The team members and their parents were staying at the Gateway Hotel in Eau Claire for the weekend.

The team lost their first game, to Durand, Wisconsin, 52–42, but bounced back to beat Altoona, Wisconsin, 55-52, on Saturday night. This put the players in the consolation championship game on Sunday against Prescott, Wisconsin.

Saturday night the kids were swimming in the hotel pool about 11 P.M. I had just sat down alongside the pool to watch my son, Andy Kiedrowski, and his teammate, Craig Brommerich, play catch with a tennis ball. They threw the ball over the water, jumped out and caught the ball in mid-air, and landed in the water.

Suddenly Craig shouted, "I think there's a body down there. I'm not kidding."

Andy recalled, "I thought he was joking, but when I looked into his face, I knew he was serious."

Andy instantly dove down, but came up empty-handed. I thought Craig must have been mistaken. Andy dove again, deeper this time, to the bottom of the deepest part of the pool. He sprang to the surface with Stevie, limp in his arms.

I shot from my chair and pulled Stevie up onto the edge of the pool. I said, "Craig, call 911. Andy, go get your mother." (Andy's mother is a nurse.)

As I started CPR on Stevie, my head told me it was too late, but my heart wouldn't listen. He was not breathing. All the time, I was thinking, *This can't be happening, he's got to make it. Is this a dream? No, it's a nightmare.*

The front desk clerk from the hotel took over the CPR. Soon, the paramedics arrived. They worked on Stevie as they whisked him away to the hospital. My wife, Peggy, and I, and Craig's parents, Betsy and Glenn Brommerich, went to the emergency room with the Komperuds. We were in the waiting room only a short time when Ernie Jr. came out and said, "Well, he didn't make it. Stevie's gone."

It was the saddest moment of my life.

Saturday, I was up all night with the players, parents, and police.

Stevie had had a great time watching the boys play basketball. He'd been our biggest fan. We all loved Stevie, and then he was gone, forever. It was hard for the ninth-grade basketball team to understand why and how it happened. Stevie's siblings were there, too. Ernie III, then fifteen, Margo, thirteen, and Andy, only eight. Lessons in life can be so harsh and unfair. Stevie was only eleven years old.

Sunday morning, most of us gathered in one of the hotel rooms to get ready to go back home, to Galesville, Ettrick, and Trempealeau, to try to heal our faith. We were going to forfeit our final game to Prescott. The boys on the basketball team had a bigger burden to bear. It was time to head home and search our souls.

Just then, Ernie Jr. stepped into the room. Stricken with sorrow, he said, "You know how much little Stevie loved to watch you guys play basketball. He would want you boys to play your game today. The family and I are going back home to Ettrick, and we'll call you tonight."

With that, he turned and walked out the door. Nothing was said for several minutes. Finally, one of the fathers who was also a coach, Dave Robinson, stood up and said, "Well, you heard Ernie, let's suit up and go play basketball." Even Stevie's brother, Ernie III, decided to stay with his teammates and play.

Andy Kiedrowski said, "We didn't feel like playing the game, but we thought if Ernie could play, then *we* could play. Ernie wasn't usually a starter, but in a gesture of true sportsmanship, Craig Brommerich sat on the bench and let Ernie take his starting position.

The referees and the Prescott players and coaches were told of the terrible tragedy and told to be ready for anything in case some of the kids broke down during the game. Emotions were running very high. We knew we didn't have a chance against the bigger and more experienced Prescott team. The disastrous death of Stevie was the only thing on our minds.

Some things cannot be explained. But our team didn't play like fifteen-year-old boys that day. They played like men on a mission, with the memory of one small child as their charter. The G-E-T ninth-grade basketball team defeated Prescott, 51–43. Everyone played the game of their life that day. Diligent defense, teamwork, and courage were on display.

When the game was over, we held our heads high, with pride, and then low, in prayer. How many tears can a team cry? As parents, we were proud of our kids. They won it for Stevie. It was a gallant effort.

The team took home third place, with a record of 2–1. Andy Kiedrowski scored a total of seventy-three points in the tournament and blocked six shots in the last game. The Komperud family wanted to give Andy an award for what he did that weekend, but he refused. I think our boys grew up a little that day in Eau Claire. The spirit of Stevie is still with us all. They wouldn't have won without it.

Today, the Komperuds have started several scholarships in memory of Stevie. A scholarship of $150 is given to the freshman boy and girl who show the most support for the G-E-T basketball team. A commemorative plaque is awarded to them in their freshman year and the money is given in their senior year at graduation.

Ernie Jr. said, "It's our way of remembering Stevie. Even his bedroom is still the same. We haven't changed anything."

Renee said, "We donate books to the elementary schools on behalf of Stevie. Books on cars and sports, things that he liked."

Basketball is something that Stevie liked, also. The G-E-T basketball team gave him the final gift, a win. They felt that with Stevie watching, they couldn't lose. After all, he had the best seat in the house.

# A Letter to My Californian Family, February 2002

## Lucinda A. Gray

**Editor's Note:** *This is a letter from Lucinda (Lucy) to some of her relatives in California a while after she and her immediate family moved to Wisconsin.*

Dearest Family and Friends—

Greetings from the Grays, and a Happy New Year! It doesn't seem like winter in California, does it? Not in Wisconsin, either! Wouldn't you know it, after we survived last year's worst winter in forty years, we are having the mildest winter ever. Not one day below zero, and that's just okay with us. A few inches of snow here and there, followed by a meltdown every two weeks, has made winter wonderful—compared to last year, when we didn't see our lawn for six months.

Sandwiched between the seasons of spring and fall is the most celebrated season of all, summer. It is the most fulfilling season in the Midwest—besides hunting season, of course. All is lost for commitment and productivity. There's a "Gotta go and do all you can" mentality—we attempt to jam everything into three months of sun and fun. Early signs of winter's surrender come in the assortment of shapes, sizes, and colored bulbs seen in bright, colorful groves. This brings most hearts a sigh of relief and rekindled hope for longer and brighter days. Experienced gardeners have systematically planted for uninterrupted blooms throughout the early spring, summer, and late fall. Equally impressive are the wildflowers on the country roads; as one dies out, another arrives. Weather permitting, I travel to the office through the country—not a traffic jam in sight, no stoplight delays, or threats of road rage. It's just the flow of the road and God's creation as far as one can see. Life is a picture, and you become a camera. Everything is to be breathed in and absorbed into one's being. Simple is seen as sensible, and is appreciated in the energy spent and saved in practicality.

We had the best summer with family this last year. Before our guests arrived, John and I prepared our home to accommodate four more children, my mom, and my sister, Auntie Sue. There was always a plan for the day, food was consumed in massive quantities, and signs of life littered the laundry room. Our travels took us to museums, logging bunkhouses, the famous Noah's Ark water park, and every Dairy Queen along the way. We all know Grandma Woodson secretly supports and owns stock in Dairy Queen. Her weakness is our delight. Thanks, Grandma, for the delicious treats! Every time we see a Dairy Queen, we think of you.

John's brother, James, and son, Jeremy, also have become residents of the state of Wisconsin. John flew back to California one morning and had James packed and ready to go the next morning, after a very brief visit with their folks. He made record time—three days! This flashback seemed minor in comparison to our relocation memories. James and Jeremy were able to settle into an apartment house just down the road. Within a day or two, I'm sure John will be available for moving assistance, if any of you'd be interested by spring. Thirty days notice is still requested, even for family members.

The children are doing great. Samuel is bound for a pulpit: he never stops talking and the volume is definitely there. He excels in his school academics, and always seeks out friends for the love of sports. Angela putts around at most things. Life is slower, thorough, and more meaningful for her. She has great depth and insight. We jokingly called her Cinderella, because she is truly a mama's helper around the house. Ian is who he is. To know him is to love him. Ian can make anything he does fun. Honestly—he can make cleaning bathrooms and emptying trash fun. He sees things that most of us would just look at. All of our children have greatly contributed in our learning more about ourselves and the continual need for God's guidance, creativity, wisdom, and encouragement.

We hope to get to California this summer. We're planning to attend the Annual Sierra Nevada camp event at Lundy Lake in mid-July. Time permitting, we'll head south into San Diego County and try to touch base with additional family and friends. This is also John's busiest time of year, so a lot of planning and prayer are necessary to make this trip a reality.

We are always excited to hear from you, and the Christmas cards were a special treat during the holiday. Hope to see most of you this summer,

John, Lucy, Samuel, Angela, Ian and Beauty (the Super Pup)

*Loneliness without a cause is lonelier than with a cause.*

# SECTION 5
# HOLIDAYS & SEASONS IN AMERICA

Andy (5) and Ryan (10)
Kiedrowski, Christmas, 1985,
Trempealeau, WI, courtesy of
Steve Kiedrowski, their father.

# A New Awakening
### *Helen Bolterman*

I look out the window and I am awed by the sight
of spring's beginning as winter loses its bite;
dormant grass turning from brown to green,
gently caressed by morning's dew.
Tulips penetrating from winter's cover,
bursting forth color in every hue.
A mourning dove sending his love song to his mate,
the tender notes so mellow.
A saucy little finch feasting at our feeder,

its feathers turning a brilliant yellow.
The tree's leaf-buds bursting in the morning light;
I pause in wonder at such an inspiring sight.
Mother Rabbit provides soft fur for her nest to form,
to shield her babies from predators and keep them warm.
The squirrels dig for nuts from last fall's bountiful fare,
dashing around the yards and treetops without a care.
The flight of the new arrivals, Mr. & Mrs. Robin Redbreast,
busily gathering grasses, twigs, and mud to form their nest,
for Mrs. Robin to lay her eggs and shelter them with her
warmth for life so new.
Spring happenings—Is it magic or God's gifts?
I'll leave that decision up to you.

## Gardening Is Forever
### *Robert (Bob) Smith*

I glance at the picturesque calendar hanging on the kitchen wall. The date is January 3rd, and it is bitterly cold outside. We are in store for another dark, dreary, very cold, mid-winter Wisconsin day. The entire area is covered with a heavy blanket of snow that has been growing almost daily. Our view of the neighborhood is blocked by steep snowdrifts. From our living room window, the only signs of color visible are the stately, snow-covered evergreen trees. We thank God for evergreen trees, for without them, many of our little feathered friends would suffer heavy losses.

I take another look at one of the numerous clocks scattered between the kitchen and living room. Our most dependable clock indicates it is now 1:30 P.M. I find myself patiently pacing back and forth, from one end of the house to the other. The reason for all this energy and anxiety is that I am waiting for "Sam the Man." As prompt as a precision timepiece, Sam, our very dependable, friendly mail carrier, is now approaching our house.

For me and most other seniors, waiting for the mail delivery is one of the few highlights of each day. This event is especially exciting and gratifying during the dull, cold, drab days of winter. What a dramatic disappointment it would be if Sam passed by our house and failed to leave some mail. I don't recall this ever happening, but if such a catastrophe *would* happen, it would be quite difficult to deal with. Sam understands how important our mail is, and if his mailbag did not contain mail for our address, he would probably take a piece or two of his extra junk mail and stick it in our mailbox. He would do that just to please us, because he knows it will be another twenty-four hours until he makes another appearance. For us, one piece of his extra junk mail can certainly ease the pain.

However, today is a very special mail delivery day, because our calendar indicates it is January 3rd. Good old Sam knows he will brighten the lives of many folks on his route this day. Also, he knows that many stops on his route will greatly reduce the volume and weight of mail in his load. I watch as Sam turns and trudges up our walkway. My heart is pounding with anticipation of today's special delivery. Sam is spending more time than usual at our box. He is very busy unloading all of our spring and summer seed catalogs. Before Sam can finish filling our mailbox, I rush out the door so I can retrieve all my beautiful catalogs.

Protruding high out of the mailbox, I spot my favorite—House of Gurney. I also spot the glossy, brightly colored covers of Jung Seeds; Park Seeds; Henry Field; Ferry Morse; the ever-popular Michigan Bulb Company; and another perennial favorite, Northrop-King. Wow, what a catch for a single day!

As I glance at my armful of catalogs, one thing really confuses me. I wonder how in the world all of these seed companies discovered that I have in my possession only a tiny, twelve-foot-by-twelve-foot backyard garden plot. When I search my memory, I recall ordering seeds each year from the same company. Yet here I find myself on all of these mailing lists. I am not complaining, by any means, because I really enjoy all of them, but with my miniature garden plot, one catalog would be more than sufficient.

Once the catalogs arrive, we can begin planning our vegetable and flower gardens. All the tempting pictures and graphic descriptions of the vegetables, flowers, berries, trees, and bushes bring spring right into the living room. For the rest of January, only gardening occupies our thoughts. The seed catalogs are always kept within easy reach. I believe God created seed catalogs so we can enjoy the inspiring thoughts and pleasures of springtime.

Despite all the dreaming, with its anticipation of enjoying the pleasures of retrieving fresh produce daily from a backyard garden, there is also a downside to this yearly project. I promise our grandchildren each year that we will give up the time-consuming gardening chores. Then we will have more time in the summer to spend vacationing with them. Since our grandchildren live a good distance from us, a visit generally means spending three or four days. We enjoy watching their summer soccer and baseball, swimming in their pool, and attending a Brewers game together. Our other grandchildren live four hours away, up in Minnesota, so we need extra time for traveling and enjoying our visit on their farm.

For us, though, that plot of ground we refer to as "our garden" creates quite a summer dilemma. The need for seeding, watering, and fertilizing means almost constant maintenance. Hanging baskets, large potted geraniums, several large flower gardens, care of lawn, birdbath, and bird feeders, portend daily chores. Every living plant needs water, and for some strange reason, ours seem to require it every day. As a result of all this, our backyard nature center limits summer travel and visitation to some very short trips.

Once a person decides to spade, till, or plow up a garden area, it is almost guaranteed to become a lifelong project. A beautiful lawn will never again replace your new, back-breaking, leg-cramping garden commitment. For many others like myself, the thought of a bountiful supply of Big Boy tomatoes, long, slender, burpless cucumbers, perfect bell peppers, and rows of both green and yellow bush beans, drives and motivates them to continue growing.

The joy of gardening also requires skill and persistence to overcome adversities. These include both weeds and pests. Over the years, I have discovered and perfected a number of proven methods that avoid the use of dangerous sprays and chemicals. The various methods used I did not originate, but were shared by friends, relatives, and neighbors.

For example, I plant a small clump of dill, a dozen or so sweet basil plants, plenty of garlic cloves, a row of onions, and then set several dozen marigolds in and around the bases of tomatoes and peppers, and maybe all around the border of the garden. This effort always does the trick for us. All of these very simple ingredients seem to help ward off most of the destructive bugs, yet will not disturb the good, beneficial insects.

I believe, from experience, that gardening can be both a hobby and sometimes a small source of income for homeowners. For many, it represents fresh produce, much-needed exercise, and a very good reason to go outside and enjoy the fresh air. This is all well and good, since I have enjoyed these pleasures for years. Now I feel it is time to give up this commitment, and from now on I will just drive down to the farmers' market each Saturday and purchase beautiful, freshly harvested produce. I plan to make gardening a memory. All this can surely happen, if Sam will remember next January 3rd to toss away all my seed catalogs.

## The Olympics and Gold Medals
### *Robert Cook*

Fourteen years ago, the Olympic Games were played in Calgary, Alberta, Canada. As always, the events, the performances, and the heroics were spectacular.

I remember them so vividly because my mother was dying at the time. She had undergone her last surgery and was bedridden. Fortunately, with the assistance of home health care services, Mother was confined to a bed in her own home. My four brothers came as often as they could from various points on the globe—California; Appleton, Wisconsin; Bangladesh; and Virginia—all to be with her in this sacred time of dying. I was the lucky one to be living in La Crosse, Wisconsin, where my mother lived. The dining room became her bedroom. Here, where she had served so many splendid meals, nurtured her family, and welcomed so many guests, we treasured her last days. Here, we could return her nurturing.

One evening, she wanted to rest, so we retired to the den to watch the Olympics. Brian Boitano, the American figure skater, was flawless. When he finished, he knew he'd done well! We all cheered for this willowy athlete as he claimed another gold medal for the United States.

Mother was just waking from her rest when the contest ended. She would sleep again soon, through the night. "What have you been watching?" she asked. "The Olympics," I replied. "We watched an American win the gold medal. There's a gold medal being won here in the dining room, too," I added. She chuckled. She liked being teased like that.

Mother died one month to the day after the Olympic games started that year. Between their start and her death, another gold medal was won by her youngest son and daughter-in-law, who gave birth to their first child. Mother was glad, very glad, for this sign of new life in the family near the time of her dying.

Heroism wears bright colors at the Olympics; it wears earthy colors in the people around us every day. We should be certain to recognize it when we are in its presence.

# A Summer Remembered
### *Mary Claire Fehring*

"You mean you don't know there are two leagues in baseball? Didn't you ever hear of the World Series? Anyhow, that sure was a good game this afternoon. It's too bad you don't know beans about baseball. You don't know what you're missing."

Maybe I didn't, but I was not about to care. I just knew a date with a fellow who had my mother's approval would amount to a big zero. We had not even reached the edge of Rockford on our way to a movie in Mason City on this, our first date, and already I was feeling that I was going to be bored with baseball talk the whole evening.

That summer of 1941 was between my sophomore and junior years of college, and spending the summer in my small hometown in Iowa didn't make for exciting times. One did not have to have a lot of dates in order to exhaust the supply of eligible men in Rockford. I did have several friends in nearby towns, so I was hoping the summer would not be a complete dullsville.

When Bob Yenerich called me in June of that summer and asked me to go to a movie, I did some thinking. I had known him all my life, but I didn't know a lot about him. He was a little more than a year older than I, had played football and basketball in high school, and had been good at both. He was well-liked by everyone and I didn't recall ever hearing any derogatory remarks about him. He didn't run around with any crowd, and I didn't remember that he had ever been the object of any girl's conquest. He evidently spent most of his weekends with his mother and his brother and his brother's wife.

His father had died before he entered high school, about the same time that mine had.

He was good-looking, even though his face was broad. His chin was firm, and he was always neat. He was probably just too good to be true and no fun at all. His preoccupation with baseball made me feel that was a pretty good assessment. But then he asked, "If you never listen to baseball, what do you do all day?" So I told him about doing the household chores for my mother and brothers, helping Mother in her store, and doing quite a bit of reading. I was just getting well into Sigrid Undset's *Kristin Lavransdatter*. He really seemed interested in this story of medieval Norway.

The movie starred Victor Mature, but that's all I remember about it. Bob held my hand during the last half. That was the beginning of a glorious summer.

Besides going to the movies, we went dancing at the Surf Ballroom in Clear Lake. When we danced, he held me as if I were someone special—not too close, but close enough. On the way home, we'd sing tunes like "I Don't Want to Set the World on Fire," "Dolores," "I Don't Want to Walk Without You," "This Love of Mine," and "You Are My Sunshine." We didn't exactly sing them, because he couldn't remember the words and I couldn't carry a tune. So while he hummed the music, I said the words. It worked great.

We went swimming down by the bridge, but mostly just sunned ourselves along the riverbank.

There were times when he came to our house unannounced and sat in the kitchen while I finished the evening meal's dishes. Then we'd walk downtown for a Coke. Some of our conversation must have seemed rather odd: Two people in their early twenties asking each other, "Do you remember when . . .?" Those reminiscences were about the Legion and Auxiliary get togethers, and all that good food.

"You're kidding! You really mean you can't go off-campus unless you wear a hat and gloves?" He had a hard time believing the strictness of the rules at Saint Teresa's College.

His courses at the University of Iowa were similar to some of mine. He planned to ender medical school, and I aimed for a degree in dietetics.

But when it came to baseball, I turned into a very good listener. He seemed determined to enlighten me, and I soon learned that all I had to do was act as if I were taking it all in, while I was really studying how his eyes crinkled when he really got going on the action of the most recent game he'd heard. We never went out together on Sunday. That was "baseball day" on the radio and the day he went out with his mother to eat or to visit his brother in Mason City.

We rarely were off by ourselves, but there were a few times when a lingering kiss began to develop into more than we intended. It was amazing how much a shared cigarette could give us the time we needed to get back on a fairly even keel.

It was not as if I didn't date others or spend time with friends from school days. If Bob called when I was not home, Mother was sure to tell me, even though he never mentioned it. Mother seemed to be pleased when she told me that one of the town elders had stopped her to say, "Well, Mrs. Unger, I see that your daughter is going around with that Yenerich boy."

So went that summer. We did not mention love, but by September, when we both returned to our studies, he seemed to be quite attracted to me. I thought he was the greatest! We wrote, but not long and passionate missives.

Then came Pearl Harbor.

He joined the Air Force.

We saw very little of each other at Christmas, except with his family or mine, and it was just too cold to sit in a car very long. He was home for only three days.

"You'll write?"

"Of course, I'll write. You'll have to let me know where to send my letters."

"I will as soon as I can. I'll miss you."

"Me, too. I wish you didn't have to go."

"Some of us just have to."

Such ordinary and unsatisfactory conversations. No declarations of undying love. I suppose he didn't want to commit himself. I know I didn't.

Our "good-bye" was anything but private. My relatives all shook his hand and wished him well, and watched, and cleared throats as he put his hands on my shoulders, kissed me briefly, and whispered, "Write."

His letters were full of his activities and some treasured references to the good times we had had together and how much I meant to him. He began signing them "With love." I tried to match his tone in my answers. Soon I received a picture of him in his uniform. There was no crinkle around his eyes. He looked so solemn, but so handsome. I displayed that picture with much pride. He wrote that he was a bombardier and what a very important job that was. Then there was an APO address. His letters did not come regularly and had little information.

After another summer and winter passed, I received a letter from Mother telling me

*Arlington Cemetery, 2000, Arlington, VA, by David J. Marcou.*

that Bob's mother was notified that he was "Missing in Action over the Mediterranean Sea." I was thankful she had let me know, instead of my reading about it in the weekly paper from Rockford that she sent. There was still hope—and I hoped and hoped. But little by little, the news gave confirmation that the plane on which he had served had been shot down, and no survivors were ever found.

I felt a deep sense of loss. I had enjoyed his company so much that one short summer, and I would never feel his arms around me again. I cried. And cried. And cried.

My life has gone on, but every year there is a baseball season, and every year I am reminded of a fellow who really loved the game. When I go to the cemetery on the outskirts of Rockford to put flowers on my parents' graves, I pause at the next plot and look at the stone that reads:

"In Memory of Lt. Robert E. Yenerich
Feb. 25, 1920—Apr. 28, 1943
Lost in combat mission of the
376th Bomb Group AAF
At Rest in Mediterranean Sea"—

Then it is that I really know a part of my youth and a corner of my heart lie deep in the Mediterranean.

## When Autumn Has Me Spellbound
### *Donna Huegel*

There's work here all around me,
and it's about to get me down.
But how can I ever get it done,
when autumn has me spellbound?
I can't take my eyes off the glory
of the trees in every hue,
or the sky that in autumn
turns so intensely blue.
The leaves float down around me,
like gifts from God above,
sharing with me their wonder,
of God's unbounded love.
Spectacular in colors:
scarlet, rust, and gold . . .
one last display of a year of life
from meek to mature to bold.
How can I attempt to work,
when fall I wish to ponder?
For work is here forever,
and the days of autumn are yonder.

## First Hunt
### *Evelyn Wilhelm*

As most wives and mothers know, if you have a hunter or fisherman in the family, the stories never cease. They always begin several weeks before opening season and go until the next season—with new ones added in as the seasons progress.

My favorite story of all time is about my oldest grandson, Alex. The year Alex turned thirteen, he went deer hunting for the first time. He had taken the gun safety classes as required, and with the help of his grandpa, uncles, and stepdad, he had his license, hunting gear, and hunting clothes. He was all ready to join the orange army the first day of deer hunting, hoping beyond hope that he would get a deer—a buck.

The day finally arrived. Early in the morning, when it seemed more like night, they were up. They dressed in their hunting clothes, ate their breakfast, and traveled to their

*Buck heads, 2001, home of John and Lynn Sattler, by David J. Marcou.*

hunting spot. They had previously gone to the place several times to scout for deer and acquaint themselves with the lay of the land. At first light, they went to the spots that had been assigned to them. No deer sightings happened all morning, although there had been several drives. They headed back to camp for noon lunch, all a little disappointed that no one had even spotted any deer. After they had something to eat and drink, they went back out into the woods.

Alex was continually scanning the area with his eyes, keeping his body still—hard for a young person to do—but it was one of the rules. About mid-afternoon, he saw some deer in a clearing across the way, got his gun in position and waited until they came closer. He kept them in his sight; when they were within shooting distance, he took aim and shot. One deer went down, and so did the one standing next to it. The bullet had hit the first, went through it, and downed the second. Two bucks, one shot. He couldn't believe it, and neither could the others. He used his own tag for the first deer, and his stepdad had to use *his* tag for the second one—much to his regret. Some years have passed since that time. The members of the group all continue to hunt, and the wives and mothers listen as new and old stories are told. And this grandma still delights in the story of one glorious first hunt.

# Cantigny Day, 1938
## *Sam McKay*

As was the custom in my family when I was growing up, we all ate our meals together at the dining room table. All big announcements were made at the breakfast table, before my father ran to catch the 8:06 train to Boston and my brother and I dashed off to school. On one such occasion in early May of 1938, my father told us that he had made plans to attend Cantigny Day at Camp Devens, in Ayer, Massachusetts, which became Fort Devens in World War II. He said he was taking us all with him.

Of course, after listening to his many stories about World War I—again and again—we knew what Cantigny was all about. It was the first entirely separate engagement by a U.S. Army division in the war—and, more crucially, the first victory. My father was really proud that he had played an important part in it. The best division in the whole Army was the First Division—the Big Red One! The best field artillery unit in the division was the Sixth Field Artillery, and the best battery in the unit was Battery B, of which my dad was assistant commander.

Every year, the surviving officers of the First Division from World War I, along with current and past officers who belonged to the First Division Officers Association, held a reunion. Usually, it was held in New York City at the Waldorf Astoria Hotel. This year was the twentieth anniversary of the battle, and the reunion was being held at Camp Devens, where the First Division was stationed.

After relating again some of the stories, my father remarked that it didn't seem like twenty years since the historic battle. I jumped up from the table and ran off to school, eager for the chance to tell all my friends what we were going to do.

Finally, the day arrived—May 28. It was a beautiful day for a parade. We all hopped into the 1935 Plymouth and took off for Camp Devens. It was in the central part of the state, about an hour and a half from home. When we arrived, a sizable crowd was already gathered. The soldiers had set up displays and were there to greet the vets and answer questions. I could see the memories flashing through my father's eyes. The uniforms were much the same, including the flat-brimmed steel helmet and the soft sombrero. Also, the insignia—the red one on the shoulder patch—brought a tear to his eye. Gone were the horses, the caissons, and the wooden-spoked wheels of the "French 75s." (As my father's unit was one of the first to go to France in the fall of 1917, they were trained at a French artillery school; hence the use of the French 75mm cannon.) The old equipment had been replaced by jeeps (a recent development), trucks, and rubber-tired 80mm U.S.-made artillery pieces. My father wanted to spend all his time greeting old comrades, some of whom he hadn't seen for twenty years, and that upset me, because it meant I couldn't go over and look at all the neat stuff—tanks, machine guns, howitzers, and half-tracks, just to name a few.

Camp Devens was typical of the old Army posts. There was the big parade ground with the "Officers' Row" of brick houses on one side, and the "Sergeants' Row" on the other. There were none of the two-story wooden barracks that became such a familiar sight during World War II. Most of the men were quartered in big square tents with wooden floors. For this special day, they'd erected a reviewing stand for the vets and their families in front of Officers' Row.

After an Army-style lunch was served under a huge mess tent, we all went to the reviewing stand. There were many celebrities and high-ranking generals running around, and I didn't know who they all were. Their names didn't mean anything to me, so this was a major learning experience. A few speeches were made from a stand in front of us, and I would surely think that General John J. Pershing was one of the speakers. He had been the supreme commander of the AEF in France during the big war.

Soon, the parade began, led by a unit of the division band playing "As the Caissons Go Rolling Along." Everybody sang the lyrics, much to the delight of the wives and kids. Now I got to see all the neat stuff, and rolling they were. Half-tracks with machine guns mounted on them full of men; jeeps with machine guns mounted on them, pulling rubber-tired howitzers; half-ton trucks loaded with ammunition and shells; $2^{1}/_{2}$-ton trucks with their canvas furled, loaded with men, pulling large, rubber-tired artillery pieces; and, finally, the tanks, which, as I look back on it, shouldn't have been part of the First Division, but perhaps were there for the celebration.

That was the end of the rolling equipment. Now came the infantry, marching to a peppy march tune—perhaps a Sousa march—played by another unit of the division band. This was my first live view of soldiers marching in ranks, and I was really impressed. When they got in front of us, the flags dipped, the officers saluted, and the men did a snappy eyes-right in honor of the vets and their families. I don't know how many units there were, but it seemed to go on forever.

At the end of the day, we were all tired and glad to get home, where my grandmother had prepared a fine meal. For the next few weeks, all I could talk about to neighbors and the kids at school was Cantigny Day. I am saddened when I look back on it, because the First Division was almost wiped out during the North African Campaign in World War II, four years later.

# World War II Memorial
## *David J. Marcou*

A war was fought over most the world,
that made it possible for those so dear
their flags truly clearly to unfurl.
What would become of them,
few people would know,
till guns were silenced,
and peace they would sow.
Before the peace, though,
millions died, both near and far,
and deadly witness had been given,
roundabout, by basic stars.
To defeat Fascism, much was sacrificed,
and much has since been repaid,
but freedom is not free,
no matter the place.
So go no farther
than to your neighbor dear,
and thank God and them, to make life clear.

From left: Iwo Jima flag-raising statue, 2002, Arcadia (WI) Veterans Park, by Steve Kiedrowski; The Eiffel Tower, 1990s, Paris, by Emma Bader; Statue of General Dwight David Eisenhower, 2002, Arcadia (WI) Veterans Park, by Steve Kiedrowski.

## Christmas Joy
### Yvonne Klinkenberg

Shining faces all aglow,
shoppers racing to and fro,
bells ringing, church bells chime—
It's nearing Christmas time.
Little girls and little boys
wishing for a lot of toys.

Ribbons curled, gifts to wrap,
children sitting on Santa's lap.
New snow falling, kind of slow,
wanting the entire world to know:
It is time for all to say,
"Have a wonderful Christmas day."

## Swedish Christmas
### Mary Lou Ryan

The snow swirled around Kari as she rushed from the brightly lit house and dashed headlong into the storm. Tears streamed down her face, and their heat formed a cloud of vapor around her head. She ran toward the shelter of the barn, pulling hard on the door that was almost snowed shut by the swirling flakes piled against it. As she entered, she was greeted by the soft nickering of the horse stabled there. She shivered and reached over for one of her brother's padded work jackets that hung on a peg by the door, before slumping down on a straw bale.

The two-hundred-mile drive to the farm from Center City had been uneventful. She and John had spent the time going over the news they had received the week before from the family doctor and telling each other that life would go on, that everything would be okay in spite of their news. And Kari tried not to cry. There was no sense in adding to John's burden.

*So why am I isolating myself? Why am I dissolving in tears now? This is Christmas Eve— I should be in there rejoicing with the rest of the family!* As she sobbed, she turned over in her mind the incident that had sent her on this headlong rush into the elements. It was the vision of Kristen, her five-year-old niece, walking toward her wearing the Lucia crown that stirred up the old worries. Her beautiful, blue-eyed, curly-haired blond niece, Kristen, carrying a tray of saffron buns, kringle, and Christmas cookies, reminded her of what would never be for Kari. To never have a daughter! To never have a daughter to carry on the Lucia tradition!

The honor of wearing the Lucia crown always went to the youngest female member of the family—at least in this family. Some families honored the oldest daughter. Some families still sent their Lucia to awaken folks in the wee hours of St. Lucia's feast day. But Kari's family chose the youngest, and had their Lucia pass out the traditional goodies on Christmas Eve. Kari had been Lucia when she was a child. All the women of the family had their turns, and then their daughters inherited the honor. And that was the source of the tears. Kari could never have a daughter. The tears continued in profusion, and the wind howled outside the barn.

*How often in my childhood did I seek the shelter of this place?* Kari asked herself. *I was born here and grew up here. This is where I came to cry when the horrible news of Papa Rolf's and Mama Sigrid's untimely deaths reached the farm. My beautiful little Swedish mom and my tall,* handsome Swedish dad had been off celebrating their twenty-fifth wedding anniversary. They had left eighteen-year-old Klaus in charge of the farm for two weeks while they flew to Stockholm. Rolf wanted to show his American-born wife the country of his birth. They were sailing with some cousins in a small boat on the usually calm Baltic when a storm came up. Only one cousin survived to tell the tale.

Kari thought about all the times she had come out here to pray or to cry out loud in anger at her parents for deserting their ten-year-old daughter. That was twenty years ago. In spite of the time that had passed, and although the healing of time had occurred, Kari felt the loss of her parents particularly strongly at the Christmas holidays. It had been such a special time when she was growing up. Both parents taught her the family traditions of the old country. She could hear Rolf's voice saying, "Now, my beautiful little Kari! We will sprinkle the clean straw beneath our 'Jule Tre' and all sleep here while we await the 'Jule Bruck' that brings the presents." And the whole family would bring quilts and sleep under the fragrant branches of the tree, and awake in the morning to see their gifts beneath the tree alight with real candles.

That "straw" custom was discontinued abruptly by Tante Anna, a sister of her mama's, who came to live and keep house after her parents' deaths. She observed some of the Swedish customs, but sleeping on straw was considered fanciful nonsense by Tante Anna. She said she didn't hold with the old pagan customs that lead children to believe in spirits and ghosts. Because, she said, "If you are under the tree to give your bed up so your favorite ghost will be comfortable, just remember . . . there are no ghosts! It's all just superstition! A waste of a good, warm bed!"

Some Christmas Eves during her high school years, Kari would steal out to the barn to sleep on the straw, hoping the old tales were right—that if you slept on the straw, ghosts of loved ones would come to use your bed, and they would be pleased and speak. *Maybe the ghosts of Mama and Papa!* Many a dream had been dreamed here.

Coming home from college for the holidays to be with Klaus's growing family and Tante Anna's brood had been so important to her. And now, after eight years of marriage, the doctor's words had left no doubt that none of the new scientific techniques for conceiving a child were open to her. Her problem was unique: she had a complete set of reproductive organs, but in miniature. She would never be able to bear a child. What a bitter pill to swallow! John was so good to accept it—he never spoke a word of blame. But Kari blamed herself. And so she wept and shivered in the cold barn.

The door creaked open, and she saw her brother, Klaus, framed against the white, swirling snow. "Kari, Kari, are you here?" he called.

She tried to stem the tide of tears. "Yes, Klaus, I'm here."

He approached, and in the dim light he could hear, rather than see, her crying. "Kari, little sister, why the tears? This is Christmas Eve, our happy time! Why did you run away?"

And so she sobbed out the story of John's and her unsuccessful attempts to be parents, and the awful sentence the doctor had delivered to her last week. "So you see Klaus, your little sister is a freak of nature. I'll never be a mother!" And the flood of tears began anew.

Klaus put his arms around her. "Quiet now, little sister. Perhaps there is a solution. Perhaps sooner than you think. You see, your John has been so worried about you that he called me last week. And I've been inquiring around here. I asked Dr. Larsen, and old lawyer Svenson, and I have found out you can be a mother very soon if you really want to be. Doc has a fifteen-year-old patient who wants to arrange a private adoption. No agency, just a lawyer and the new parents. The only requirement is that Doc has to find a good home with people of Swedish background. The parents of the girl want their grandchild brought up properly. I think you qualify quite well. Will you think about it? I had planned to tell both you and John about this together tomorrow, after the tree, but now it seems this news shouldn't be kept."

Gradually the sobbing slowed, then stopped. "Adopt, Klaus? Do you really think they would approve of me?"

"What's not to approve of, Kari? You and John have a solid marriage, a nice home in the city, and you both have good jobs."

"Oh, I'd quit my job in a minute, if this could really happen," Kari said quietly.

"Let's go back in and join the caroling. They'll be sending out a search party if we're gone much longer. You just think about what I said. You have two months to wait, and that should be long enough to make up your minds!" Klaus pulled Kari to her feet.

"Lucia, the bringer of the light, the bringer of the spring," chanted Kari. "Oh Klaus," she said, with her voice full of wonder and excitement, "I wonder if it will be a girl?"

# Gifts in Life
## *Lucinda A. Gray*

When my siblings and I were children, Christmas mornings always seemed to start with begging, dragging, and nagging Dad from his bed. Next, we shredded gift-wrap down to the cold, hard facts: what we saw was all we got. Within days, we were thinking about what we didn't get for Christmas instead of being thankful and enjoying what we had received. This must have been an annual heartbreak for our mother, who literally made Christmas seem like a supernatural event. There was no salary paid to a stay-at-home mom, and we felt the pinch as children in our humble lifestyle.

We broke from tradition one year when our family had Christmas at our grandparents' house. Spending Christmas with them meant a two-hour road trip, with four children on the back bench-seat of our two-door coupe. Peace had no room with arguing and bickering so practiced and polished. Upon our arrival, the hugging, kissing, and greeting ceremony took place. We were finally released to run to the local school and exhaust our two hours of stored energy. Shortly after dinner, we were talked into an early bedtime for what seemed to be a long winter's nap. After all, it *was* Christmas Eve.

All tucked into bed, we quietly wondered what Christmas morning would be like if there were no presents under the tree. Even though Grandma and Grandpa had a Christmas tree, it was unlike anything we'd ever seen. It resembled a tree only in its shape. It was made of oversized silver pipe cleaners and displayed a collection of perfectly matched blue bulbs that reflected onto the fringed branches. The tree earned a position on a table in the front living room window. Grandma and Grandpa talked about their exceptional tree more than they talked to each other. Maybe only children could notice the real difference between their tree and others. It was obvious to us that there were never any presents under their cold and lifeless idol of a tree. Would we have to wait until we got back to our own home to open our presents? My dad was quick to recognize our concern. He reminded us that Santa knew we weren't home and made special deliveries in such cases. Eventually, we fell into a sleepy slumber, only to awake to a well-planned surprise. Mom had made arrangements ahead of time to have all our presents at our grandparent's house for Christmas morning. Silly Dad, he still believes in Santa Claus.

Long ago and possibly the only time I can remember, my grandparents agreed about something. They agreed to give us the same gift each Christmas. It was a dollar-sized envelope with an oval opening under an over-sized flap. George Washington's face peeked through the opening to reveal the cash gift. Each grandchild always got three brand-new dollar bills. With this common knowledge, we had already calculated it into our total Christmas cash count. Our parents each received a Lincoln bill at Christmas. I often wondered why my Grandma saved the Christmas wrapping paper we'd used for the gifts that we made for them. Every gift they gave fit exactly into a dollar-sized envelope. And so the lack of surprise and uninterrupted tradition went on until this one morning.

After all the gifts were opened, Grandma looked far behind the tree, and said, "I think we forgot one. Who could this be for?" Since my birthday was eleven days before Christmas, it was often lumped together with Christmas or rushed right over. I wondered if the gift could be for me. Every eye tracked Grandma's moves as she reached for the package. Each heart was gripped with the same thoughts and possibilities of receiving it. In my anxiety, I took a quick inventory of the gifts we'd already received. If this was mine, I would be one up on the other children. It would be just a minute before they came to the same conclusion. All favoritism is punishable in the secret society of sibling rivalry. Still, I couldn't conceal my excitement.

The sizable package had been carefully wrapped in Grandma's recycled Christmas paper and crowned with a delicate bow. Grandma stood up to read the tag. I caught my breath as she finally announced, "Why, this one is for you, Lucy!" I wondered who could have forgotten my birthday. This could be the only explanation that would spare me from the cruel sentencing for being shown favoritism.

All eyes were on me as I opened the gift. A crushing blow followed instantly. The gift was meant for no one other than myself. It was my favorite powder-blue, shag-textured sweater. It used to have a pale shimmer that added to its elegance, but now it appeared to be a mere rag. I'd worn the shine down to dullness, the texture was napped together, and the sleeve seams were unraveled. It was the same sweater my family accused me of never taking off. For so long, my identity seemed to be wrapped in this sweater; we were inseparable. I must have left it at Grandma's house during a summer visit earlier in the year. While I did miss my favorite sweater, I had given up looking for it as the weather warmed and the need seemed to vanish along with the sweater.

It was like an old friend that I hadn't seen for some time, and I stared at it. I was speechless. Suddenly, laughter penetrated my thoughts. Apparently, I'd brought some cheer to the adults as they realized what Grandma was up to. My siblings exploded with uncontrollable joy. "Life is fair after all," they chuckled under their breaths. Not facing defeat so graciously, I thanked Grandma profusely and excused myself from the room, trying to disguise my disappointment.

Without denial, my powder-blue sweater had become a rag. Certainly, this is how others had seen it long before I would admit it. Initially, it had been an irreplaceable piece of fashion. It represented my presence in a crowd—my individual style and good taste. It made me feel confident and secure. Now I was looking at a memory in time, collected in a sweater. It was a time when I was a teenager, searching desperately for my identity.

The shimmer had gone from my sweater, but a brightness shone through the awkward process of self-discovery in the midst of family. I love to recall the echoes of laughter. I treasure the thoughts of traditions. I miss the personalities of my heritage that have already passed on. Our family journey greatly contributed to my growth in confidence and security. I grew to trust that my delicate dreams would fall deeply into the gracious hearts of my family, my unfading gift of love.

## Wisconsin Winter

*Yvonne Klinkenberg*

You talked about your weather
and skies so bright and blue,
but I'll take Wisconsin's winter,
I'd miss it—why—don't you?
The snow is white with glory,
the sky is hazy gray,
but when the sun comes shining
   through,
it's such a wonderful day.
The kids scream with laughter
as down the hills they slide,
as in the snow they tumble,
after their hilarious glide.
I wouldn't want it ever to change
before the winter's through—
What would the kids do without a sled;
what would they do?

The sleds would die of loneliness,
before our very eyes.
I love the white, fallen snow
that comes from graying skies.
So keep your ever-warming days,
without any snow to fall,
and I'll take the children's laughter,
as through the snow they call:
"Bring your sleds and ice skates,
hurry before it's too late."
Only once are they children,
with no worry about their fate;
so let the snow keep falling,
for too soon, it'll melt away,
just like dreams of childhood,
it's never here to stay . . .

## Give Me Forty Acres and I'll Turn These Skis Around

*Donna Huegel*

When you live where there's snow, sometimes you get cabin fever. On a perfect winter day when mine set in, I decided to try cross-country skiing. How hard could it be? Using my experience from downhill skiing attempts as a child on toy skis, I decided to walk down the hill and put the skis on at the bottom. This went fine—well, until I had to actually get my boots clipped into my husband's skis. I figured out how to do it, but the snow was slippery and the snow pants I had borrowed from my son were tighter than I expected. This made it quite difficult to bend over. After several futile attempts and much grunting, the task was accomplished. Poles in hand, I slid forward and was off! Left, right, left, right. So far, so good.

Then I encountered my first hill—a bump, really. I was going to just slide down it, but spied the tracks of a cross-country skier there before me. They were not straight anymore, but sort of crosshatched. *Oh, yeah, 'snowplowing'*, I thought. I was suddenly impressed with the skill of this anonymous skier!

Somehow a childhood technique of moving my tongue around my lips in times of particular awkwardness seemed to help. (So that's why skiers use so much Chapstick!) I attempted the V marks in the snow, as I'd seen before me. The only problem was, I made an X. It was then that I learned V's are good; X's are bad! Making an X means you have crossed your skis, leaving you virtually unable to move, or you have turned yourself into a human pretzel! Fortunately, I was able to shift my weight to my left foot (the bottom ski) and slide my right ski back off. *(Aha! So that's what the poles are for—maintaining balance in such a predicament.)* I gingerly laid my right ski in the snow again, being careful to form the V pattern. The key to this technique is to be pigeon-toed. Otherwise, it's fairly difficult to do. Tongue engaged, I made it down the bump, congratulating myself on my fine mastery of a new skill.

With another bump just ahead, I decided to go for the thrill of downhill skiing and just slide down. Suddenly finding myself lying in the snow, I recalled a former skiing adventure with some of my family. There, in my mind's eye, was my adult sister, lying in the snow with her skis to one side, flailing about helplessly and yelling for help! She was as stranded as a beached porpoise! The scene was pathetic.

I vowed to get out of this pickle myself. (Besides, if I waited for help, I'd likely become a pitiful ice sculpture, since not a soul was around!) Then that stupid TV commercial flashed into my head: "Help! I've fallen, and I can't get up!" Digging the poles into the snow on the side I'd fallen on, I gave a mighty push, which helped me align my body over the skis. Handy things, those poles! Moving them to either side of me, I straightened up and was back on my feet again. *All right! I am resourceful . . . I am competent . . . I am independent!* I thought.

*Time to turn around . . . hmm . . . such a simple thing to do—without six-foot boards stuck to the bottoms of your feet! What to do?* I pictured a move my brother once showed me in skiing. Let's see . . . to turn, you leave your left foot on the ground, lift your right foot high enough to plant the back of the ski on the ground, so your leg is straight out from your waist; then, let it fall to the outside, turning your leg backwards. That was just step number one, and it sounded way too painful for me! For step number two, you merely lift your left foot and ski up and turn it in the direction of your right foot.

Yeah, that could work . . . if I'd been trained in advanced yoga! I contemplated jumping in the air and twisting my body around to get turned the other way, but I worried about the landing. Knowing I had to get back to work with bones intact following this little escapade, I opted for the simpler tiny-baby-steps-sideways technique. Ninety-six tiny steps later, I was pointed in the opposite direction. No wonder they make cross-country ski courses so big! People can't turn around on these things! Pondering my tracks, I discovered how crop circles are really created! U.F.O.s—Hah! It must be farmers practicing ski turns in the middle of their fields where people can't see them!

Working on my last skill of the day, I stepped sideways, up a small hill. It took forever. I finally took the skis off and walked back. Next time I have cabin fever, I'll just make a snowman!

# Winter Sense
## *Lucinda A. Gray*

See the grave of winter, settled on motionless stones.
Gray, gaunt, and leafless trees stand still in the wind,
breath expelled in a puff of heated vapor.
Winter is felt in the bite of a gust.
Waterfalls suspended into a frozen cascade, waiting;
bearded hillsides of whiskered trees.
In the squeaky crunch of ice-packed snow, winter is heard.
Crashing, spearing dives of icicles giving way,
noting the random song of a winter-winged resident.
Smell winter all around within a crisp, deep breath.
Smokestacks billowing with demands for warmth.
The chill of winter is most sterile of all—
To taste the death of winter would be an announcement
into eternity.
Frozen tears and infinite rejoicing released,
salted, it thaws and the winter withdraws,
surrendering to spring . . .

# The Disappearance of Minnesota
## *Joyce Crothers*

Minnesota has disappeared;
it must have fallen off the earth.
At least that's how it appears
when I look out from my back porch.
On a clear day I can see it well,
in all its Midwest beauty;
sunlit snow upon the hills
and traffic on I-90.
But with all the cloudy weather
during this El Niño winter,
I haven't seen an awful lot
of our Minnesota neighbor.
Yesterday the sun was out;
I could see 'cross Old Man River.
Today the snow's blowing about,
seems it's disappeared forever.
Spring is right around the corner,
I've seen the signs already.
Geese are flying overhead,
lake ice is melting quickly.
Shovels will be put away,
green grass will be here to stay,
flowers will push through the
   ground,
and all the birds will be around.
But for another month or so,
I'm sure we'll get a bit more snow.
I'll watch the Gopher State appear,
Then fade into the atmosphere.

*Iowa farmstead in mist, taken from a Genoa, WI overlook (with a 1,200-mm lens), 1990s, by Gerald A. Bonsack.*

# In Praise of Winter
## Joyce Crothers

I love winter. The fresh, crisp coldness of the air and the glistening beauty of the snow make a winter wonderland. Snow falls gently—fluffy and white. It sparkles in the sun like millions of sequins on a dressy white gown. It lies on the land like a giant monochromatic counterpane. It bends the boughs of evergreens with its heaviness and paints the trunks of trees with white. It lies in wires of fences, giving them an ethereal quality.

I love to watch my grandchildren lie in the snow on their backs, as they flap their arms and legs making snow angels, their breath white in the frosty air. They build mighty forts and long tunnels in the huge piles of snow beside the driveway. Fat snowmen appear, with colorful scarves and Dad's old hat.

I see cross-country skiers on the bike trail below our house and cars on the highway with skis on their roofs, heading for the slopes of Mt. La Crosse. I can hear the whine of snowmobiles in the distance, as they head out on the many trails in our area. And out on Lake Onalaska, icehouses appear in profusion; later, after the ice thickens, the fishermen are out on it with their vehicles.

The hill in the park near our house is dotted with children on sleds, all bundled up and happy. And once in a while, you might see my friends, Norma and Ken, running their dogsled team of Samoyeds on the bike trail or across the backwaters in Goose Island Park, or skijoring those same areas.

My husband, Bill, may be out using the snowblower and waving to neighbors doing the same. Our dogs, Reggie and Samantha, love to frolic and roll in the snow and push their noses down to the grass underneath, snuffling and sniffing for new scents. Samantha runs to get her Packer football as it is thrown, and slides in the snow, coming up with a white moustache on her face.

It's fun watching nature in winter. I've thrilled at seeing eagles on the edge of the ice on the Black River and Lake Onalaska, watching for fish or soaring in languid circles overhead. I've observed a herd of deer along the road in Goose Island Park, calmly watching me watching them. Many birds flock to our feeders and feed especially heavily when there is snow on the ground. Cardinals, chickadees, purple finches, juncos, bluejays, and sparrows peck at the seeds, sending some down to the ground for the doves and squirrels underneath. Deer visit our compost bin at night to feed on peelings from last night's supper—I see their tracks in the morning. Rabbits leave tracks everywhere, and the dogs follow them to the bushes and hedges where they hide during the day.

Winter brings the beautiful holiday of Christmas and many colorful lights radiate softly across the snow, adding to the beauty of the season.

One night, Bill and I decided to take a walk before we went to bed. It had been snowing for a while, and there were about five inches on the ground. We bundled up and started out. The snow muffled the sound of the traffic on the highway, and we felt like we were walking down a country lane. The snow stuck to our eyelashes and felt soft underfoot. It enveloped us in its whiteness, and after a while we resembled one of its own.

And what could surpass a winter night when the moon shines through the trees, casting a filigree of shadows on the snow, and the night is so bright that it resembles daylight?

Some days, when the weather is frigid and blustery and not fit to be out in, I stay inside, fix a cup of hot chocolate, curl up in a big stuffed chair, and pore over the multitude of seed catalogues and plan my garden for the coming spring. Winter is also a wonderful time to work on puzzles, read that book that I have been meaning to get into, get sewing done, and start a quilting project. It's a time to go through magazines, saving what I want and discarding the rest. It's a good time to clean out closets to get ready for a rummage sale in the spring. And on those cold winter nights, nothing beats the warmth of a wood-burning stove. You can feel the warmth right down to the bone. The dogs love it, too, and curl up as close as they can get.

More scientifically, I've read that research shows cold is a mind stimulant. Our brains function best at air temperatures around twenty degrees Fahrenheit. Also, there are no mosquitoes and flies to bother you the minute you walk out the door. Now there are some positive aspects of winter! Winter brings many opportunities for us to be out and enjoy the things it has to offer. Snow is the "frosting on the cake," so take advantage of this wonderful season.

P.S. This was written a couple of years ago in response to all the complaints I usually hear about winter. This past year, however, with the warmer temperatures and lack of snow, I haven't heard as many complaints.

## Easter
### *Yvonne Klinkenberg*

Easter is not a rabbit, hopping down a bunny trail.
It's not the fancy card we get in the mail.
It's the rising of the Son,
to show that what's been told is True.
It's a special gift,
given by Love, just for me and you.
To reach out with spreading arms,
to gather all within,
no matter if we live in cities or on farms,
it is a special gift freely given,
by One's Spirit, who passed from earth
to His Father's heaven.
So please take this gift from above,
that was given by our Heavenly Father,
filled with His perfect Love.

## The World Celebrates
### *Doris Kirkeeng*

The earliest observance of Easter occurred in the second century. Easter has been observed following the first full moon after the sun crosses the celestial equator, when the days and nights are equal, between March 22 and April 25.

What is this celebration all about? Jesus Christ, who lived on this earth, had been accused of blasphemy because he acknowledged he was the King of the Jews. In obedience to his Heavenly Father, he was crucified and died. The Easter celebration is about his resurrection to life—gone from the tomb and walking on this earth. Many people celebrate this church holiday by having a beautiful service at sunrise on Easter morning to recall that happy occasion. In 1921, the most elaborate celebration was at the Hollywood Bowl in Hollywood, California. Still today, about 20,000 people come to the Bowl around midnight on Easter Eve. In front of the band shell are 50,000 calla lillies. As the sun rises over a mountain, a choir of 250 teenagers and 100 adults, accompanied by a symphony orchestra, burst into the music of the "Hallelujah Chorus."

In parts of Africa at 3 A.M., a bell is rung and people go to a hill for sunrise service. They march singing, and have special music. The minister closes the service with an Easter meditation. Later on, young people present a dramatization of Easter events.

In Matendaze, near Mutanibra, six groups go out in different directions, singing the great news, accompanied by a *hostos* (African rattle). After visiting homes and villages for twelve hours, they all meet in a central place for an Easter service.

The traditional Easter rabbit is closely related to fertility (new life) and the new moon. Japanese artists paint its figure across a moon disc. The Chinese represent the moon as a rabbit pounding rice. Europeans have all sorts of fantasies connected with the moon, but the most accepted is that it represents fertility. Children like to believe that on Easter Sunday a rabbit, after a long winter sleep, lays bright red, blue, yellow, and purple eggs in new grass. In Germany, the Easter Hare brings eggs to hide in the house and garden for little children's searching. Nests are prepared with moss and grass. The Germans are also well-known for eggs made of sugar, with little scenes inside that can be seen through a transparent window at one end. In Slavic countries, eggs are hand-painted with traditional designs, and inscriptions are etched into each egg's surface. These are then exchanged. Romans, centuries ago, gave eggs as prizes for races run on oval tracks.

Breakfasts with hot cross buns are often served following sunrise church services in America. Egg hunts, at private homes or on public grounds, are popular. Even an underwater hunt has been shown on TV. Egg rolls are another interesting pastime in honor of Easter, with the goal being to roll the egg the longest or the farthest. The most famous egg roll and hunt takes place on the White House lawn, where hundreds of children participate, and the President of the United States and others join in the fun.

As we in America dress for the Easter Parade, entertain with the Easter Bunny, and attend sunrise services on Easter Sunday, we can recall that many cultures and peoples throughout the whole wide world will be celebrating, too, in diverse ways.

# A Promise

*Barbara A. Pauls*

You sent me a promise, my love,
when the white lilies came . . .
A promise of hope, love, and faith,
as plain to see as the lilies white.
They speak of promises made and
    kept
by someone greather than you or I.

A symbol of love, so pure and true,
this Easter that we celebrate.
I too, will wait, for the day ahead,
when we together can celebrate
the day our Lord showed to all of us
the truest meaning of love on earth.

*Stained glass window, 1986, in a church in The Philippines, by David J. Marcou.*

SECTION 6

# AMERICANS AT WORK AND PLAY

Art Hebberd with his famous No-Crack hand cream, 2002, La Crosse, WI, by Rick Wood, courtesy of the **Milwaukee Journal Sentinel**.

## Cracked Skin and a Note Make Hand Cream a Hit (or, No-Crack Hand Cream: How Great Thou Art)

Rick Romell, of the **Milwaukee Journal Sentinel** staff

La Crosse—No cracks, please, about No-Crack. It's the lucky little hand cream that could.

They cook it up here at the Dumont Co. in an unmechanized process that, on a slightly smaller scale, might be duplicated in your kitchen—five-gallon kettles on a stovetop, ingredients poured from glass jars, globs of lanolin added with what looks like an oversize butter knife.

The formula was concocted forty-five years ago by a local druggist who's now ninety-two and no longer owns the business, but who calls every morning at ten minutes to eight—sharp—asks if any big orders have come in, greets the crew over the speakerphone, receives a collective hello in return, then says good-bye until the next day.

They don't advertise. Their label design is from just this side of the Great Depression. Counting the co-owners, their full-time work force totals all of six people.

And they just happen to be a big hit at Restoration Hardware, the California-based retail chain that targets prosperous baby boomers with pricey, retro, home-and-hearth luxuries.

**A Popular Product**

"We don't talk specifics about dollar amounts it generates," said Restoration marketing director Dave Glassman. "I can tell you it's been one of our most popular products, week in and week out."

For that—and for the more-than-40-percent of Dumont's sales Restoration has come to represent—credit a basic marketing tactic, a truckload of art bound for Oregon, a single, determined consumer, and a powerful but seldom-discussed element of business success—luck.

Dumont didn't woo Restoration. In fact, until Restoration called four years ago, Dumont co-owner Paul Meyer hadn't even heard of what is now his largest customer.

"Never," he said, sitting in the firm's office, with its utilitarian metal desks and vinyl flooring. "I had no clue who they were."

Enter Victoria Beal, who had no clue about Dumont. Beal is thirty-four, a friendly, garden-loving Chicagoan and a former art student who, in April 1997, was in the middle of a brief stint as a curator that saw her organizing a show in Portland, Oregon.

Headed west in a truck with her mother and the artwork, she pulled off I-90 at the edge of the South Dakota Badlands for a stop at Wall Drug. There, beyond the rattlesnake ashtrays, lizard skin cowboy boots, and jackalope hunting permits, she saw it: No-Crack hand cream.

Beal had never heard of the stuff, but she liked the simple label with its World War II-era aesthetic appeal, and she liked the straightforward name.

"My husband is a woodworker," Beal said, "and so he literally has cracks in his hands. And it said 'No-Crack,' and I thought, 'Well, that spells it out.'"

**Discovery Retold**

Beal bought some and loved it. But back in Chicago, she couldn't find the hand cream, so she wrote to Dumont and ordered a supply via mail.

And in an inspired stroke of self-interested consumerism, she also dashed off a note to the headquarters of Restoration Hardware—one of her favorite stores—suggesting that it carry No-Crack.

"I wanted the little company from Wisconsin to do well," she said, "but I also wanted to be able to get my hands on the stuff without having to write away for it."

Six months later, Beal walked into a Chicago-area Restoration outlet and, to her surprise, found not only a supply of the hand cream, but a promotional sign mentioning her by name and telling of her discovery.

"It's my claim to fame," Beal said.

And it's been Dumont's ticket to growth. For fifty years, the company was among the smallest of small businesses. It's hardly big now, but its $1 million to $1.5 million in annual sales is a huge advance.

"We never went over $100,000," said Dumont founder Arthur Hebberd.

A portrait of Hebberd hangs on a wall at the company. He was middle-aged when it was painted. Now he's very old, and when he greets a visitor, he shakes with his left hand. A stroke nine years ago weakened his right arm.

Hebberd visits Dumont once every six weeks or so, but mostly he stays in an assisted-living center called Meadow Wood. He's lived there since Mary, his wife of sixty-three years, died three years ago.

Outside his door is a small watercolor of an Irish cottage that he painted. Inside, the walls are decorated with seven other framed watercolors he did. Each portrays one of the deadly sins, though Hebberd doesn't take a rigid view of the subject.

Envy, for example, isn't so terrible, he said. Lots of people feel it. Lust, too.

Hebberd was born in La Crosse, went to the University of Minnesota to study pharmacy, and returned home. His father had bought a downtown drugstore around 1890, and Hebberd, too, went into the business.

**World War II Producer**

He was in his thirties when World War II came and tightened supplies of things like shampoo and lotions. Hebberd decided to start making them.

He learned about production by reading trade journals such as *The American Perfumer* and through research at the public library. Before long, he was turning out deodorant, cologne, hair rinse, lipstick, and other items.

Most of it sold pretty slowly, but Hebberd drummed up enough business to close the drugstore in 1957 and concentrate on production. It was about then that he developed what would become Dumont's signature hand cream and, walking home one night from the library, thought of calling it No-Crack.

No-Crack didn't make Hebberd much richer than his earlier formulas did.

In his last year at Dumont, the company netted about $11,000. But his wife was a teacher, he could fill in at area pharmacies, and the couple owned an apartment building.

"We didn't starve, but it wasn't very lush," he said.

Hebberd sold Dumont Co. in 1993 after his stroke left him no chance of returning to work. From his hospital room, he struck an agreement to sell to Meyer—the son of a Dumont employee—and Meyer's brother-in-law, Jim Ames.

"If somebody couldn't have taken it over, it would just have been lost," Hebberd said.

Meyer and Ames, a former chemistry professor who left a tenured post two years ago to work full-time at Dumont, have tweaked the No-Crack formula a bit. They've played a little with the typeface on the label.

Basically, though, they've let well enough alone.

But it's not as though they've simply ridden a horse Hebberd saddled.

It was Hebberd who started what remains the firm's principal marketing technique —mailing free samples to potential customers. That's how No-Crack landed in Wall Drug, where Beal found it.

### Samples Sent to Chains

But Dumont's current owners have taken the strategy to a new level.

Where Hebberd sent samples primarily to independent pharmacies, Meyer and Ames have targeted chains, too, and succeeded in getting into some Walgreen's and CVS outlets, among other places. All told, Meyer said, Dumont products now are sold in about 1,700 stores—more than double the number of five years ago.

None, however, approaches the importance to Dumont of Restoration Hardware, the account that sprouted from Victoria Beal's road trip to Oregon.

Helpful as it is to have such a large customer, it also means that your business fortunes can ride on theirs. And Restoration, which went public in 1998, has lost money in eleven of the last fifteen quarters.

But the 104-store firm last year hired a new CEO, announced plans to reposition its merchandise assortment, and saw investors bid up the price of its once-battered stock —all of which gives Meyer confidence in his business partner.

"I'm not concerned about them," he said.

As for Beal, she's just glad to have helped, and she recalls getting a nice thank you letter from Dumont. Her hopes for easy access to her preferred hand cream, however, didn't quite come true.

What Beal really likes is the "All Purpose" variation of No-Crack, a thick, pink concoction that to her smells like carnations. That's what she recommended to Restoration Hardware. What the store decided to buy, however, was the lighter "Day Use" version.

"Which is white and doesn't smell like carnations," Beal said resignedly. "So by necessity I've become used to it."

*Copyright 2002, Journal Sentinel Inc. All rights reserved. This story and photo are reproduced here with proper permission.*

## Ordinary, Humble Work

### *David J. Marcou*

My teacher wrote to me the other day,
that I needed no more education, in his way.
He said I needed ordinary, humble work,
and with the latter, came a smirk.
Until I thought of Jesus and what He did,
and suddenly my thoughts were fully rid
of arrogant temper and mighty misdemeanor.
Today, I labor plainly, and am happy more.
Labor hard, labor long, if you must;
and think only heavenly thoughts about the dust.

# A Well-Earned Tribute to Public Servants

*Doris Kirkeeng*

One Sunday in January, a couple of years ago, it was made clear to me, as I watched out my window, how deserving the public servants of La Crosse are of a tribute. As I sat in my home, I heard a siren close by. I put aside the book I was reading and looked out the window just in time to see a fire engine pull up to the fire hydrant near a house located at 29th Court and East Fairchild Street.

I saw dark brown, almost black, smoke rolling from my neighbor's house, so dense that it engulfed nearby houses and the fire engine that was first on the scene. By this time, another fire engine and three other fire vehicles carrying supplies were arriving.

I didn't think the people were home, as their decorative Christmas lights hadn't been on the night before. As I prayed for the people, bright orange flames shot up in the air. The firemen, decked out in their waterproof, fire-resistant garb, desperately attempted to squelch the fire. Two of them ascended to the roof with an ax. After the hose was attached to the hydrant and pulsated with water, the garage was quickly hosed down and the hose was handed to the men on the roof, who were faced with smoke rising to the sky in two areas.

Since it was January, the sub-zero weather and snow buildup on the roof threatened the safety of the firemen. They scooped snow and debris off part of the roof with a shovel and into a garbage-can-sized container. In the meantime, on the ground, a man struggled with a chain saw that wouldn't respond. Perhaps that, too, was affected by low, low temperatures. Another brave firefighter was being strapped into two oxygen tanks and a mask. He disappeared into the smoke.

Even though a fire department rescue squad was already in place, a Tri-State ambulance joined the group of vehicles standing by. Two electric company trucks, two cable TV trucks, and a telephone company van stood by, as well, waiting for the firemen to finish their work and allow them to take over.

Assuming that the owners weren't home, I pondered their anguish and saddened hearts when they arrived there and found their home charred and water- and smoke-damaged. Where would they stay? What about their precious family treasures?

I recalled that my son had a friend whose home had burned, melting his cherished state champion wrestler trophy. How painful to a young high school student who worked so hard to win this award! To him, it was more than just a material item.

As two white police cars with flashing red and blue lights controlled traffic, two little boys walked toward the afflicted building, thrilled with the excitement of fire trucks in action. The littler one was dressed well, but it looked as though the bigger boy had become impatient and had grabbed the jacket of another member of the household. He wore no cap, and his jacket was open, with the sleeves hanging way beyond his hands. Down the street, leading his little charge he went. Much to their disappointment, one of the officers on the scene rerouted their visit, and they immediately were headed to the safety and warmth of their home.

Nearby neighbors stood outside, bundled up in their warmest clothes, and watched for a short time. Soon the cold weather made them retreat to warmer spots, where they watched out of windows. Others, from outside the neighborhood, chose to take the route down East Fairchild Street to walk their dogs—and perhaps satisfy their curiosity.

A white sedan labeled L. F. D. made its appearance. Three people from the media with cameras, tripods, and notebooks were in action. Of course, the white vehicle with "News you can count on" printed on its side was there. The last arrival on the scene was the mini-van of the Inspection Arson Board.

"A young boy's dream," Matt Marcou waves to a Fire Department truck, Labor Day Parade, 1991–92, La Crosse, WI, by David J. Marcou

At 1:55 P.M., almost three hours after I heard that first siren, the smoke subsided and the men climbed down from the roof and carried their ladder away. Electric company representatives were elevated to their posts and repaired their wires, and cable TV linemen followed. Telephone workers carried out their expected duties and left the area.

Everyone was gone. The garage was charred and stood open, no longer able to shelter the automobile it had held during the fire. The house looked so alone and pained. I couldn't stop wondering about the people who lived there. How would they take the heartbreaking news when they arrived home?

The 6 P.M. newscast's "Top Story" revealed the disaster as it was filmed earlier in the day. It also communicated that the owner reported the fire and all occupants were safe. This was welcome news. I no longer had to be concerned about my neighbors being confined within the burning building or coming home to a deplorable, heartrending situation. They were safe, and later on, the fire engine drove by their home to be sure the fire was definitely out.

We in La Crosse, like residents nearly everywhere, thank each and every one of our public servants for being there when we need you.

## Memories of a Milkman

### Steve Kiedrowski

*Reprinted from the **Winona (Minnesota) Post**, with the paper's and author's permission.*

"Milkman, milkman." Those were the words that Ed Gilberg would say to introduce himself into hundreds of homes in the Galesville, Trempealeau, and Centerville, Wisconsin, areas from 1934 to 1969.

Gilberg, seventy-five, was born in 1923 in Galesville. In 1934, at the age of eleven, he went to work for the Frenchdale-Guernsey Dairy in Galesville. The business and dairy farm was owned by Arnold (Mon) French of Galesville.

"Old Mon French was a great guy. You worked hard, but he treated you fair," says Gilberg.

When he was first in the business, Gilberg started at 6 A.M. and worked a few hours before going to school. He was a helper for the full-time milkman, Carlyle Cory.

Besides milk, they delivered cream, buttermilk, chocolate milk, and orange drink, all in glass containers, which they had to clean when they got back to the farm. All of the dairy products had to be packed in ice bags to keep them cold.

The customers left lists of what they needed for the day outside the door, and the milkmen let themselves into the house with the announcement, "Milkman, milkman." The items were placed on the kitchen table. Sometimes they were left on the porch where Gilberg picked up the empty bottles. But there was a small problem with that.

"The kids in the neighborhood would take the bottles because they could get a nickel for each one at the local grocery store," said Gilberg.

In 1939, Gilberg took over the milk route full-time himself. He worked seven days a week, sixty hours a week, at $60 a month.

"We had to pasteurize the milk to 171 degrees, let it cool, pour it into big vats, and then bottle it. I can remember cleaning those bottles in the barn during the winter, when it was thirty-six below zero. We were freezing," he says.

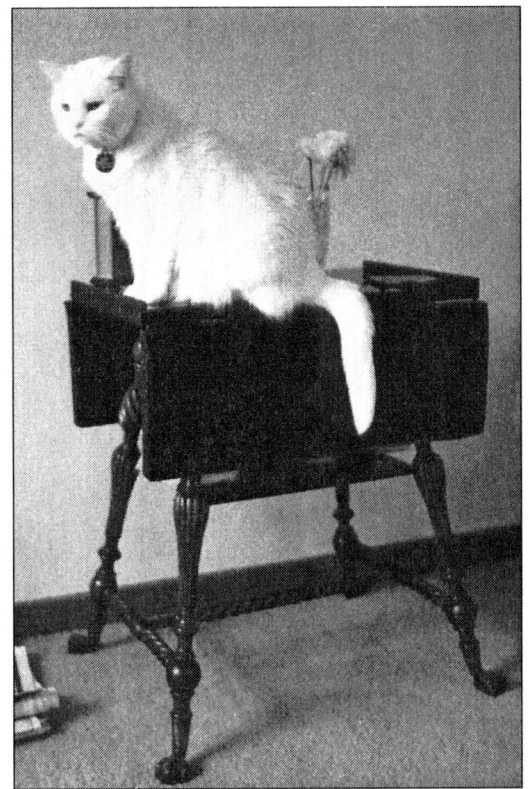

*Smoky the cat, owned by Sydney and Larry Wangelin, 1991, Pittsburgh, PA, by David J. Marcou.*

On what kinds of cows produced the best milk, Gilberg replied, "Guernsey over Holstein, any day."

Because he started so early, 6 A.M., his day was done by 2:30 P.M., so he took a part-time job delivering groceries in the Galesville area for five local grocery stores on Tuesdays and Saturdays. It took him about three hours each day to make his rounds.

In 1946, Gilberg left the Frenchdale-Guernsey Dairy and went to work for Marigold Dairy in Winona. It meant more money, but a lot more hours.

"I would get up at 2:30 in the morning, be in Winona at Marigold by 3:00, and work till 6:00 at night," he said.

That year he also moved to Trempealeau and married Lois Papenfuss. "He worked such long, hard hours," said Lois.

Ed has an overflow of high excitement and goodwill. He always has a friendly smile and a handshake for everyone. "He has a gift for gab," said Lois.

In 1952, Marigold purchased refrigerated trucks, which made life a lot easier for Gilberg. Then he could drive the truck home after filling it full for the next day and plug in the generator to keep things cold. In the morning, he could start his route right away instead of driving into Winona to pick up his truck.

"I could sleep an extra hour in the morning," he laughed.

His daily route covered Trempealeau, Marshland, Bluff Siding, and Centerville. He delivered all the different kinds of milk, plus ice cream, butter, and eggs. He even picked up people along the side of the road and gave them rides to Winona.

Ed delivered to our house in the early 1960s in Centerville. My buddies and I used to cling to the back bumper of Ed's truck as he backed out of our driveway. It was our thrill for the day. Then Ed would tell us to jump off, and he was on his way to the next house. My older sister, Ruth, worked then in the office at Marigold in Winona.

Gilberg recollects, "One time when my daughter Sandy was young, I took her along with me on the milk route. We'd just left Winona and, as we got over the Mississippi bridge, the truck caught on fire. The emergency brake was stuck and somehow started a fire. We put it out by throwing milk on it. Sandy said it was the last time she was going to ride in the milk truck with me," he laughed.

Gilberg was paid a straight salary plus a commission, based on a point system. If he could sell more than what the customer ordered, he got more points and more money.

He even demonstrated new products, like the special bottles that bulged at the top to collect cream. He also collected the money customers owed at the end of the month. "That was always an extra long day," he sighed.

The Gilbergs have two children, Sandy, forty-eight, and Gary, forty-nine. "You know, to this day, Gary will not drink milk," laughed Ed.

Lois Gilberg worked as a cook at the old Trempealeau High School from 1955 to 1969, when she retired. Ed also retired in 1969 from Marigold, after twenty-four years with that company. He was forty-six at the time. He then leased the Texaco gas station next to his house in Trempealeau. The building was owned by John Pittenger. Gilberg planned to have his son, Gary, manage the business, and Ed was going to get a job in the local factory in Galesville. But the U.S. government had other ideas. Despite an old leg injury from playing backyard football, Gary was drafted into the Army. So Gilberg took over the gas station himself, full-time.

When Gilberg was two years old, he'd contracted polio, which left him with a slight limp. Still, it never slowed him down. He was an excellent athlete and a sports fan. After he took over the Texaco station, he sponsored a men's softball team. When Gary's hitch in the Army was over in 1972, he played third base and managed the team. Ed and Lois Gilberg were at every ball game cheering. Team members joked, "If they won the game, free milk for everybody!" I played several years for his team.

The Texaco gas station was a full-service station. Gilberg pumped the gas, cleaned your windshield, checked your oil, and also did mechanical work. Gary was employed there, too, and Lois did the bookwork. In 1985, the Texaco station became a Conoco station. Then, in 1991, Gilberg retired for the last time—sort of. At seventy-five, he still does snow-plowing for numerous businesses, churches, and homes in Trempealeau. He and Lois spend a lot of time on their front yard, which is a showplace of holiday decorations and meticulous lawn maintenance.

It's difficult to keep a man with that much energy in one place—especially a hard-working former milkman like Ed Gilberg. Echoes linger for him and for many of us, who still can remember those time-honored cries of "Milkman, milkman."

# One U.S. View of Seoul: Namdaemun

*David J. Marcou*

Namdaemun is like a perfume
if bottled right—not uptight.
She sings and hums
all the day long,
But at night and just before dawn,
she reveals all her charms—
like a great lady's interested song.
Have you noticed her aroma
during such times of yore?
All the splendor of flowers,
and still-bright-eyed working girls,
with the way to their souls expressed in swirls
of ginger starts
and silken hearts.

*Korean vase, 1985, Icheon, South Korea, by David J. Marcou.*

# Boxing: The Ancient Art of Pugilism

*Steve Kiedrowski*

"Put up your dukes!" That battle cry of boxing has been heard for centuries. The art of pugilism goes back to 800 B.C., where it was practiced by the nobility to demonstrate physical fitness. And at the third Summer Olympics, in St. Louis in 1904, there was a boxing contest for the first time in modern Olympic history.

In 1869, the implementation of the Marquis of Queensberry Rules changed the brutal contest of boxing with regulations that provided for, among many things, padded gloves, three-minute rounds with a one-minute rest between rounds for the groggy fighter, and no wrestling holds. Boxing had become somewhat civilized.

When I was growing up in Centerville, Wisconsin, in the 1950s and '60s, my dad (Art) would take me to the Winona (Minnesota) Athletic Club on Mankato Avenue to watch the boxing matches on the third floor. In those days, Winona was the axis of boxing in the area. Many good fighters also came out of Rochester. Watching live boxing was both exhilarating and exhausting. We cheered till our voices disappeared. I felt the urge to partake in the sport.

In Centerville, our family ran a tavern called Art's Bar, now known as the Sand Bar. Next to it was a garage and gas station that my uncle Frank Kiedrowski owned. In there, the neighborhood kids held boxing matches. We always wore oversized sixteen-ounce gloves to lessen injury. It didn't always work. Many times I beat a path home with nothing but a bloody nose to show for that midday battle. A little blood, sweat, and tears were lost in Centerville during those formative fighting years.

*The author, Steve Kiedrowski, in a boxing stance, 2002.*

My first three years of schooling were at the old Centerville School, along Highway 54/35. After that, the students were bused to Trempealeau Elementary for the continuing grades. I discovered in the fourth grade that the Trempealeau School had a carnival every year in the gymnasium. One event was a boxing match. Perfect, I thought—a chance to put on the gloves again for a little controlled pugilism. But wait—my opponent was the undefeated, three-time champion, Barry Eichman. We went toe-to-toe the first three rounds. Barry had a bruising right hand, but I caught him with a right uppercut, and it was all over: a TKO in the third round. To this day, we are still good friends.

After that, my interest in boxing began to slide a bit. Then along came Cassius Clay, a.k.a. Muhammad Ali. On May 25, 1963, at Freedom Hall in Louisville, Kentucky, he upset Sonny Liston to win the world heavyweight title. Ali was electrifying. I've followed his career ever since.

So last year, when *Ali*, the movie version of his life story, came out, I naturally went to see it. The film, starring Will Smith, rekindled the flame in this former fighter to lace up the gloves again. I feel that your body responds to your attitude. Maybe it was a case of myopic vision or some sort of rite of passage, but whatever it was, I wanted to box.

I contacted the Winona Athletic Club; however, they had stopped having boxing matches in the mid-'90s. Next, I tried the Lion's Den Boxing Club and Youth Center, in Winona. At the time, they were temporarily closed for remodeling, but they hope to reopen by mid-March 2002. The group is led by Dale Johnson, Larry Johnson, and Stu Goodwill. All are sanctioned, certified, USA Boxing coaches.

Dale said, "We get fifteen to twenty kids a night who are boxing and working out."

Every kind of boxing equipment, weights, speed bags, heavy bags, even a boxing ring, are used there. The old boxing ring was moved over from the Winona Athletic Club. Boxers range in age from twelve to twenty-four, but all ages are welcome.

Stu said, "We hope to do more things than just boxing. We want the kids to get involved with community projects, food drives, charity work, even maybe Bible study on Saturday mornings. Our objective is to develop well-rounded young adults."

Donations are needed, as are coaches. The long-range plan is to start having boxing contests back in the Winona Athletic Club again, possibly by the end of the year.

Winona mayor Jerry Miller said, "We may even have some outdoor boxing matches for Winona Steamboat Days this summer!"

With the Lion's Den not opening till mid-March, my next step was to call the YMCA in La Crosse, Wisconsin. I was fortunate. They were starting adult boxing classes in January at their Holmen, Wisconsin, site. So, for the last two months, on Monday nights, I've been boxing once more.

Our instructor was Bill Anderson. The first thing he said was, "I'm going to teach you the science of boxing."

He was an incredible instructor. The fifty-year-old fighter started amateur boxing when he was seventeen. He spent twenty-six years in the Army and retired an officer in 1999.

He stated, "I took up boxing to defend myself and to stay in shape. I got into a lot of scrapes when I was young."

Bill has yet to be beaten in the ring. He has a master's degree in Business Administration and hopes to teach school someday. Another of his goals is to revitalize the sport of boxing in this region. His two young sons, Joe, nine, and Sam, eight, show promise in their boxing skills.

Bill said, "Boxing has been a lifetime passion for me. It gives you power, agility, fitness, speed, and self-confidence. To understand the real science of boxing is a great way to stay in shape."

In our boxing class in Holmen, there were both men and women. One woman, who is a professional fighter, is Lorie (Klomsten) Mueller of Holmen. She grew up in Trempealeau.

Lorie said, "I started watching boxing on TV several years ago with my husband and father-in-law. One night I stated to my husband that I would like to try boxing."

They contacted the Winona Boxing Club in 1999, and with the help of instructor Larry Johnson, Lorie started training. Her first amateur fight was in the Twin Cities in an Upper Midwest Golden Gloves contest. She won! Lorie fought one more fight before turning pro. Her first professional fight was in Rochester last July. Her total record is a sparkling 3–0.

The thirty-one-year-old boxer said, "You really have to be dedicated to the sport because of all the time and traveling involved."

Lorie's four-year-old son and her husband go with her on their long journeys on the road.

"My husband is almost like my manager, too."

Boxing can be a family thing. It's an ancient sport that has been overshadowed by karate and Tae Kwon Do. But remember the old "one, two punch." That comes from boxing. Every punch has a number—for example, the one, two, three, five, and six (there is no four). Odd number punches are thrown with the left hand, even numbers with the right.

Boxing is a true one-on-one sport. I want to go the distance—to be the comeback kid. Maybe it's time to bring back boxing.

## Muhammad Ali: Champion
*David J. Marcou*

We remember you now,
not for your stand against the draft,
which was not wholly right,
but rather for your lightning speed,
your savvy style, your great showmanship.
You were, and are, the epitome of what boxing
should be all about, even though you might
not have survived Rocky, in his prime.
None other could have beaten
you, in your prime, though.
And the Olympics? You
deserved everything you received from them.
Youth should be knighted so incredibly,
even when it is no longer so ebullient.

## From the Series *Syracuse West*, "Part II: Recruitment"
*Jim Rodgers*

It was about the March mid-point, almost the onset of official spring, as I recall, that Admissions had scheduled a series of recruiting junkets to various locales that would, hopefully, serve to fill our student slots for academic year 2000-2001. Nothing all that unusual about this; such efforts take place every semester each year. However, this year, several multi-state excursions by various faculty and staff had been scheduled to occur simultaneously. As it turned out, the "Swedish Bachelor" contingent of the faculty (which, in fact, included several non-Swedish bachelor professors and one married one) was scheduled to travel to New Orleans for a visit to several prominent high schools, in search of new scholars.

Over the same weekend, Professor Larry Kristoferson, the University on the Mississippi (UOM) designate raconteur and theatre director and educator, was to travel to the sunny climate of California to rake in those hardy fruits— and even a few nuts— who would drop from the abundant trees of the university's brother and sister schools in San Jose and to visit with the great university alumni from that area.

Let me describe the New Orleans excursion to provide a full picture of how the natural or supernatural forces that oft accompany the vernal equinox played havoc on the best recruiting plans of the UOM faithful. The plane ride to New Orleans—the Queen City of the South—was uneventful, and it seems that the mostly bachelor professors got to their appointed hotel by cab without incident. The group had time for a fine Cajun-style meal and several drinks before retiring for the evening, doing so fairly early, in order to make their rounds first thing the next morning to the vital high schools that could serve the university as a supply source so well. Professors Bjorn Anders and Ben Samuelson were ensconced in one room, while down the hall, professors Jon Stensgaard and Morgan Longman were about to turn in for the evening.

Samuelson, a professor of criminal justice—one of the most popular and, in the twenty-first century, one of the most promising majors at the university—unfortunately discovered upon unpacking that he had neither suit coat nor tie, nor any other real semblance of formal attire for the morrow's presentation to the Young Catholics for Freedom League at St. Xavier's High School. Samuelson's dear wife, Melissa, had listened to her husband explain in detail how his chum and colleague, Kristoferson, had planned on going to California, complete with golf attire, and how the folks there were planning to entertain with several informal faculty-student outings, including a pig roast. Well, Melissa heard her husband say that it would be great to go with Larry, and knowing that Samuelson had a trip planned, mistakenly assumed he was off with Kristoferson on the apparently "informal" way to San Jose. She had not heard correctly, of course—Samuelson had said it would be great to go with Larry next year—two missing words of explanation that meant a world of difference, among other things. She had loaded the suitcase with all manner of golfing shirts, shorts, loud polyester pants, and not a dark or beige piece of clothing in the mix; plus no ties.

In horror, Ben looked at his roommate, Anders, and asked pathetically, "What am I going to do for tomorrow?" Checking the room clock, which read 10:10 P.M., Anders indicated that most clothing stores were probably closed by now, but that they should call the Hotel Randolph's bell cap and inquire as to what might be procured within a reasonable distance of this fine, genteel establishment. Following the bell cap's specific instructions, Anders and Samuelson proceeded to secure a cab for a drive from the Hotel Randolph to Simon's Fine Tailoring on Royal Street, in downtown New Orleans. Now the Randolph was on St. Charles Street near Lafayette Square; as such, the trip to Royal Street, a one-way thoroughfare, required that the cab travel down the infamous Bourbon Street, a one-way street parallel to Royal in the center of the Big Easy. Samuelson had once been on the great "Bourbon," when on his senior trip in high school, he and three other friends got roaring drunk and ended up spending a good part of the night throwing up in an alley outside one of the city's sleazier bars. About 4 A.M., the local constables had rounded them up and, in a spirit of genuine New Orleans kindness, escorted them back to their hotel, taking, of course, all of the $200 in cash the three had on them. Anders had never been to New Orleans, much less Bourbon Street.

As the cab traveled on toward its destination, Samuelson could see in the near distance many flashing blue and red lights and vehicles blocking the street ahead. At first, he thought it must be an auto accident, but as the cabbie slowed down upon nearing the commotion, he discerned that it was more serious than that.

Suddenly, from the side of the street, a scantily attired, orange-haired lady, mascara still thick, though melting in the humid heat, stumbled over to the idle cab and began screaming at the top of her lungs, "It's him! It's him!" This was said outside Samuelson's window and gave him quite a shock. Just as he tried to refocus, a rather rotund and graying police officer came over and motioned for all, including the cabbie, to exit the vehicle.

The officer, pad and pen in hand, began to interrogate the unfortunate trio as to their whereabouts and activities over the past hour and a half. As the three, beginning with the driver, recounted their innocent doings, Samuelson glanced over to the nearby street lamp, where he again saw the agitated lady of the evening and noticed that a young paramedic had handed her an ice pack, which she placed on her neck and chin. Just below those two, on the pavement, he could barely make out the silent shoes of an apparently well-dressed man, to whom oxygen and other more serious therapies were being administered.

Our Minnesotans plus unlucky cab driver were soon to discover that what had happened was a bit of a turf war between rival pimps. It seems that Boston Johnson, the unfortunate man lying on the wet pavement of this muggy night, had had his clock cleaned in a most effective way by Black Belt Willie, and Willie had thrown in a few chops and leg kicks to Johnson's now petrified harem. None of this should have been of much concern to two gentlemen from Minnesota on their way to buy a new suit of clothes, but the persistent questions of the stern policeman unveiled some dramatic coincidences. Ol' Willie liked to wear golf shirts and loud pants, seeing as how he had once been Southeastern Conference golf champion, in 1978 for LSU. Willie had a black belt in karate and liked to hang out at the karate and judo gyms when he wasn't seeing to his street operations. Further, Willie had black, gray-streaked hair, a moustache, was about six-feet-two-inches in height, had a bit of a paunch at 215 pounds, and usually looked as if he needed a shave, as did Samuelson. Willie, it so happened, had been born in Duluth, and had not migrated south until his golf scholarship in the 1970s. He liked to use phony IDs around the city and area, so the cops had difficulty pinning him down. Also, he rarely made street appearances himself, but usually relied on his ex-con surrogates to put the stiff on clients or ladies. Putting all this into perspective and relying upon the ever-honest answers of Samuelson, the police officer concluded that there were too many matches between Willie and Ben, so he needed to go back to the Hotel Randolph with the pair of Minnesotans to see if he could verify who they really were.

All might have been fine at the hotel, but Longman and Stensgaard had long been asleep by this time and, due to the Richter-scale snoring of Stensgaard, could not be roused even by the insistent cop. Trying to verify the Minnesotans' room reservations, time of arrival, and so on, also proved futile because of the night clerk's inability to comprehend the policeman's questions and the fact that he also did not know how to use the Randolph's antiquated computer system. Seems the clerk was a recent arrival from the not-so-sunny streets of Haiti. So, the policeman insisted that he be allowed to search Anders and Samuelson's room. Upon entering and finding a colorful array of golfing attire fit for any champion of the Southeastern Conference, and with description matches in every other category of appearance, the now surly gendarme stiffly arrested poor Ben and whisked him away to the local establishment for incarceration with the city's finest folks.

Anders proclaimed loudly that he would secure the release of his sad friend, and he was soon on the phone to Minnesota, hailing President Arnie Beauchamp in the middle of the night with his tale of woe. The next morning, a call from Beauchamp to a Bishop Whittaker, and a further call from Whittaker to Bishop Rochambeau in New Orleans, finally got the wheels of real justice moving in Ben's favor. Anders went down

*The thin blue line during Coon Creek riot, 1991, La Crosse, WI, courtesy of the La Crosse Police Department.*

by cab and picked Ben up at noon from the local icebox hotel. He later indicated that he would never forget the dazed, glassy-eyed look on Ben's face as one of his cellmates called after him, "Bye-bye Ben, Baby! Y'all take care of your sweet fanny, Baby Boy!" Ben apparently kept that dazed look throughout the long plane ride home and for two weeks thereafter.

Oh, yes, about the recruiting to St. Xavier's: Longman, although he is an instructor of international studies, had to give the presentation on criminal justice. Answering questions as to the whereabouts of the real Criminal Justice professor proved a bit more embarrassing than Longman's attempts to answer other questions. Of course, the *Daily Report* got the story of Samuelson's mistaken identity and highlighted the mug shot of him and the incarceration on the front page of their Sunday edition. Much embarrassment came the way of UOM, and many gloating chuckles came from a neighbor school, Riverside State Teachers College. A strange, but typical, note on the whole affair was the statement made to President Beauchamp by Professor Stensgaard, of the Statistics Department: "Ya know, Arnie; you sent three single men and one married one on that trip to New Orleans, and look who got into trouble. That tells you something, Arnie." (The trip, for all of its problems, brought about a record number of applicants in the criminal justice program; Ben's courses were filled to overflowing with fearless freshmen—future cops—the very next fall.)

## Connecticut and the Leaf Peepers
### *Nelda Johnson Liebig*

In 1992, my husband and I enjoyed a week of hiking in the Catskills of New York. Instead of heading home to Wisconsin, we journeyed east toward Litchfield, Connecticut.

"This is a good opportunity for you to visit your fiftieth state," Carl said, handing me a brochure. Carl was a history major, and when I married him, I knew my life would include travel and impromptu history lessons. In less than forty years, we had visited all but a few states. Now, in 1992, Connecticut was to be my fiftieth.

I browsed the brochure Carl handed me. "Oh—the state is only seventy-three miles north to south," I said, "and a hundred miles east to west. We can drive through it and be on our way home this afternoon."

Carl's silence told me he had other plans. I couldn't imagine taking more than a few hours to see a state that was one-twelfth the size of Wisconsin. At the New York-Connecticut state line, we stopped for the traditional snapshots of each other at the state sign. Another sign caught my eye. "You didn't tell me that the Appalachian Trail cuts through Connecticut," I exclaimed. It was a dream of mine to add segments of this famous trail to my backpacking adventures. As we crested a hill, we were greeted by gold, orange, and red foliage. The trees were near their autumn peak. Glancing down at the brochure again, I chuckled. "The locals refer to the thousands of autumn visitors as 'leaf peepers.'"

We made a stop in Litchfield. Old but immaculate New England homes and businesses surrounded the historic village green. The scene was much as it had been in 1800. As we drove on, NO VACANCY signs adorned every motel. I was glad we were camping.

We pitched our tent in a state park near Derby on the Housatonic River, in a serene rural setting, complete with cows and large, stately barns with windows. It would not have surprised me to see them adorned with gingham curtains, tied back with ribbons. I was falling asleep when I heard drums. Native American drums. I sat up listening. Carl read my thoughts and explained that it was a gathering of several tribes—an annual tradition, he told me. My Cherokee heritage welled up within me. I wanted to leave the warmth of my sleeping bag and attend the event, but I reluctantly agreed that wasn't feasible. I listened to the magic of the drums well into the night.

The next morning, I glanced at the state map Carl was reading. My husband reads road maps like normal people read the morning newspaper. "See," he said enthusiastically, pointing to the map, "this will be our route. Down to Bridgeport, then up to New Haven, then to Wallingford for a lunch stop. We will sightsee for a few hours in Hartford. Then, I'm saving the best for last."

"And what is that?"

"Mystic Seaport."

In the coastal town of Bridgeport, we saw numerous manufacturing plants. "The state is known as the 'Gadget State,'" Carl offered.

"Gadget State?"

"Small things have been invented here, including the first copper coins and handy kitchen tools. Also, the first stone crusher. The first football tackling dummy was created at Yale University in New Haven. The first American-made steel fishhook was invented here as well. And not just gadgets! The first submarine torpedo boat was built here in 1775."

I was duly impressed with the creative minds that called this little state home. We drove through Wallingford and its bountiful orchards that produced apples, peaches, and pears, wishing we were here at harvest time.

At Rocky Hill, we visited Dinosaur State Park, the site of dinosaur tracks over two hundred million years old. "Give or take a century or two," quipped Carl. I begged to linger at the park, but Carl's internal clock had our day planned.

Two rolls of film later, we left squeaky-clean Hartford and its immaculate white business buildings. "So Mark Twain really did write *Tom Sawyer* and *Huckleberry Finn* here," I mused. "I always think of him as writing in Hannibal, Missouri. And to think that President Bush's father, Prescott Bush, was a United States Senator from Connecticut. He was born in Hartford." Little did Carl and I know in 1992 that our forty-third president would be George W. Bush, also born in Connecticut.

Our station wagon, now stuffed with souvenirs and tourist brochures, moved along over hill and dale toward the southeastern corner of the state. As we went by Groton, on the Atlantic, we passed the submarine base. "The first nuclear submarine was launched from here," my tour escort informed me.

"How do you remember so much?" I asked. Then I saw the Groton brochure on the seat next to him. Again he had done his homework while I had browsed the gift shops along the way.

We dropped down into the seaport town of Mystic. Could that really be a three-masted wooden vessel at the dock? Carl caught my look of disbelief. "That's the *Charles W. Morgan*, an 1841 whaling vessel that sailed to the Arctic and the South Pacific." He handed me another brochure. "This is the Mystic Seaport Museum. I thought you would like it." I reached behind me and gathered a handful of pamphlets from the back seat. So much information about one very small state! Small? Well, maybe in land mass, but quite an impressive one in its beauty and accomplishments.

I breathed in the crisp salt air. "Let's stay another day."

Carl pulled into an information center to ask directions to the nearest campground. *(See photo of a famous Lebanon, Connecticut, church steeple on the back cover.)*

# Between the Lines

## *Jim Rodgers*

Between the lines, the game is played.
Within these lines, the best of baseball plans are laid.
When the boys of summer give way to the men
of fall, the game is played between the lines.
Between the lines, October winds push uncertain
hits here and there.
Between the lines, the heroes of old—Koufax,
Drysdale or Mantle, so bold—give way to
Schilling, Johnson, or Jeter, we're told—
new heroes who compete between the lines.
Between the lines, may the game be played,
This year and always, the Series for the
World, between the lines.

# Blue Laws
## *Ida Hood*

I will take you back to Sundays in the 1940s, when I was growing up. In our small community, Sunday was a day of rest. Church service in the morning was the start of the day for a good many people. Then came Sunday dinner at home, or an occasional dinner invitation to family or maybe friends, an afternoon of visiting, or a drive to see the countryside. This was our Sunday routine. Shopping on Sunday was not done—we couldn't, because stores were not open. I recall mention of Sunday Laws or "blue laws" as the reason for businesses being closed on Sunday.

Reference material defines blue laws in the United States as Sunday closing laws—forbidding labor, business, and other commercial activities on Sunday.

There is a history to Sunday legislation. It has been cited that in Rome in 321 A.D., Constance the Great commanded judges and city dwellers to rest on Sunday. England's Henry III, in the thirteenth century, forbade frequenting of markets on Sunday. In the early 1400s, Henry IV prohibited the playing of certain games on Sunday, and bodily labor was outlawed on Sundays by Edward VI in the mid-sixteenth century.

In America, soon after the settlement of the colonies, the Puritans had restrictions on Sunday activities, motivated by religion and as a means of regulating moral behavior. The term "blue laws" first applied to laws enacted by the Puritans in a New Haven, Connecticut, colony in the seventeenth century. An example of a 1653 Puritan blue law spoke of regulating activities "which tend much to the dishonor of God, reproach of Religion, and Profanation of his holy Sabbath."

In the late 1700s, after the American Revolution, the influence of Colonial Puritanism was not as strong, and blue laws were often abolished or not enforced. The Prohibition movement in the late nineteenth and early twentieth centuries revised the laws regulating moral conduct. There were bans on sale of cigarettes and alcohol; amusements and unnecessary labor on Sundays were prohibited; and there was local censorship of arts and entertainment. In the mid-1900s and after, blue laws were again ignored or repealed.

But why the term "blue" laws? One claim is that they were originally printed on blue paper—but no one has turned up with seventeenth-century sheets of blue paper or blue-bound books containing these Puritan laws. A more likely reason for the term is that the word "blue" is a belittling reference to something seen as "rigidly moral." A "blue nose," for example, is one who advocates a rigorous moral code.

An appropriate description of blue laws—or Sunday laws—today would be "deregulated," that is, restrictions have been removed. Take a look around at our local communities today. Shopping is a Sunday pastime, a time to get things done. I could speculate on reasons for the change in Sunday activities during the late twentieth and early twenty-first centuries. It could be the growth of suburbs with shopping complexes and malls, increased consumerism, and the change in values and lifestyles. In a word, Progress.

# Regis Takes the Trophy
*Virgene Nix Oldenburg*

**Editor's Note:** *In March 1952, the Eau Claire (Wisconsin) Regis Ramblers' high school basketball team won the state parochial school championship at St. Norbert's College, DePere. Nixie, who graduated that year, wrote this spirited poem later. (The first team Regis played was not mentioned by name in the poem, but it was Fond du Lac St. Mary's Springs.)*

The score was 50–52, with but seconds left to go,
when Kolstad called time out, and prayers were whispered low.
Nothing but a miracle could save us now, we knew,
but the fight was there within us, as our old anxiety grew.
We took the ball out, and dribbled it in the backcourt . . .
We stalled—as seconds grew so short . . .
Then all at once, Miller dribbled up the floor,
and as the bell was ringing, sank a two-point score.
St. Norbert's all went crazy, and the fact will still remain,
of miracles that happen, for a miracle saved this game.
In our overtime, we were perfect, for we built up quite a score.
We were in the tournament now, and sure to win a couple more.
We took Aquinas the next night, with a fight up to the last,
and the final game ahead crept up on us awfully fast.
St. John's marched onto the floor, averaging all of 6-feet-4,
but our team was tops and beat them, by a humiliating score.
And when the game was over, and we saw what had occurred,
we had barely won the first two, and easily won the third.
We were "State Champs" all the way, and glad as we could be,
that Regis took the trophy, for all Wisconsin to see.

# A Good Day to Greet a Friend
*Yvonne Klinkenberg*

Winter winds are starting to blow
trying to bring the glittering snow.
Leaves are dead on the trees
and letting go before the winter freeze.
The cold winds blow the chilly rain
to bang against my window pane.
The furnace comes on with its comforting heat;
I'm glad for the phone, my friends I'll meet.
We can yak a minute, or an hour or two,
talking over with them, the old and new.
So let the winter's blistering cold wind blow
'cause on the other end you're there, I know.

Top: Students and friends of the photographer, 1997-99, Ardie's Restaurant, La Crosse, WI, by David J. Marcou.

Right: Leno Lewis, a good man at an auction, 1980-81, Columbia, MO, by David J. Marcou.

Bottom: Newsman Charles Kuralt speaks on the night he was presented with the Pope John XXIII Award by Viterbo College (now Viterbo University), 1990, La Crosse, WI, by David J. Marcou

# Part II

# During September 11th, 2001

"The wise man looks into space, and does not regard the small as too little, nor the great as too big; for he knows that there is no limit to dimensions."—Lao-tse.

*Two boys on Liberty Island, September 8, 2001, New York Harbor, courtesy of Anna Muktepavels-Motivans.*

SECTION 7

# EYEWITNESS

*Twin Towers burning, September 11th, 2001, New York, NY, by Rick Wood.*

*Policeman comforting 9/11 victims, September 11th, 2001, by Rick Wood. Both photos are courtesy of the* **Milwaukee Journal Sentinel.**

# Eyewitness
### Charles Nierling

I go to work at the Mercantile Exchange just before 8:30 A.M., a bit earlier than usual. The report comes over the news that a plane has struck the North Tower of the World Trade Center at about ten minutes to nine, so some of us get a cup of coffee and go downstairs and watch. We are down there for about ten minutes, watching the flames spread and small pieces fall away from the building, wondering if the market will be shut down as this is such a horrible thing. I'm glad my former roommate is in Tokyo now, instead of on the 105th floor. People are casually chatting, wondering how the control tower and pilot could have erred so badly that this could happen, as it is obviously an accident. A whine starts and grows, and it sounds like an airplane coming in low. There is a very short moment to have the thought, *Uh-oh*. And then there is a fireball blowing out the north side of the South Tower. This is the most horrible moment for us there. Someone starts screaming, "Terrorists! Terrorists! Terrorists!" However, many thousands of people standing in the Winter Garden Plaza make a mob and dash toward the river, since the ferry to New Jersey is right there and appears to be—right then—the only way off the island and away from the machine guns that the screaming fellow must have seen.

This minute is still echoing inescapably through my mind. First the buzz, then the explosion, then the screams. I suppose this is the ideal goal of terrorism. I'd never seen it before, and terror is a truly unique thing. (In retrospect, I and the people closest to me were in no danger at that moment; but believe me, we thought the next attack would be directly into the New York Exchange.)

Of course, there is really nowhere to go in a hurry, with the water on two sides, a pair of burning 110-story buildings to the east, and a mad crush of insane people all around. We look back to the buildings as we shuffle, trying to exit through the park along the river. A body is floating down, almost too slowly, and you can practically hear the person screaming. It's one body out of how many hundred or thousand that must already be dead, but we see this life ending. It punctuates the degree of the situation. Someone chooses an 80-story free-fall over whatever it is like up there. For both men and women, previously dry eyes are welling up with tears. Another plane going over sends a spook through the crowd, but we take comfort that it is a silver fighter plane at high altitude. A fellow in a floor trader's coat is telling how he has just come down from the 70s in the South Tower. They were informed that a plane hit the North Tower, but that they were fine in the South, and there was no need to evacuate. An old black lady suggests that we all better leave, because if those things come down, they're coming down on us. She is being dismissed; they will never come down; they'll be there after the pyramids are gone. Ah, New York hubris.

The next worry, though, is that there may be poison gas canisters laced through the garden and park that would be an easy and effective way to exterminate all the people trying to get off the island, or just away from the scene, but thankfully the attack hasn't been coordinated in this fashion. The crowds, however, are impossible to escape. On the West Side Highway, a bus stops and lets out its passengers, an elderly group. One fellow is explaining to a local man that they are tourists, headed for the observation deck at the top of the North Tower. Another adds in a questioning tone, "Maybe we came on a bad day?" From this vantage point, there's a clear view of the first hit, and you can see the silhouette where the fuselage struck and the angle of the wings, spanning almost the entire width of the building. The light nature of the fellow's comment breaks the grimness of the moment, and I have time to be happy that I took this job instead of the one on the 79th floor. Another explosion brings me back to where I am, though, and I start moving inland.

Out on the street, someone passes in a car, yelling, "They hit the Pentagon! They hit the White House! The Mall is on fire! We're at war!" This becomes quite evident, as the military helicopters start to buzz the Hudson. This is the first opportunity we have for anger to mix into disbelief, but it can't last long. Somewhere in Tribeca, about ten blocks north of the towers, a car stops in the middle of the street with the radio on, so I stop to listen to the news. We're standing there watching the towers burn, and some lady is being interviewed over her phone on the radio, when she starts screaming. The fire blowing out of the second tower is replaced by a dark pillar, due, as we learn shortly thereafter, to the fact that it has collapsed. There are no screams this time. It seems that even the sirens stop for a moment as the world goes into disbelieving shock. (There was always a chance that someone would fly a plane into one of them, a very slim chance that terrorists would fly a plane into one of them—but next to impossible they could hit both of them, and no way they could ever take one of them down. That was proven in 1993, wasn't it?)

A minute later, people manage to start breathing again, but there is still silence, for the most part, from the onlookers. I continue my trek, hoping to make it to safety in the relative seclusion of the far Upper Eastside. Two miles away, I find a pair of pay phones that have only five people waiting. "We're sorry, all circuits are busy." I get a phone card and manage to leave a choked message to my mother and one to a friend. It's another hour before I can use the card again, as cellular service is out and others have turned to this method as well. A bit freer to concentrate on the situation, I stop to get cash. This network goes down shortly thereafter, leaving people not only stranded, but broke as well. I make it a mile east, through Union Square, before stopping again. At a café, the news comes on that the North Tower has come down. There's really no new feeling to have at this point, though. The dead horse is being beaten. I'm far enough away, by this time, that the character of the people has changed. Everyone has fear. The island has been completely closed off. Most businesses have shut down, dumping commuters onto the street with nowhere to go. We're all trying to avoid landmarks, so the usually sparsely populated areas are now dense with the aimless march. They all have fear, but there is no terror, which is a comfort in a way.

I stop at a pay phone and meet a woman I used to work with. She now works in this area, has been discharged, and is trying to figure out how to get to Brooklyn. She is shaking, and neither one of us can talk much. I manage to speak to my father here before making the last push. Sneaking between Grand Central and the United Nations is a mess, as these would be the best land-based targets—the center of the city and the center of the world. If there are guns, this is where they'll be. Another glut of people is at 59th Street, the bridge that goes into Queens, where they are letting people cross by foot. Everyone from Queens, Brooklyn, and all of Long Island, is trying to make it off Manhattan across there. But the character of the people has changed again. It's now mostly wonder and anger about the inconvenience. It's so far from the attacks that no one has seen it except on the news. I make it to a bar on the Upper Eastside, around 87th and 1st, before stopping to wait for the friend I intend to stay with.

I'm about seven miles away from the towers. I am not able to contact my friend, and wonder if he was with a client in the towers that morning. Phones are busy well into the night, and most cellular service for the city has gone down with the North Tower. But at least it is over for the moment. The people have become academic on the subject to an almost offensive degree, with apprehension about what will come next. Nothing so far. Subway service has resumed to a degree, but not to the south of Manhattan. I can't imagine that the trains I take to work have survived, as they are in and next to the towers. Life is resuming, although you can now discern three specific types of people by looking at them—people who have been down there, people who have lost someone, and people who are concerned. There's no telling now what will come next. I'm a long way from having been in the worst of it, and even I can't put real words to the situation, much less the implications that you'll have to decide on your own.

**Author's note:** *The city has changed. The world has changed. The meaning of life, I might venture, although could not argue, has changed. Except for sore feet, I'm fine today, although beyond shaken. Thank you for your prayers to date, but please continue them for the innocent victims and their families, the hundreds of rescue workers who have already given their lives, and those who continue to face the danger.*

*New York policemen marching on St. Patrick's Day, circa 2000, New York City, by Barbara A. Pauls.*

## Midst of Silence
### Lucinda A. Gray

Dim the lights of an amplified world. Melt the driven soul of commitments and obligations. Release the cursed spirit of guilt and shame. Be still and welcome the deep, hollow boom of silence that becomes an invited guest of suspended peace. It rises up in one's heart, a query of just how silence exists. Initially, there would be a special notice of its arrival. As it approaches, slowly gaining magnitude, it stills the breath that had previously roared in it. There is a spaciousness that has no beginning or end; its presence surrounds every particle of transported dust. All of a sudden, it is just silent. Trappings of the world slip slowly away, and its abruptness fades completely. Silence is rarely heard and nearly always ignored. The minute clash of a whisper, a gentle motion, or simple thought, are huge in comparison. The rising volume of silence comes when the spirit rests and peace becomes the aching ear's attempt to hear it. The roar of silence, in the midst of itself—depth, width, infinite!

## My City—New York
### Charles Nierling

The night of the eleventh, I was sitting in a bar with a friend. A friend of his had come to join us. This second fellow had struck up a conversation with a very attractive brunette at the end of the bar. I was rather absorbed in thought at the time, but my friend made time to comment on how lucky this fellow was. Around midnight, the brunette came to me, wiped away a tear that was sneaking unnoticed down my cheek, and kissed me. Although I was in no condition to reciprocate, I've never known a kiss so soft, so warm, and so perfect. She kissed me, and then walked out the door.

I wish people could know New York. I have received correspondence from friends all over the world, asking what hell we're going through here. I don't quite know how to respond to any of them. To know what we do and how we are now, to know what we feel and think, you had to know New York before.

My image of New York formed the same as virtually everyone else's—what one can see on TV, what one reads in the papers, and stories from someone who has a friend who visited there once. It is Babylon. The intense pursuit of money and sex reign over all other considerations, including such quaint trivialities as food and sleep. This image was confirmed with each of my early visits to the city, even during my first time living here in the mid-nineties. Three of these visits stick out in my mind. One trip involved a club with a sixty-dollar cover charge. A group of us walked into this place in semiformal attire. The first floor looked like us, with coats, ties, and dresses everywhere. The second floor was smoke and strobe lights—a standard club crowd. The third floor looked like a Nine Inch Nails video, and we'll leave it at that. The second trip involved visiting friends who had recently moved here. They took me to Times Square just because they thought I needed to see it. Nothing for entire blocks but neon advertising peep shows— and prostitutes carousing in that unnatural light. The third trip involved visiting the Salomon Brothers trading floor, the scene of the book *Liar's Poker* and the source, along with Drexel Burnham, for all the cultural mentality of junk bond glory and Wall Street dreams that persists from the 1980s. Even on my December 31st visit, calm as it was, you could hear the steady ring of thousands of cash registers going off, one after another.

I love and cherish my memories and my image of New York. I still keep them near the forefront of my mind. But my image of New York is not my reality of New York, or that of anybody who still lives here. The wild images remain alive in popular media because the outlandish reality of what once was, still sells, and any of these things can be found if you're willing to look, but they are no longer the norm.

It's hard to say why it happened, but the pre-September 11th New York had changed. The current mayor, Rudy Giuliani, has played a large part in it. He, his policies, and his police force—that have been criticized in the media more than praised—have made New York one of the safer metropolitan areas you can live in. Times Square is now owned primarily by Disney, and hordes of tourists now bask in the lights from the flagship stores and offices of any number of reputable national names, including Nasdaq and MTV. The Internet has scattered the money to be made in the market across the earth. In spite of this niche disappearing, many more have appeared in its place, and New York has benefited greatly from the Internet—there was plenty of money, and the talent was willing to chase it here to make the new dream a reality. With the work of the newcomers, the money has turned to wealth. This has been a new wealth, though, spread across a much larger part of the population.

The city is a macro-economy unto itself, and nearly everyone has benefited. For a nice, but simple, two-bedroom apartment, my roommate and I once paid $2,300 a month —a bargain for a pair of middle-income males in the staid business of finance. Everyone made money, everyone was trying to make more, but everyone was very nice about it. Shallow as it sounds, money freed the population. We could do what we wanted instead

*Ice skaters in Central Park, 1990s, New York City, by Barbara A. Pauls.*

of what we had to do, and this made us even more money that gave us more freedom to do what we wanted to do. To describe any aspect of New York, I usually compare it with Los Angeles. I think that in Los Angeles everyone has a story. Here, though, everyone *is* a story and a work in progress. Even with the economic downturn, this sentiment has remained. We are no longer so much in competition with each other. Each of us, doing well, helps everyone else to do well, which, in turn, helps each of us again. So we support each other, since this is what got us where we were. We did well. We were doing well still, in early September 2001. We could afford to be proud.

The pride of the entire population had a single expression. Traveling down the New Jersey turnpike sometime during my college years, I looked out the window for my first glimpse of the Statue of Liberty. The absurdity of a huge copper woman in a toga, looking out from an otherwise worthless island, was far outweighed by the symbolic significance of Her, a significance that can perhaps be conveyed only by a huge copper woman in a toga looking out from an otherwise worthless island. The Lady remained a symbol for me for quite some time, until I was walking to an interview in the city one day and looked up. And then, from there, I looked up again. And I kept looking up, farther and farther. And then I looked over. There were two of them! I had my new symbol. I had been infected with the thing that held all of New York in its grip.

I've since spent time in all of the buildings that have fallen or are being demolished. Looking out from a floor high in WTC7 was the most profound experience—only because it was a windy day and the entire wonderful view nearly made me seasick with the swaying of the building. The Cotton Exchange floor in WTC4, where cotton, orange juice, cof-

"Lady Liberty," June 2002, New York, NY, by Barbara A. Pauls.

fee, cocoa, and some metals are traded, was next, because it was just as hectic as are the other open outcry floors you see on the news, but it was incredibly cramped for the activity. Nothing in either of the towers—WTC1 or WTC2—was profound. All I ever saw were offices and more offices, no different from anything I've seen in Iowa, besides the view. There was a mall underneath the complex, with no stores of particular note. The buildings themselves were not ornate or pretty. The lobbies were far from impressive. The buildings themselves in their entirety, though, more than anything *the idea of them*, was one of the more beautiful things you could ever behold. They were our freedom. They were our strength. There were two of them! They looked out over the world, in not just one direction, but in four, and said calmly, because they did not have to scream: "Look what we are; look what we can do."

With the events of the eleventh, nineteen men said, but did not scream: "Look what *we* are; look what *we* can do." We have two problems now, living in New York and being a part of this. I have not conveyed, and cannot appropriately convey, just what these buildings were. I can say I no longer cry, but I do occasionally find a tear running down my cheek for losing these buildings that were so much more than buildings—that were the center and expression of pride for a population more than five times greater than that of the entire state of Iowa. I have seen this same phenomenon of the random tear, and an occasional scream of "They're gone!" from the homeless or borderline population of the city, who shared the same pride in their presence as those who owned multi-million-dollar companies in the buildings.

This is the first problem—simply that the buildings are gone and, unfortunately or perhaps fortunately, this is something that cannot be understood by anyone who has never lived here. The second problem involves the way they were taken. Five times the population of Iowa sustained the idea of these buildings and all of the dreams they represented in fulfillment or in promise, for thirty years. Ten men took them away in twenty minutes. These most incredible of all things were taken away. The second problem we face, then, is that no matter what we do, no matter how great the accomplishment, it can be taken away. We no longer have the freedom to take an idea and change the world, because we are not safe or secure to do what we want. This speaks nothing of the seven (or is it three?) thousand who are certainly dead, and their friends, or what may follow in the amorphous pseudo-war we are at the edge of. This is just the account of a New York mind as a New Yorker.

We have stood together as New Yorkers to create the good times. We all have the infection I spoke of. We were here together in health, and we are here together in our sickness. Our presence in this city is a choice, and it's the strongest marriage that can be imagined.

We are returning to work and life. It's not the same, and we can't see it ever being the same, but we are there for each other. We live together, just as we did at the club I described earlier. I went back to the Mercantile Exchange to retrieve personal belongings. There were an additional six mandatory security checks to enter my office besides those that were in place before, and rows of police officers and army guards stood between us and the site. I have never been called Sir with such sincerity so many times in all my life. My offices have moved, so that I am now a few doors over from the New York Stock Exchange. Troops in riot gear roam Wall Street, and this is actually a comfort. If the wind is wrong, you can barely breathe there, as the rubble continues to burn, but everyone is happy to be alive and back to work, including the floor traders, who wait in line for hours in the haze for their security inspections each day. My manager, who was a very successful securities trader and someone you would expect to be very level-headed and rational in any situation, has rearranged her wedding and honeymoon plans because she will not fly. For a brief time, *The New York Times* shifted gears—from reporting on political and economic news to profiles of the people who died on 9/11.

Ten days after the attacks, I was meeting a friend at a bar in the Village. I stopped to talk with a long-haired fellow wearing a black tee shirt and a large silver belt buckle, who was sitting at the bar, shaking his head, crying, and muttering, "I don't know, I don't know." I moved to Brooklyn earlier this year, where previously I could get only a nod out of people I passed on the street. I now get, "How are you?"

The night of the eleventh, I was sitting in a bar with my friend, when a girl I'd never seen wiped a tear from my cheek, kissed me, and then walked out the door. This is what life is like in New York after the attacks.

# Tragedy

*Blaine R. Thorson*

Life provides many avenues of travel—
a lot of mysteries to unravel.
Many will cause our faith to stumble,
if we don't sort out the rubble.
If, in a tragedy, some live and some die,
it's all right to wonder why.
But it is certainly ridiculous to think or
   say,
God made it happen that way.
To save some and destroy the rest
is not God or His test.
He doesn't choose or separate anyone,
nor is it His will that it be done.
His love and grace for us is always at a
   peak,
providing strength when we are weak.
If you escape mortal death with another
   chance,
make the most of it without a second
   glance.
*(Matt 5:45: Eph 6:9; Col 3:25; James 2:1;
I Pet 1:17; Acts 10:34)*

**Author's Note:** *Often, when a plane or train crashes, someone will survive or miss the connection and explain, "It was God's intervention." Or, "By the grace of God, I was spared. God was looking out for me." While faith is a good thing to have and hold onto, I think it is a stretch to believe that one or two were spared and God let the rest perish. Events happen in our lives that are sometimes unexplainable, remaining mysteries that escape comprehension. But they are just that; God neither wants nor deserves credit or blame!*

Mother Teresa (R) and fellow Sister whispering in chapel, 1985, Anyang, South Korea, by David J. Marcou.

A statue of Thaddeus Kosckiusko, Polish patriot and general during the American Revolution, 2000, located in Lafayette Square, Washington, D.C., by Tom Marcou.

*How long is forever, in the universe of time?*

SECTION 8

# HEARTLANDERS' IMMEDIATE RESPONSES

Jet on display, circa 2000, Arcadia (WI) Veterans Park, by Barbara A. Pauls.

America's tallest building, the Sears Tower, 2000, Chicago, IL, by David J. Marcou.

# Trapped
*Mark D. Smith*

Trapped in the stairway! Not by the sheer fact that it is narrow and steep—too narrow for one person to comfortably pass another; steep enough to be more like a ladder than stairs. Trapped! Not by the fire blazing in the room at the top of the stairs, its searing heat keeping the man ahead of you from advancing., the dark smoke not letting you see the flames, much less anything else around you. There is only the blistering heat threatening you, holding you back.

Trapped! Not by the crew of men trying to advance up the stairs behind you, unable to feel the intense heat. Unknowing, they curse the fact you have stopped them. Cramped themselves, they still try to move forward.

Trapped! You came here for what you thought would be a worthy cause. You came here, willingly following the order, "Come with me!" You came here, knowing a small child was somewhere in the room above, trapped. You had no way of knowing that you also would be trapped. Now you wish only to get out.

Trapped! Not by the fire that blocks your advance. Not by the plug of other firefighters that block your retreat. But trapped, just the same, by the thoughts now running fast-forward in your head. The knowledge that advancing means possible injury, and retreat most certainly means humiliation. Every insecurity about who and what you are is racing through your mind. All this, and you are still trapped.

Trapped! Your frustration overflows, and you scramble past the man ahead of you. The heat is intense, but not like that which retreat would bring. Someone is yelling, "Don't go!"—but you push ahead, mad at yourself for even being there. Trapped!

The fire is out now, and everything has gone dark and cold. A new family has lived in the house for several years. They know there was a fire there once and that a small child died. They know that you are still following the order, "Come with me!" They don't know that you were once . . .

Trapped in the stairway.

# September 11th and Photos in My Mind
## *Karmin Van Domelen*

The day began like any other for me. I shut off the alarm clock and suited up for my morning run. It was a beautiful September morning, and the run just felt good. Once back inside the house, I switched on the TV to catch the morning news. The lead story comprised the burning questions surrounding Michael Jordan's return to basketball. Would he or wouldn't he come out of retirement again? *Hmm, a slow news day,* I thought, shutting off the TV to continue with my routine. I could never have imagined how very wrong that thought would be. Some of our worst fears would soon come to life—and death.

After dropping my son off at school, I returned home and switched on the TV again. This time, I tuned in to discover the morning news team reporting on a plane that had crashed into one of the World Trade Center towers. I remember distinctly the clear blue sky behind the burning building as the reporters scrambled around to get details about the crash. The questions began to mount. Did something mechanical go wrong? It seemed unlikely that it was weather-related. Then the phone rang. It was a secretary from one of the elementary schools, asking me to work in the office for a few hours. I accepted the temporary job and dressed to go, with the news from the TV droning on in the background.

On my way to work, I turned on the car radio. "The south tower of the World Trade Center and the Pentagon have also been hit by domestic airplanes," said the voice over the airwaves. *Did I hear that right? Did he say the Pentagon?* I pulled into a church parking lot to listen intently to what was being reported. As the news rolled in, the faces of our family and friends flashed through my mind. *Where were they right now?* I couldn't help but wonder what was next. "More news at the top of the hour," said the reporter. With that, I realized it was time for me to drive on or be late for work.

As I entered the school building, the news of the collapse of the south tower was pouring in from a TV in the principal's office. Gasps of disbelief filled the room as we watched the destruction rage on. It was then that I noticed a sort of numbness setting in. For a moment I wasn't sure whether I was breathing. I couldn't feel my legs beneath me. All I could do was raise my eyes to the sky and choke out a prayer—a plea—"Please God, make it stop." Yet it did not, and at 10:30 A.M., the north tower of the World Trade Center collapsed, and, shortly afterward, we learned of the fate of Flight 93 in Pennsylvania.

*Troops marching, Oktoberfest, 1990s, La Crosse, WI, by David J. Marcou.*

As the day progressed, I watched the children running around the playground, some of them practicing soccer skills or throwing footballs and others hanging upside down on the equipment, while the fate of our nation hung in the balance. Again I prayed, "Please God, no more." At two o'clock my shift ended, and I drove across town to pick up my son from school. I met him as he ran from the building hollering, "Mom, a bunch of really bad guys slammed a plane into a big building in New York City and lots of people have died. We have been praying hard all day." I'd wondered how much he had been told. Apparently, enough to know that it was necessary to gather for special prayers in a small, Catholic elementary school.

"Why did those guys do that with the planes?" he asked. "Does this mean war like we see on the history channel?"

I found myself struggling to come up with a simple, reasonable answer, but I couldn't. I shook my head and said, "We don't know why just yet, honey. We will have to see what happens." He seemed satisfied with the answer, but in his eyes, I could see the confusion he felt.

Back at home, the painting contractor we'd hired over the summer was finishing up for the day. As I walked up the back steps, the song "I'm Proud to be an American" was blaring from his radio. I stopped to listen, and as our eyes met, he asked, "What is happening to our world?" We stood there, holding each other's glance, fighting back the tears as the lyrics played on. It struck me that it was the first time I'd really looked at his face, even though he'd been around the house all summer long. I'm not sure what was said to finally break the silence once the song's final refrain drifted away, but the look on his face stayed with me.

I stepped inside the door to check the answering machine and discovered six messages blinking back at me. I played the first one. It was my mother-in-law wondering if my husband was traveling. For the first time that day, it dawned on me that my husband was supposed to be in New York City for meetings, but they had been canceled the Friday before. *He's dodged a bullet,* I thought. One by one, the messages played on, each of the callers asking the same question: "Where is Gary?" The usually impromptu travel required of his job was cause for concern for many family members that day.

We left the TV off until the very end of our day. I hesitated to watch the destruction being replayed, but somehow I felt I needed to face the grim reality of it all and share the grief of our nation. As I watched the horrible images churn from the screen, the lines of distinction between our lives and those around the world who face the possibility of this destruction every day were suddenly blurred. Could this really be happening to us, in New York City, and at our capital? As I continued to watch, I took some comfort in seeing the love and kindness coming from everyday people like myself. It quickly became apparent what is most important in life and just how entangled our lives really are. Still, I went to bed wishing I had just left a movie theater and Hollywood had created the drama.

Since that day, many ordinary or familiar things have taken on new meaning. For instance, American flags have gone up all around us, and our definition of a true hero has been revised. No longer do we judge a day good or bad based on the rise and fall of the stock market. We have returned to our places of worship and take comfort in standing shoulder to shoulder in prayer. For many, life has slowed down, and we take pleasure in the simple things around us. For me personally, each time I hear a patriotic song being sung, the images of that day float on the words like a series of snapshots, and the feeling of sorrow lingers about like a ghost. I guess it's true that time heals all wounds, but I will never forget that day as long as I have a heart and mind to hold its memories.

# The Immediate Effect 9/11 Had on Me
## *Joyce Clason*

OUR WORLD HAS CHANGED FOREVER . . . and where was I when our world forever changed on September 11, 2001? As usual, I was up early, had taken my husband's first morning medications to him, had brought in the newspaper, and had drunk my coffee. The TV was tuned to ABC. The early news and weather report led into *Good Morning America* at 7 A.M. As I scanned the newspaper, sipped coffee, and moved around with my daily activities, the relaxed camaraderie between Charlie Gibson and Diane Sawyer changed to that of an impending serious news announcement . . . A little after 7:45, I believe, we heard and saw news of a plane hitting one of New York's Twin Towers. That day I had a golf tee time, and was readying for that, placing items in my car and doing other mundane things. While Diane and Charlie were speculating about the size of the plane and the probability of an accidental occurrence, a second plane hit the other tower. My oldest daughter and her family live two houses away from me, and I had to call her. She did not have the news on. She did call her husband at work, and then went walking. When she returned, the towers were down. Because it was Tuesday, and time for our area refuse collection, I was moving our garbage containers from garage to curbside, as was our neighbor across from us.

I said, "Do you have the news on?"

"No," she replied.

I said, "Our world has changed forever. New York's Twin Towers have been hit by planes and are aflame."

This is close to the context of my reaction, because there was no longer any doubt of the impact of this attack. *My God*, I thought, *it seems like yesterday that I stayed in the Marriott Hotel within the Trade Center with a group from Aquinas High School.* What a time for a news freak like I am to have to leave, but I had an appointment; my golf partners had worked on the Awards Day lunch meeting, and I couldn't let them down. En route, news of the towers coming down was startling—so much happened in so little time. When a third plane hit the Pentagon, and later a fourth crashed in Pennsylvania, it was a scenario of such magnitude. No one wanted to be away from a news source. If I had been at home, I would have been watching intensely. But I went on to another meeting, and the leaders were so sad, but they felt obligated to attend and carry on.

So much happened that day, with so many feelings and awareness and sensory changes—the very skies echoed the silence, as air traffic subsided for days. In the late night sky, a falling star was a cosmic occurrence and not what could have been a plane, as it moved on its way in the evening sky. 911, 911, 911 . . . Help, help . . . our world has changed forever.

# The Sky Was So Blue

## *Sharon Swenson Schmeling*

September 11, 2001, dawned sunny in the Coulee Region, with an autumn sky of pure blue. I remember thinking, as I stepped off our farmhouse porch, how good it was to be alive, and how lucky I was to be living where I could see so much of life. On this fresh Tuesday morning, I'd intended to be up and out even earlier, a list of busy errands running through my head. Already, it was almost eight o'clock, and I knew that the hardware store, the grocery store, and the lobby of the post office had been open for some time. I got into the Explorer, drove the six miles to town, and parked in front of the local hardware store.

Hurrying toward the entrance, I saw a business friend doing the same. Or so I thought. Actually, it was me he was hurrying toward.

"Your husband," he called, "where is he? He's out of state, right? He isn't flying back today, is he?"

I looked at him, puzzled. He seemed to be trying to rein in his expression, yet his words were oddly insistent. I replied with a smile, "No, he's not flying today, he's still in Kentucky with our son. Why?"

"Oh, thank God," he said; then his words rushed out. "Do you know what's happened?" he gasped. He half pushed me through the door of the hardware store. He was telling me something about a hijacked jet being flown into the World Trade Center. I could hear a newscaster's loud voice saying the same thing. Standing open-mouthed in the aisle were two clerks and a handful of customers, staring at a demo television turned on high volume. They were frozen into profile, watching the demo with their hands to their mouths, saying things like, "Oh, my God! Oh, dear God! I don't believe it!"

I could not seem to get my mind around what was going on. I remember asking, "What do you mean a jet was hijacked? You mean an ordinary passenger plane with people on it? It crashed into the World Trade Center? On purpose?" No one answered me. They were as one, watching and listening, in frozen profile.

Suddenly, a newsman was yelling, "It's happened again, they've just crashed a plane into the South Tower!" *Who did?* I wondered wildly. *Who is doing this? Isn't this just an ordinary day, a sun-filled day in September?* In front of our eyes was this horrific picture of the Twin Towers of the World Trade Center exploding in flames, the black smoke billowing against the pure blue sky of New York City.

We stood in that store in that little Wisconsin town, and we were stunned, unable to comprehend. When I made myself glance at the others gathered around, I realized that we all had the same look on our faces. I don't recall how long it was until the first person moved to leave. With reluctance, shaking, I too pulled myself away.

I got into the car and went to the post office, but I never got to the grocery store. I felt numb. I wanted to go home. I couldn't get there fast enough. Back in my own house, surrounded by my own things, which were miraculously as I remembered them, I turned on the television set and sat horrified and glued while the tragedy kept compounding itself: new footage of people jumping from the towers, new footage of the planes crashing into the towers, the sliding collapse, of first one and then the other, the mushroom of cataclysmic ash that clogged the mouths and noses and eyes of those running away from the towers, the rescuing firemen and policemen presumably lost as we watched, the crashes of two more jets into the Pentagon and the Pennsylvania countryside, the subsequent official and ominous grounding of all air traffic, and the President's orders to shoot down any stray aircraft headed for Washington D.C. or New York City. The order of it all was jumbled then, and it is jumbled to me now.

I sat there, alone. The unbelievable magnitude of this morning-gone-wrong was staggering. I could not—would not—imagine how hellish it must be for those directly involved. My mind would go just so far and then refused to go any further. I remembered that our two sons-in-law were on business trips, and my heart especially raced for the one whose home office is in Boston and who might well have been flying out of Logan International on this fateful day. I put in calls to our children—four calls to four states—and not one of them answered. What to do? I called my mother, concerned that she might be alone. My youngest brother picked up her phone. He was as emotional as I. We spoke harshly to one another, lashing out at this nightmare that we could not control. My mother spoke in measured tones; she said that she was all right.

Back I went to a television that I couldn't bear to watch and couldn't bear not to. The day had lost its perspective. My phone rang. It was one of our daughters, quickly followed by a call from another. Their husbands were safe, grounded in obscure places, said their anxious wives, but safe. The phone rang again. It was my own husband. Finally. We clung to each other over the distance of four states. I knew that at last I could weep. *We couldn't believe it, We couldn't believe it, We couldn't believe it,* we told each other. But then, before September 11, who could?

# September 11th, 2001
## *Joyce Crothers*

People in my generation used to ask, "Where were you . . . When Kennedy was shot . . . When Man landed on the moon . . . When the *Challenger* blew up?" The question for people in the current generation will be, "Where were you when terrorists hijacked planes and flew them into the Twin Towers of the World Trade Center, the Pentagon, and the Pennsylvania countryside?"

My mother called the morning of that fateful day and told us to turn the TV on—she knew we didn't watch TV during the day. My niece, Kim, was visiting us from Atlanta, and we watched the coverage all day and night. We cried in horror and disbelief as we watched and tried to understand how this could have happened. We cried for all those innocent people in the buildings and on the planes who lost their lives that day.

How could four planes be hijacked simultaneously in this country? How does someone brainwash another person to commit suicide by flying a plane into a building? How could anyone dare to attack the United States like this, killing so many people? We get insensitive to the accounts of violence in other countries that we see on TV every day because it has been going on for years, and sometimes centuries. But the United States had been fortunate up until now to have been virtually exempt from terrorism. Not any more!

Since all U.S. flights were grounded after the attacks, Kim was unable to fly home on September 12th, as planned. She did manage to get a flight back by the end of that week, but we were afraid to let her fly. She insisted and got home safely.

It seemed so quiet in our area across Lake Onalaska from the airport. We have gotten so accustomed to planes flying in and out over our house that when they were grounded, we really noticed their absence.

Since 9/11, I've become much more patriotic. Two days after the attacks, Kim and I decided to make pins—red, white, and blue ribbons with stars and hearts on them. Everyone else in town must have had the same idea, as we bought the last of the needed supplies. We made as many as we could and gave them to friends so they could show some of their patriotism.

I used to fly the flag just on Memorial Day, the 4th of July, and Flag Day. Now I fly it every day when we are home, except in inclement weather. It is getting faded and tattered, but it still waves proudly in the air.

One thing that scares me is that those terrorists lived among us, shopping, playing and working, and no one knew who they were. They shared our freedom and way of life, then turned around and attacked us.

How do we trust people again? How do we look at a person from a Middle Eastern country and not think that he or she might be a terrorist? When Kim flew home after 9/11, there was such a traveler on the plane, and everyone was nervous and kept looking at him. I know that this all really happened, but sometimes it seems like a horrible dream I could wake up from, and find out it really didn't happen. It is hard for me to believe that two huge buildings like the World Trade Center's Twin Towers could be reduced to metal scrap and dust.

One can't help but feel pride in the heroism that occurred that day—especially the heroism of the firefighters and police officers who put their lives at risk to help others, and the men who fought the terrorists in the plane that crash-landed in Pennsylvania, preventing it from hitting its target. Their families should be very proud. I wonder how I would react in a situation like that.

I know our world has changed forever. We will be suspicious of many things that we weren't before 9/11. Hopefully, we will be less concerned about "me" and more concerned about our families and other fellow human beings. Hopefully, we will consider each day we have on this earth a blessing and get the most out of it that we can, because we don't know what the future will bring. I, for one, will try do what's needed.

## Two Days to Remember
### *Aggie Tippery*

This week has been a time for grief, terror, and prayers, and of watching the TV news. Those of us not directly affected at this time have prayed and donned red, white, and blue, flown our flags, and let it be known that we are in this together. We can all help, in one way or another. The Red Cross can use blood, and if not blood, then money for expenses.

We will always remember this day, a fateful Tuesday—where we were and what we were doing when the news came to us. I was lying in bed, waiting for my husband to come and help me to my wheel chair. (I'd just come home the day before from the hospital. I had broken my ankle and had been hospitalized for two weeks.) My son Tom called and told me the World Trade Center had been hit. I reached for my clock radio and punched the On button. Minnesota Public Radio was reporting the events.

Soon, Ivan came back from his bus run and rushed into the bedroom. "Did you hear the news? We have been attacked by terrorists!"

I wheeled into the kitchen to watch the events on TV, and noticed the holes in the shattered windows of one of the buildings. They were shaped like angels in flight. It was as if the souls of the victims left their images as they floated through the holes and into God's light.

I remembered another day, sixty years ago, as vividly as if it were yesterday. I was twelve years old when Pearl Harbor was bombed. After our Sunday dinner, Dad had said, "I think we can go to a movie today. Babe is old enough to sit still and watch." Babe was my little sister, Ella Mae. That day, December 7th, 1941, was her second birthday. Marian and I could hardly contain our excitement. We hadn't gone to a movie since Ella was born. We piled into the car and headed for Caledonia and the theater. We didn't know what was playing, and I still do not remember.

Afterward, we went next door to Colleran's Café for a treat. The minute we entered the building, we sensed an air of excitement. "Bill, have you heard the news?" Charlie asked Dad.

"What news?"

"The Japanese bombed Pearl Harbor today. It's in the Hawaiian Islands. They've hit our ships in the harbor."

Others at the bar chimed in: "Listen to the radio—the President is going to speak."

There was silence in the café as we listened to the radio. We were at war! At twelve years of age, I didn't know how my life would be affected. I don't remember worrying much about it. If I asked questions, I was told to "shut up and listen." No grief or fear counseling in those days. Another thing I remember about that day at the café were the young men talking about joining the Armed Forces as soon as the offices opened the next day. It seemed as though everyone there wanted to enlist.

Today, I pray for our children. They are so protected from life. We have bent over backward to keep them safe from dangers of the mind and body. They have not learned that life is not fair—that it can be dangerous and unjust. These kids are the ones who will suffer the most now. There may be hardships and shortages of things they take for granted.

If young people have a grandma, grandpa, or older neighbor close by, they could visit with them. Ask for advice about what they (the children) can do in this crisis. The oldsters have been through the Great Depression, World War II, Korea, Vietnam, and the Gulf War. They have more than stories to share. Ask about letter-writing, helping the Red Cross, prayer, and church services. The youngsters will keep busy and help others, and they will not have time to be afraid. They will show that their pride in the U.S.A. is more than just wearing red, white, and blue.

As I write this, I have recovered from my broken ankle—just use a cane now. My husband and I are still watching the news every day and feel somewhat paranoid, but we also enjoy each day so much more. Life is precious, and we realize it now more than ever. We go out often to eat or to a special event, or just to take drives on a sunny day and enjoy our beautiful Midwest scenery.

We survived World War II, in which Ivan served in the Army in Germany; we were depression babies; we married after the war; and we contributed our share to the "baby boom" generation with five sons. We had very little extra money in those days, but learned to have fun anyway with the boys.

As our lives are bringing us closer to death, we are glad we are the age that we are, and we are not afraid of whatever is in store for us. We are survivors! God Bless the U.S.A.

# How September 11th Changed Our World

## *Helen Bolterman*

My husband, Wes, and I, as retired senior citizens, were engaged in our second leisurely cup of coffee and watching television on the morning of September 11th, 2001, when the tragic news flashed across the screen that changed our world as we know it. One of the Twin Towers in New York City was hit by an aircraft. We didn't realize the magnitude of it until the second tower was hit and a later announcement was broadcast that the Pentagon, in Washington, D.C., had also been hit by an aircraft. I felt a chill come over me as I thought, *How can this be happening? We have always felt so safe in our country.*

Terrorists had hijacked aircraft, four planes in all, with the fourth passenger plane having circled over Pennsylvania in what was feared to have been a plan to destroy the

White House, too. All subsequent flights over the United States were directed to land that day. A directive was given that if any aircraft proceeded toward the White House, the only alternative would be for a U.S. Air Force plane to shoot it down. This would have been a difficult assignment, since it would have meant the loss of lives of American passengers aboard the airplane.

Several passengers on the ill-fated airplanes became aware of other terrorists' attacks via plane that day through cell phone contact with their families. Thus the plan was conceived by some of the men in the airplane over Pennsylvania that they would try to overpower the terrorists and take over the airplane, one of the men being a skilled pilot. I and other Americans prayed that plans like the ones of those innocent passengers would be successful. As we later learned, in spite of these brave men, the airplane crashed, and all passengers, including the terrorists, perished.

*Old wagon wheel, 1990s, western Wisconsin, by Jim Solberg.*

We viewed the panic of people as they streamed from the towers. We viewed the rescue attempts by the brave firefighters and police officers who put their safety aside and worked to direct people out of the buildings. When the landmark buildings collapsed, many firefighters and police officers were among the casualties. We were elated when several firefighters were brought to safety from the collapsed buildings, with the hope that there would be many more survivors. But with the intense heat from the oil-fueled fires and the immense rubble, that was not to be.

We watched and hoped, but the numbers of casualties rose, and hospitals were reorganized to care for the many injured and burned survivors. Through the following days and weeks, we listened to the many stories from survivors. We revisited the events of September 11th, hearing the story about the blind man who was led to safety by his dog, people struggling down smoky and blinding stairways, and the businessman on the 90th floor who lost his own brother and all of his employees that day, but who courageously worked to get his company afloat again. We relived the stories of the brave airline passengers who died in their attempt to foil the terrorists.

The shock was great, and we asked, in our hearts, how these terrorists could be so willing to sacrifice their lives in their attempt to destroy America. Was their hate that intense? Who were these men, and how did they manage to hijack the airplanes or go undetected so long? It would later be learned that a number of them had false identities and were illegally in our country. They were trained and financed by their leader, Osama bin Laden, and the Taliban leadership in Afghanistan.

President Bush declared the attacks "an act of war," and vowed to find the terrorists who were responsible. Congress declared war against Afghanistan. President Bush gained the full support of the government and the American people in this action.

War is a frightening thing—to those of us who lived during World War II, did we not think it was the war to end all wars? We would now be fighting a different type of war —we would be fighting against people who place no value on human life. What will this mean in loss of American lives forced into combat? How will this affect our country's ability to fight back, and how long will the struggle against terrorism last? Fight back we will, in a unified America. American flags fly everywhere. Volunteers have come from all parts of our country to help in the cleanup at the disaster sites. Money has poured in from American citizens to aid the families who lost so much in lives, property, disruption from lost jobs, etc. May the world take notice—we will not succumb to the acts of terrorists. We value our freedom too much to let such acts of barbarity continue to occur. United we stand!

## Twin Towers Retrospective
*Mary Lou Ryan*

I awoke today,
haunted by the look of glee
on the face of an Afghan woman,
dancing in the street to celebrate our loss.
I ask myself: Why? Why the hate?
And the answer comes back to me
from vignettes on CNN, of little boys
throwing stones . . . who are answered
by tank attacks and air attacks upon their homes.
And the answer comes back from Michener's book,
*The Source*, which documents hate in Palestine
for generations and generations, long before Christ
brought his message of love.
Why the look of glee?
Whether right or wrong,
she must believe that we are the source of her sorrows.
I will never forget the sickness of soul I felt
as the Twin Towers burst into flames, and before my eyes,
imploded and fell.
When, oh when, will love replace hate?

# September 11th, 2001: A Poem
## *La Vonne Woodhouse Mainz*

Side by side, they stood proud and tall,
and watched the city from overall,
the ebb and tide of humanity.
The World Trade Towers, refined urbanity,
the powerful reached for them,
desiring to link with this gem.
In alliance they, too, were strong,
touching the world with its prong.

Hijacked planes struck from the skies,
as we watched with screams and cries.
Terrorists wielded their terrible crime,
with ugly hate none can define.
As millions watched the fatal strokes,
the Towers came down in flames and smoke,
falling—falling—falling down,
the Twin Towers crumbled to the ground.

Screaming throngs were trapped inside,
the crumbling Titans' downward slide.
Their souls were gathered, heaven-bound,
as America watched, aghast, spellbound.
Soon thereafter at our nation's seat,
hundreds died in one heartbeat.
A hijacked plane with innocents aboard,
crashed the Pentagon, untoward.

Ungodly fiends were not finished yet,
they commandeered another jet.
But heroic men took matters in hand:
They fought the evils o'er Pennsylvania land.
Bravely fighting till they crashed to the ground,
ending the flight that was Capitol-bound.
They gave their lives so that others may live,
American heroes, so much did they give.

Thousands and thousands came to search,
while countless others prayed in church.
Searching and praying for those to survive,
but so very few were found alive.
It is hard to fathom this hateful fact,
The purpose behind this cowardly act.
How could anyone plan this evil deed
to innocent people in our land of the freed?

For three decades, this sculpture stood in the plaza of the World Trade Center. Entitled "The Sphere," it was conceived by artist Fritz Koenig as a symbol of world peace. It was damaged during the tragic events of September 11, 2001, but endures as an icon of hope and the indestructible spirit of Americans. The Sphere was placed here on March 11, 2002 in memory of all who lost their lives to terrorist attacks at the World Trade Center.

*Barbara Pauls and "The Sphere," Ground Zero, 2002, New York, NY, by Barbara A. Pauls.*

# Part III

# After September 11th, 2001

"When I return to U.S. soil after having traveled abroad, it always feels good to hear an immigration agent say, 'Welcome home.' It feels good because in that moment, I have been identified as an American with rights and privileges."
—Roberta H. Stevens

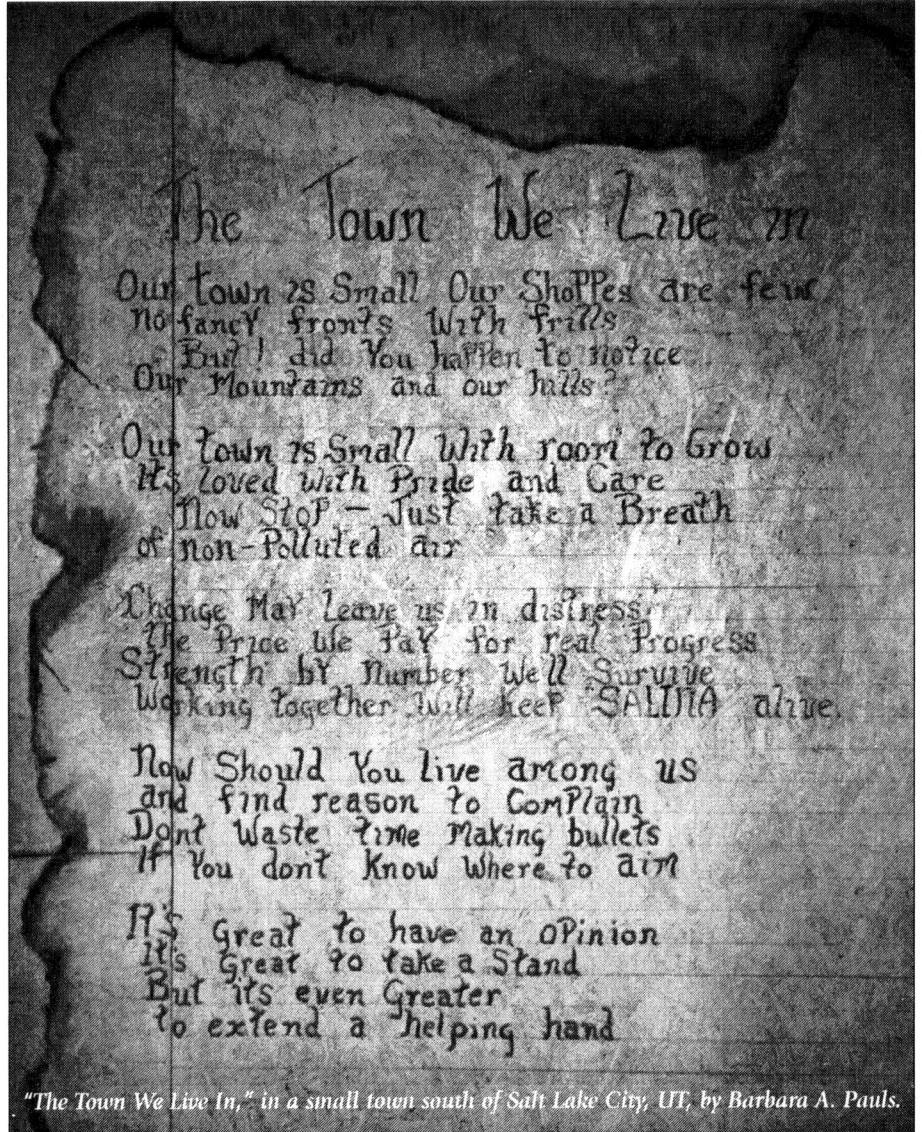

The Town We Live In

Our town is Small Our Shoppes are few
No fancy fronts With frills
But! did You happen to notice
Our Mountains and our hills?

Our town is Small With room to Grow
It's loved with Pride and Care
Now Stop — Just take a Breath
of non-Polluted air

Change May leave us in distress,
The Price We Pay for real Progress
Strength by Number We'll Survive
Working together Will keep "SALINA" alive.

Now Should You live among us
and find reason to Complain
Don't Waste time making bullets
If You don't Know Where to aim

It's Great to have an Opinion
It's Great to take a Stand
But it's even Greater
to extend a helping hand

"The Town We Live In," in a small town south of Salt Lake City, UT, by Barbara A. Pauls.

SECTION 9

# HEARTLANDERS' CONSIDERED RESPONSES

Right: Detail of Thomas Hart Benton mural at the Truman Presidential Library, 2001, Independence, MO, by David J. Marcou.

Below: Insignia of the many police and fire-fighting units from around the country that volunteered in the rescue and recovery effort at Ground Zero, 2002, New York, NY, by Barbara A. Pauls.

## American Heroes
### Mark D. Smith

*"Someone a person might call a Hero or Coward is often defined only by the moment they chose to run."*
—Firefighter EMT Mark D. Smith

I believe every firefighter who has ever responded to an emergency call has them: little scars on his or her soul. Like turned-down page corners in a book. They mark references, in our minds, to people or events on the job that have changed us. I can think of nothing that could make a greater mark than the death of a fellow firefighter.

The events of September 11th, 2001, were such events. The death toll suffered by New York City firefighters at the collapse of the World Trade Center towers was devastating. It brought to the public eye the reality that firefighters have always known: Ours

*Friends of the photographer on the grounds of the Statue of Liberty, 2000, New York Harbor, by Barbara A. Pauls.*

is a dangerous job. Firefighters have been injured and killed working in the Fire Service since it was founded. Only when the loss is high does it seem that the people they serve take notice.

Support for firefighters was never stronger than in the days that followed the terrorist attacks. People waved at us, shook our hands, and expressed condolences for fallen brothers of the New York Fire Department. All this came to us in Wisconsin, although we are safe and half a country away from New York City. Now, months later, it seems that people have for the most part gotten back to their normal lives, but words of thanks still come in more often than before. The waves on the street, however, are almost back to pre-September 11th days.

I'm sure the lives of the men and women who worked at Ground Zero have forever been changed. The survivors will carry a burden in their hearts only those who worked there could know. Will it be unlike the burden carried by firefighters who respond daily to emergency calls all across our country? For the individual who handle the calls, I don't believe so. Are the lives of the public they serve different now? I believe they are.

The terrorist attacks on America affected everyone who cares for the values of our country. The firefighters who worked the scenes of the terrorist attacks will carry another scar on their souls. This time, though, they will share that scar with the people of an entire nation.

# Letter to the Editor about Transplant Patients and September 11th

*Jim Solberg*

To the Editor, *La Crosse (Wisconsin) Tribune*,

I know I speak for all Coulee Region Transplant Support Group members when I send my sincere condolences to all who lost loved ones or were harmed in the terror attacks of September 11th, 2001. We will all stand firmly behind any rational efforts our country and the world will need to take to root out the fanatical perpetrators of such unspeakable horror.

As organ transplant recipients, we thank God daily for the tremendous value placed on human life by our nation and our people. We are grateful for the tremendous effort, expense, and sacrifices that were made to preserve the life of each and every one of us. It is almost incomprehensible to us that anybody, much less groups of thinking, planning human beings, using the modern financial and technological assets of the very world they seem to hate, could value human life so little. Surely, the God they claim to represent will see them as the worst sort of evil, not as the saints and martyrs of their own delusional madness.

After September 11th, we truly live in a different world. It didn't just change on that Bloody Tuesday—the evil has been lingering there all along—but our national perception has changed, and our need to react to this threat has become clearer. We can no longer pretend that we as a nation are safe from barbaric human brutality.

In spite of these sad circumstances, though, we as organ recipients still know and treasure one unchangeable fact—human beings in this world can create miraculous good as well as evil. We have hope that just as we recipients have survived illness and certain death, our great nation will also survive the challenges ahead, and will be even better for the effort.

Sincerely,
Jim Solberg

*(Jim Solberg is a co-founder and facilitator of the Coulee Region Transplant Support Group. Jim received a liver transplant at University of Wisconsin–Madison Hospital & Clinics in 1992, and now lives in La Crosse.)*

# The World After September 11th, 2001

*Bernard McGarty*

New York City lost two towers. I lost two friends. One was Richard Madden, my cousin. The other was John Hart, a parishioner. Whenever I see pictures of the smoke billowing from the two towers, I think of these two friends.

Michelle McGarty Madden is my first cousin. Richard, the third of Michelle's five children, age thirty-five, was married to Maura, and he was the father of Tricia, seventeen months. When the first plane hit, there was no room for Richard on a crowded elevator. The announcement "The building is safe, return to your workplace," was Richard's death knell. In the mid-1970s, John Hart was a blond, smiling adolescent at Saint Patrick's Parish, Eau Claire, Wisconsin. In class, his hand was always up, offering correct answers. In church, he sang loudly and prayed reverently. At age thirty-eight, married, and living in California with four children, John was visiting New York on September 11th, conducting computer seminars in the South Tower.

As earthly life was terminated for my friends, everyday life was changed for a nation. On September 10th, we groused when standing in line or stalled in traffic. On September 11th, we were patient in line and traffic. On September 10th, we worried about our stocks and bonds. On September 11th, we worried about our souls and eternity. On September 10th, we felt safe in mid-America. On September 11th, we felt vulnerable anyplace in America. On September 10th, we were at peace. On September 11th, we were at war.

On September 10th, we criticized our government. On September 11th, we sang "God Bless America." On September 10th, we bickered with family. On September 11th, we hugged family. On September 10th, we thought only of ourselves. On September 11th, we donated blood. On September 10th, we forgot about friends and relatives in New York and Washington. On September 11th, we telephoned the same friends and relatives.

On September 10th, the words Islam and Muslim meant little to us. On September 11th, we needed to know volumes about them. As we read the biographies and histories of the terrorists, we ask the perplexing question, "Why did they hate us?" I know five reasons why they hate us.

When the religion of Islam was beginning, from 622 to 632 A.D., Christianity was six hundred years old. In the following four hundred years, Muslim armies conquered countries with Christian populations in Arabia, Spain, North Africa, the Holy Land, Syria, Lebanon, and Asia Minor—which is one reason some Westerners hate Muslims, even today.

The first reason "they" hate "us": In the reign of Caliph Al-Hakim, 996-1021 A.D., the Church of the Holy Sepulcher in Jerusalem was deliberately destroyed. In response, Byzantine Emperor Alexiu asked Pope Urban II to assemble a European army to recapture the Holy Land. Nine Crusades followed, with horrible bloodshed. To Muslims, the Crusades happened yesterday.

The second reason they hate us: Islam Universities were centers of vast learning from the eighth to the thirteenth centuries. In art, architecture, philosophy, theology, medicine, mathematics, optics, astronomy, jurisprudence, and languages, they were world leaders, sharing knowledge with Europe. After 1250 A.D., Islamic leadership in science atrophied. European universities vaulted ahead, triggering the Renaissance, the Enlightenment, the Age of Science, and the Industrial Revolution. From these flowed technological superiority. Resentment lingers in Islam because of lost university glory.

The third reason they hate us: Colonialism saw European powers, like Britain, Germany, France, Italy, Spain, and Holland, invade and conquer Muslim territories. With superior battleships and guns, the European powers looked down on conquered peoples, exploited their resources, and labeled natives ignorant, lazy, and unsanitary. Resentment festered and grew among the conquered peoples. The United States is seen as the new colonial power because of our military and financial might.

The fourth reason they hate us: The wealth in Europe and North America stands in grim contrast to the poverty of many Islamic nations. The affluence of the West is seen as obscene by the Middle East. Sexual permissiveness, pornography, legalized nudity, violence, crude music and film are repulsive to pious Muslims. Our freedoms are seen as degenerate; our consumerism greedy—all fueling resentment.

The fifth reason they hate us: Stereotyping Muslims with the harem, particularly in political cartoons, evokes anger. Europeans have portrayed Muslims as libertines because a man may have up to four wives, with easy divorce. Americans publicize that Osama Bin Laden's father had eleven wives and fifty-three children. Negative events in Islamic countries dominate headlines: suppression of women, dictatorships, the religious police, political corruption, slavery, and denial of human rights are trumpeted on TV and radio. Muslim virtues are almost never reported.

When there is a clash of cultures, there is misunderstanding. The democratic process, emphasizing individual freedom, is difficult for many Muslims to comprehend. The union of mosque and state and domination of political, social, and economic life by the Quran and Sunna, is seen by the West as antiquated. Separation of church from state happened two hundred years ago in Europe and the United States. Islam sees us as greedy, arrogant, secular, and materialistic, in contrast to Muslim spirituality.

The attacks on the Twin Towers and the Pentagon, and in the airspace over Pennsylvania, arouses many reactions. One of the responses that is counterproductive is revenge. Revenge begets revenge, begets revenge, begets revenge. There are lessons to be learned from the decades of antagonism in Northern Ireland and in the Holy Land. Let us not follow those tragic models.

The world of Islam may be divided into two groups—Authentic and non-Authentic Muslims. Authentic Muslims are those who wish to live in peace with Europe and North America. Non-Authentic Muslims are those who wish to have a violent confrontation with Europe and North America. Can we in the West persuade Authentic Muslims to challenge non-Authentic Muslims to interpret the Quran and Sunna as textbooks for peace? Moderate Muslims carry the best chance of persuading radical Muslims to change their way of thinking.

In looking at the world after September 11th, 2001, we ask, "What can I do?" My answer is this: In mid-America U.S.A., most of us probably have limited contact with radical Middle Eastern Muslims. But we do have contact with our own consciences. We who call ourselves Christian must examine our secularism, materialism, greed, arrogance, sexual permissiveness, consumerism, cultural aggressiveness, pornography, legalized nudity, destruction of innocent life, despoiling of the environment, and reliance on force as solutions to problems.

If the adherents of Islam and Judaeo-Christianity fail to live in peace, we Jews, Christians, and Muslims—who constitute sixty percent of the world's population—risk the destruction—the annihilation—of our planet and its people. My friends Richard and John and thousands of other innocent people learned how hate can dissolve human opportunities for peace. But perhaps they did not die in vain. Perhaps their deaths have helped create new opportunities for peace, if we view them properly. If we Americans, including the Muslims among us, and all our allies, can wake up to the twin promises of true forgiveness and peaceful resolve, our world may grow up to a new day and to a new life, for all time and for all humanity.

# New Thoughts
## *Donna Huegel*

The terrorist attack on the United States that fateful day in September last year shocked the whole world. The ripples of it traumatized all parts of our country, even in America's Heartland, a thousand miles from the destruction. Here is the story of how it affected my small community and myself.

The first weekend after the September 11th attack was Applefest time in La Crescent, Minnesota, "The Apple Capital of Minnesota," where we've been celebrating our heritage every September for over half a century.

Should we carry on with the festival as usual or cancel it? Would canceling it mean the terrorists had won? Would anyone come if we held it? After all, airports were barely reopened, and people in America felt nervous about their safety. Would it be inappropriate to celebrate when so many innocent people had just lost their lives and the country was still grieving? Or would people be relieved to have a diversion from the tragedy?

Everything had been planned for so long that it was too late to cancel much of the event. We decided to go ahead with the festival and see what happened. Security was a concern, although terrorists had probably never heard of our small town and would have no reason to attack unless it was to make people in America feel there was noplace in the country they could be safe.

I was a volunteer for the Historical Society, which provides bus tours to the apple orchards during the festival. Although the thought had never occurred to me before, on the drive into town I regarded the other cars on the highway with suspicion. *Anybody could be a terrorist!* I thought. *They could even be driving down this very highway in one of these cars!* I knew, logically, that the chances of that were remote, but after the bizarre way the terrorists had attacked, nothing seemed improbable.

As we set up, we talked about the recent tragic events: where we were at the time, how it affected us and our loved ones, wondering whether some of our families in the military would be called to serve.

The crowd was smaller than usual, but I was surprised to see so many people. It seemed that the community indeed needed a diversion from the fear and grief that was enveloping the nation. It seemed as if they just couldn't stand to think about it anymore. Peoples' moods were sober, and they were restrained, as if at a funeral. They were polite but quiet. Nobody felt very chatty.

People on the bus tours also seemed to desire a diversion from the never-ending TV reports that brought no comfort, only fear and grief. On the tours, they heard of the distant past in the area—about happier times—times of persistence, triumph, change, and development—and stories of forefathers who made the town what it is today. The only change from previous years was that we added a moment of silence before each bus tour was on its way through town to the orchards. It seemed we had to.

The participants seemed especially appreciative of the tours, as if we had helped lift a sorrow, if only temporarily. Checking our guest book at the end of the day, we found that all the riders on our bus tours were from the immediate area, pretty much within a twenty-mile radius. There were no people from Texas, California, Florida, or Germany, as in previous years. People were not traveling great distances yet. The Historical Society also held its Art Gala, our largest fundraising event of the year. This year it seemed to be a major draw, as it displayed the beautiful and imaginative side of life and distracted people from the horrible reality of recent events.

The carnival rides were sparsely used, mostly by kids. The adults weren't ready for wild rides—it would have seemed a sacrilege. Parents stood mute, trying to smile for their children and pretend everything was okay. I looked around at the arts and crafts booths after the bus tours had concluded for the day, but there was no joy in it. Although I was going home to an empty house, with my husband out of town and the kids grown, I was almost relieved to get away from all the sad and sober faces of people still in shock from 9/11.

Once home I felt quite alone, but had planned to watch a video. I had just turned the TV on when the electricity went off! Normally, this would be just an annoying occurrence, but this time, my first thought was, *Oh my God! What if the terrorists broke into the power grid and left the whole United States without electricity!* The loss of lights, refrigeration, and TV were the least of my personal worries, but electricity also pumps our water, keeps people alive in hospitals, and keeps our factories and businesses going. Panic could set in if electricity were off for long. I dreaded all the consequences for our society and felt vulnerable, as if in a war zone. I was scared and wished my family were there with me. I checked the cordless phone to see if that still worked. It didn't! *Oh no, they got the phones, too!* I heard a plane come over and wondered if I should be afraid, since commercial planes were still scarce. But it passed over without incident, and I was thankful. I decided to try the other phones. *Hallelujah! They worked!*

Then I checked around the area to see how widespread the blackout was. Workers had been putting siding on the house the last few days. Could they have disconnected something? I looked, but that didn't make sense, since we had used electricity after they left. I surveyed the mess in the yard, with siding lying here and there, and imagined the bleak destruction of war. Finally, I called a couple of neighbors to find out if they had power. I was relieved, yet peeved to find that they did. So I called the power company to report the outage. They assured me they would get right on it.

While I waited, I sat on the front porch, watching the evening become night and the stars come out. But as it got dark my imagination began running wild and I thought, *What if there are terrorists out there? They could be hiding behind the bushes! What would I do if they came after me?* I wished my husband were home and thought of many other people who face the future alone.

I had to think of something else. I got my flashlight, a transistor radio, a lantern, and a book to read, and I lit some candles. So it was that I passed the next few hours until the electricity was restored. It wasn't so bad. In some ways it was even pleasant. Still, I was grateful that the power came back on and my life would be easy again.

It gave me a chance to think about what might come. I knew we could survive, but it would be a hardship. We all knew that life would never be the same again after 9/11. That's part of what the grieving is all about. Shangri-La was ruthlessly ripped from us on that horrible day! It's as if America had been cast from the Garden of Eden, and now life has to be hard. I still grieve for my community, my country, the world and myself for all we lost that day. The feeling of security in our communities had ceased—as suddenly as the electricity to my house stopped that day.

# Thoughts
### *Alice Cook*

This has been a year we won't forget.
And the last of the terrorism may not be over yet.
We have united together, both young and old.
We have seen the turnaround of the brave and the bold.
We do not know where this will end, or when,
but we are preparing for the thick and the thin.
Our flag has meant more in the last few months
than it ever did, just flying once.
We have prepared ourselves, our soldiers for war,
but truly hope we can just go on as we did before.
Our hearts go out to those we've lost.
In peace, in buildings, in duty, what a cost.
Many have given their lives, their family and friends,
Many have given their contributions—food, time, and stipends.
For the things that happened, we were not prepared.
The freedom, the prosperity, the peacetime we shared.
We know for sure that 9/11 was a wakeup call,
not just for you and me, the world and all.
Since then, we have heard about the stock market fall.
Perhaps we simply took for granted the greed in us all.
The lesson we learned has pulled us together,
for true Americans are like birds of a feather.
Let's hope we have seen the end of these terrorist acts,
and can go on with peace and tranquility, an American pact.
Let Old Glory fly high, her colors so true,
what an honor to be an American and fly the Red, White, and Blue.
Let's all bow our heads in prayer for all,
in memory of the men, women, and children who have answered God's call.

# My Special Place
### *Anna Muktepavels-Motivans*

**Editor's Note:** *After 9/11, we all need to find our own Special Place. Here is Anna's.*

It is sunny, crisp and calm on Sunday, September 17, 2000. I am sitting here at the edge of what used to be our volleyball court in our country garden hideaway. The net has not been stretched out this summer. The poles still stand fast in the thick, closely clipped grass. Oh, yes—my husband cemented them in really well—to last a long time!

For our family, the fall was always a time of exuberance. It used to be a time of renewal, a time for new class schedules at school and work. It was a time for all of us to get organized after a summer of scattered thoughts, trips, and sometimes days of

*Oak tree on prairie, circa 2000, Latvia, by Anna Muktepavels-Motivans.*

pleasure and rest. It was . . . well, that time is gone. Yet, every fall I feel nostalgic for the exuberant time that *was*.

This is the seventh fall since my husband died. At the time of his death, I felt as if my life had stopped, too. In the grief and sadness that followed, I learned to live on my own. My life is very different now. Yet once in a while, I still need to talk to *you*, my dear husband! I need to remember the brilliant falls when you were here, and the ones that came after you. What have I accomplished? What accounting can I give? To whom? I find that you are still my hero—nothing has changed there. When I need to talk or ask for advice, I come here. I walk on the cut grass, think, and sometimes chatter silently. I go back home refreshed and collected, to tackle any problem that comes along.

A sudden noise startles me. "Hey, there's a squirrel in the cottonwood tree!" Oh, yes, the walnut trees that you planted have grown tall and are bearing nuts already. The squirrels have a nest up in the big cottonwood, and they are quick to collect the walnuts that are all around. A few years ago, my colleague, Sister DeSales, gave me a bushel of walnuts so I could use the husks for dyeing wool. I did not have time that fall to do that, so I scattered the nuts in our gullies behind the barn. Now they are coming up as small seedlings. Someday, there might be a black walnut forest here!

I try to do my best to keep up this place. I still mow the grass with the riding mower all around the garden, the road, and the picnic area. As I feel the warm sun on my face, the scent of cottonwood leaves and the grass, I feel your presence here like a gentle hand touching me and a sound of the fragrant breeze: "It's okay! You are okay!" This feeling validates my life, and peace returns to my soul.

The sugar maples and oaks you planted have grown. Every fall their leaves turn bright oranges and yellows amongst the browns. That sight delights my heart. What a beautiful reminder of you!

Last summer there was a big storm, and many trees, especially the willows you planted, toppled over into the creek. They still are there, and I'm letting them be until they return to the earth. The creek is still running, except that the gully has become much deeper. The cottonwoods are all standing and getting to be bigger and bigger. I have read that Native Americans regard the cottonwood tree as sacred. Their medicine men still use the bark and fresh buds in the spring to heal human illnesses. They also have an inherited wisdom that the location of a cottonwood indicates that there is an underground water source close by, or underground springs. This fact has been lifesaving for people in arid areas and on treeless prairies.

The lilac and crab apple trees are overgrown. They still bloom in springtime. Some of the crab apple trees have succumbed to a disease specific to them. The birch trees are not doing well either—something makes their leaves turn brown and curl up in summer. Several of them have died. So have the Norwegian maples—a fungus under the bark killed them off. So far the sugar maples, oaks, black walnuts, hickory, aspen, and cottonwoods are well.

The grass around the fire pit has grown over its bricks. I should have cleaned it off, but I didn't. The picnic table and benches you built are weathered, and some are not too safe to sit on. Last week our friends from the potluck group gathered here for a picnic. We remembered you and Aggie's husband, Joe, who has left us, too. Yes, this place still holds the presence of you for all of us! I lit a fire, as usual, and we had good food and drinks. We did notice that our drinking has switched to iced tea and lemonade instead of whisky and beer! Well, maybe some wine, too.

I took some of the people through the prairie across the ravine. That is something new since you've been gone. No more growing corn! Instead, a wild, tall, grass prairie was introduced in 1996 and is doing well. There are many wildflowers and grasses growing now—a whole list of plants native to La Crosse County. I think you would like it. It took a lot of effort and money to establish it, but I feel justified. It definitely was worth the effort. This year, it was ablaze with shades of gold from several different sunflowers, coreopsis, compass plant, brown- and black-eyed susans—just to name a few. The Canadian rye, big bluestem, little bluestem, and Indian grass swayed in the wind.

Our friends enjoyed the walk, and everyone in the group felt well that evening. A full harvest moon rose over the hill. There were no mosquitoes or flies. Not a leaf was stirring—even the aspen stood still. It was as if you had given us that special evening.

Today, as I glance at the perfectly blue sky and the green and yellow cottonwoods against it, I feel peace within myself. Most of the songbirds have gone south already; only the winter birds are left. The silence surrounds me. The butterflies are enjoying the sun, and the bright blue bottled gentian gives a sparkle of blue to the fall grass. As I watch the bees scampering on the last blossoms of goldenrod and fall aster, I think of you and your passion for beekeeping. You wanted to try out everything that you had your mind set on, didn't you?

There again, I see a very beautiful butterfly, warming in the sun on the grass in the volleyball field! I hope you will forgive me for thoughts of building a little house here. I know—you swore my friends to this—that they should not let me build out here. You said that I would be too isolated here by myself. I can be isolated even in town—it all depends on one's frame of mind and physical ability. I want to keep an eye on that prairie! I'll be okay.

Oh, yes; the meadow across the road is all subdivided into lots. There are houses going up already. Our prairie, the gullies, and the cottonwood trees might be the only "green belt" here someday. We have to make sure that it stays that way.

## At the Edge of Life or Death
### Terry Smith

Our first responder page-out was like many of our department's medical calls. "Man down in kitchen, police officer on scene, CPR in progress." As soon as we arrived on location, two of us took over CPR from the officer. Other crew members then moved family members back into the living room and proceeded to get information on the patient and what they had witnessed.

With the weather hot and humid and no air conditioning in the small trailer home, this would become a tough call to work. After just a few minutes of doing chest compressions, the sweat from my forehead was burning into my eyes, then cascading down to my hands and pooling onto the man's chest. Struggling to maintain my hand positioning, I methodically pumped away at his heart. Any movement of my hand placement would decrease the required flow of blood to his brain. It would also increase the possibility of cracking some of his ribs, which could then puncture a lung. Whenever that happens, the snapping sound and vibration sends shivers through your body.

With perfect timing between my compressions, my partner fought to maintain an open airway so he could breathe life into the expanding lungs. Numerous times we had to stop CPR and turn the patient onto his side in order to release volumes of regurgitated liquid onto the kitchen floor. Then, with the airway cleared again, we flipped him back over and continued our rescue efforts. The smell, as always, rocked our senses from head to stomach. We mentally and visually fought off our body's natural revolt, and focused on what we had to do. Numbing your emotions at a scene like this allows you to concentrate on your work and not lose control of the situation. Learning to desensitize yourself is not easy and not without potential flashbacks.

Now, pressing on with our effort, we struggled to keep our knees from sliding away on their own, painfully balancing ourselves in a slippery pool of dinner and drink. We constantly looked up and checked with others on the location of the ambulance. Soon, a fellow firefighter bent over and wiped the sweat from my face, giving me a few more minutes of dry vision. With every stop of CPR to check for a pulse, I wiped my hands and the patient's chest, hoping for a dry, accurate restart. At this point, we were literally soaked from our heads to our feet, in both our fluids and his. I quickly glanced behind me to the family members, watching, weeping, and hoping. Slowly, I turned back to our patient, and as my eyes and my partner's met, we continued with our efforts to save him.

Suddenly, sounds of sirens echoed into the trailer. There was a grateful ringing to our ears as the ambulance arrived with fresh troops. Once inside, the paramedics put to work their defibrillator paddles and drugs of life as we watched for a good sign. After some time, with no change of luck, we loaded the patient into the ambulance while still performing CPR. Sometimes, the same crew will ride along and continue with CPR, but we were quite a mess and thankful that others made the trip. Of course, we still had a scene to clean up and family members to see off, as their terrible night was to continue.

The ride back to the station, whether short or long, can be a time of camaraderie and joking around or just the dead silence of deep thought. Usually, on a call as serious as this one, all is quiet in the dark shadows of the back of the rescue unit. Brothers and sisters, some with eyes wide open, some with eyes held shut, sit reflecting in their silent thoughts. We often find ourselves thinking back to the scene and wondering—*What had we just witnessed? What did we do? Did we do enough? Did we do everything as we were trained? What would we do differently next time?* Some of us think of our families at home, as if this had happened to them. Then sometimes, a sudden rush, a feeling of pride, sweeps through our bodies as we realize that we had done all we could, and maybe the patient will pull through.

Arriving back at the station, we snap out of our trances. Firefighters who didn't make the call are quick to help us with our gear and restock the unit. They can tell by our actions whether to tone down or keep up with their chatter. Some of the crew will stay to write up reports as others fly out the door, trying to get home before we have another call. We're volunteers, and not everyone wants to spend the whole night at the station unless we're really needed. Most have full-time day jobs we have to get to.

It's sometimes after midnight when I quietly let myself into my dark but peaceful home. Everyone is usually asleep at this time, although my wife tries to stay awake to hear how things went. After showering, sometimes twice, I try to slip quietly into bed, only to be asked, "How did it go?" So, I briefly tell my story and then slowly slip off to sleep. Deep inside, though, many of my thoughts and feelings stay buried.

Suddenly, the shocking sound of my pager going off vibrates through the bedroom—again! I leap out of bed as my wife buries her head under her pillow. I rush down the hall, banging off the walls, hopefully with most of my clothes on. Out the door I fly, pumped up like a track star, jacket and keys in hand, shoes untied, sometimes without socks. I back out in a rush, hoping the garage door is all the way up and trying not to take the side mirror off again! Miraculously avoiding the cars parked across from my driveway, I turn on my red lights and put the pedal to the metal. Before I make it to the first intersection the pager goes off again! "Onalaska Fire, you can disregard. This call is in Holmen's fire district."

So begins another day in the life of a volunteer firefighter. It is in their spirit—their calling—to risk everything to bring anyone back from the edge of death.

# Harp of Hope
## Steve Kiedrowski

*Reprinted from the* ***Winona (Minnesota) Post****, with the paper's and author's permission.*

Since ancient times, music has been associated with healing of the body, mind and spirit. Harps in particular have been shown to be beneficial to the human listener.

Harpist Dr. Diane Schneider of Winona says, "There are many different languages and people. To meet the needs of a multicultural world, we need something more universal than the English language. I found music is that universal language."

Diane plays not only for patients in hospitals, hospices, and nursing homes, but at many festive events like weddings, anniversaries, church gatherings, concerts, and parties.

Diane's pilgrimage to Winona, Minnesota, has been a protracted journey.

She was born in northern Kentucky and started studying piano at the age of nine. She graduated from the University of Kentucky and worked as a lawyer for the next ten years. While at school, she took up the harp. As a lawyer, she worked mostly with state and federal agencies, with physically and mentally disabled people as her clients. She was somewhat of a social worker for them, too. "I would hear many parents ask why their kids were disabled. I would work for their education, health plans and handicapped accessibility to public buildings."

After a decade in the field of law, Diane came to a crossroads. "I felt I wanted to spend more time with the deeper questions about God, suffering and illness." So she earned her master's degree in Theology from Xavier University in Cincinnati, Ohio.

In 1991 she received a Ph.D. in Philosophical Theology from the Toronto School of Theology in Canada. While there, she worked part-time as a pastoral theologian and chaplain. In 1995, a teaching job finally brought her to Winona.

Still, she wanted to do more. She wanted to blend her past knowledge, her experience, and her musical talents.

In 2000 Diane did a one-year pilot study testing patients' reactions to the harp in the Mayo Clinic system at Franciscan Skemp Medical Center in La Crosse, Wisconsin. The findings were fantastic! The gentle vibrations and notes of the harp helped to diminish pain and the need for pain-killing drugs. It also helped to stabilize blood pressure, relieve depression, slow heart rate, relax muscle tension, and alleviate anxiety.

In the Old Testament, King Saul called upon his harpist, David, to soothe his fears and anguish with the melody and harmony of music. The ancient Greeks and Egyptians, as well as people of Ireland, England, Scotland, and Wales, all cherished the harp as an instrument of healing. In the old Celtic tradition, the harp was known as the doorway between the worlds of heaven and earth.

Today, Diane provides therapeutic harp vibrations to patients at Franciscan Skemp Healthcare in La Crosse and at the Mayo Clinics of Rochester, Minnesota, and Jacksonville, Florida. She is continuing her study of the effects of harp therapy under a grant from the Franciscan Skemp Foundation. She works closely with the Oncology Department, ICU, and the Pastoral Care Department.

"I work a lot with people who are in pain and whose quality of life has diminished. With the harp, I choose certain strings in certain combinations, depending on the per-

*Dr. Diane Schneider playing harp, 2002, Winona, MN, by Steve Kiedrowski.*

son's condition and diagnosis. Studies have shown that the vibrations can reduce pain in a variety of patients."

One client claimed that the music of the harp took her pain level from a ten down to a two.

Diane declares, "The harp becomes my voice when I play it. We change each other by absorbing our own energy and moisture."

Sounds actually come from within the harp, not only from the strings. The flexible spruce soundboard vibrates, so most of the resonance comes from the hollow chamber at the back of the harp.

"The vibrations of the harp die slowly, and thus are soothing and therapeutic. That may be why we don't have a therapy accordion," she laughed.

In her practice, the most requested songs on the harp are "Amazing Grace," "Greensleeves," and the love theme from *The Titanic*.

Diane has recorded three CDs of her harp music, including "Harp of Hope," which is therapeutically sequenced for relaxation, anti-anxiety, and sound sleep.

Diane smiles, "The vibrations and musical notes of the harp are very healing, they give hope." The harmony of her arpeggio arrangements are heavy today with passionate hope.

# Christmas 2001

## *Donna Huegel*

Ever since the terrorist attacks of September 11th, I'd been feeling especially apprehensive about Ryan living in Los Angeles, eighteen hundred miles away from home. It was hard to see him move out there anyway, just weeks before that awful day that changed our lives forever. Sure, he'd been away at college for four years, but we went to visit a couple of times during the year, and he'd come home a few times each year. Some summers he was at home, and he'd always been home for Christmas.

But this year, he wasn't going to be here. He'd signed an apartment lease for six months only a couple of weeks before the attacks. Southern California had laid off twenty thousand people in technology jobs just before Ryan moved out there. After the attacks, Hollywood all but quit making movies, the industry Ryan was hoping to get into. Suddenly, people from the airline industry, tourism, hotels, and restaurants were also laid off. Ryan had to take any job he could find, and it turned out to be with Wal-Mart. But it was a job and would pay the bills until something better came along. He had no money to come home for Christmas, and even if he did, Christmas is the worst time of year to ask for time off in retail.

I tried to resign myself to the fact. "I'm not the first or only one to be without a loved one during the holidays," I told myself. I thought about people in the military service and about the families of the September 11th victims, who would never again be with their special loved ones during the holidays. I never fully realized the loneliness and heartache of it before.

As always in the holiday season, there was plenty to do, so I had no trouble staying busy. But the work of decorating, writing Christmas cards, shopping, and even baking, was a reminder that Ryan wouldn't be home this year. As I put ornaments on the tree, I remembered various fun Christmases with Ryan around. When I wrote the Christmas letters to go in our cards, part of my news was that Ryan wouldn't be home for this holiday season. It made me sigh with every card I sent. My holiday baking doubled, because I made duplicate recipes of cookies and fudge to send to Ryan to give him some of the home-style holiday cheer he'd be missing.

As tough as it was to be without him, I imagined how hard it would be for Ryan to have none of his family around on such a special day! He knew only a few other people in California. His roommate was an atheist, which made it especially hard for Ryan to celebrate at all. He thought he might spend the day with some friends of his roommate whom he was getting to know. They were Christians and weren't going home for Christmas either. It comforted me somewhat to know he wouldn't be alone on Christmas. I told him we'd call and secretly sent him a surprise phone card, so he'd call Grandma's on Christmas Day, where we'd be with his aunts, uncles, and cousins who could make it. He could at least take part in the revelry that way.

I shopped early for him so I could mail his gifts; hopefully, they'd get to him by Christmas Day. I worried, as Christmas approached, when I called and the packages hadn't arrived yet. It was understandable with the holiday rush and new regulations for checking mail since the anthrax scare. Still, I hoped the packages would arrive on time so Ryan would have some things to open from us on Christmas Day.

This year, I just couldn't get my fill of Christmas music. I listened to it all day almost every day in December. I don't know if this season seemed especially precious to me because of how we'd learned to cherish our loved ones since September 11th or because the traditions of the season gave us a sense of security in such uncertain times. Maybe it was both. Some songs made me sad, though, with refrains like "I'll have a blue Christmas without you," "I'm dreaming of a white Christmas, just like the ones I used to know," and "I'll be home for Christmas, if only in my dreams." Sometimes my eyes would fill with tears, but mostly I'd just sigh.

"It's life," I'd tell myself. I don't know why I expected we'd all be together every Christmas. After all, there were times when my husband and I couldn't be with our parents and siblings for Christmas. Our kids had grown up. That's the way life goes. It just seemed to come so suddenly that I wasn't prepared. I'd mention my despair to my husband, Len, once in a while. He was missing our son, too, but was more philosophical about it and would change the subject.

It didn't get easier as the holidays approached. I tried to imagine the scene of only three of us together, instead of the usual four, laughing and joking as we exchanged gifts late on Christmas Eve after church. It would still be pleasant, and we'd enjoy being together, but I knew we wouldn't be sharing the laughter we'd been accustomed to, with silly gifts as well as serious ones. How could we, when Ryan wouldn't be here to add some wisecrack to his brother Eric's jokes, like he always did? They are always so funny when they're together. It would be like hearing half of a joke this year.

Well, I tried not to dwell on it. I tried to stick to my routine as much as possible. I went dance-skating at the roller rink on Sunday, December 23, like I did most Sundays, "Family Days." In between rounds of skating, I visited with the other regulars, and we talked about the incident from the day before—the "shoe bomber" on a flight from Europe to America. Suddenly, I was glad Ryan wouldn't be flying home for Christmas. At least I wouldn't have to worry about his safety.

When I arrived home around 6:30 P.M., Len wasn't back yet from his day of last-minute holiday shopping, as was his usual way. He told me before he left that I didn't need to bother with supper, as he'd bring something home to eat. He also called Eric to come over around suppertime to help him unload something.

When the doorbell rang about 7 P.M., I went to the door to let Eric in. I opened the door, and there was Ryan, grinning and kneeling on the doorstep, like he did in high school when he went trick-or-treating with his friends! My mouth dropped open, and, there I stood, wide-eyed and speechless in my amazement. I opened the outside door, gesturing and telling Ryan to "Come in! Come in!" We gave each other big hugs, and I didn't want to ever let him go, now that he was here, safe, at home for the holidays.

When Len had asked me to write out my Christmas list for him, I wrote "Ryan" at the top of it, but like a child asking for an elusive Christmas pony, I never expected to get my Christmas fantasy! He had dipped into our savings and sent Ryan airline tickets two weeks earlier, unbeknownst to me. He and Ryan had kept the secret perfectly. Likewise, asking Eric to come to unload something was just a ruse to get him over here for a family surprise of the best kind. My heart was overwhelmed with a Christmas joy I'd never known before. It was the best Christmas present I ever got. It wouldn't be a blue Christmas, after all.

# First Year of New Millennium Was Great in Hokah

*Aggie Tippery*

Reprinted from the **Houston County (Minnesota) News** with the paper's and author's permission.

Yes, to my way of thinking, 2001 was the first year of the new millennium. My reason: I start counting with 1, not 0. Thus: 2001, 2002, 2003, etc., to 2010, would be the first ten years of the twenty-first century.

My town of Hokah, in southeastern Minnesota, was a busy town, getting ready for its 150th birthday party. New paint was applied to buildings on Main Street. The windows were decorated with scenes depicting the past. Banners and billboards proclaimed the event. Flyers invited celebrants to come to the festival. City Hall became a museum of memories of Hokah's past. The ballpark was transformed into a fun park, with games, food, music, and refreshments. A tent city with reeactments of olden days (before 1851) was erected in the swimming pool area. The fire station housed a card game on Friday night and a craft arena on Saturday and Sunday. Como Falls Park was God's own natural church on Sunday. Even the Root River got into the act, with canoes racing between its banks from Mound Prairie to Hokah. Two little children were chosen from a group of contestants to represent our town in the parade as Little Miss and Mr. Hokah.

The BIG weekend finally arrived with some rain on Friday, then clearing; and Saturday and Sunday were two days of the kind of weather Minnesotans wish for all summer. Sunny and dry, not too hot, not too humid—just perfect. Folks came home to Hokah from all around the country. There were family reunions, church gatherings, and visiting along the street, where old friends shook hands, hugged, and brought each other up to date. It represented the old-fashioned, leisurely kinds of days; everyone relaxed and just enjoyed each other and the events put on by the 150th Committee. The souvenirs and t-shirts will bring back the event in memories for years. It was a time that will be remembered with fondness.

The parade was exceptional for this small town. Units were lined up from the south end of Hokah all the way out into Butterfield Valley. Parade watchers staked out territory all along Main Street, from the south all the way to the "Y" at the north end. One watcher, unfortunately, missed the whole event except for being the first "unscheduled" unit in the parade. After I fell and broke my ankle on the way to the review stand, I was whisked away in the ambulance, not to return to Hokah until September 10th.

Then, on the morning of September 11th, the news on TV made my little injury seem very insignificant. A terrible tragedy had happened to our country. Everything that had happened in our town and around the country took a back seat to the news from New York. The American spirit soon revived itself, and we have been continuing to live our lives as normally as possible. The 150th Committee is meeting and planning a new celebration for next year. The rendezvous group is coming back again. The planners will have more of the same events that were so successful in 2001. Congratulations once again to Hokah and all its citizens. God Bless Hokah and America, and Happy Second Year of the New Millennium!

# And Now Every Day is Flag Day
## *La Vonne Woodhouse Mainz*

Our country's flag is flying everywhere these days. It waves proudly on newly erected flagpoles and from staffs projecting from citizens' homes, and it's attached to automobiles. It is displayed in store windows and on clothing. It is impossible to go anywhere without seeing this symbol of our country.

The horrific events of September 11th have sparked a new national pride in the hearts of Americans and brought us closer together, with a determination that the terrorists will not bring us down. Their actions have served only to make us stronger.

At this writing, the XIX Winter Olympics is being held in Salt Lake City, Utah. American flags are waving everywhere, and when an American Olympian is competing in an event, the crowd ripples with people waving American flags.

One of the most memorable events of the opening ceremonies was the moment that the tattered, torn, and dirtied flag that had been recovered from the rubble of the World Trade Center was reverently carried in for all to see. The thousands of cheering people in the stadium fell absolutely silent—so silent that one of the flagbearers said that all of a sudden he could hear his own footsteps. The television camera that panned the audience during that awesome exhibit revealed that many people had tears in their eyes as they viewed that special flag.

At the medals ceremony, when one of our athletes wins a gold medal, the American flag is raised and the national anthem is played, so many of the American recipients stand proud, with their caps removed, hands over their hearts, with tears in their eyes. I cannot recall that happening as much in prior Olympics.

Our medal winners are also as ethnically diverse as our country is. A Japanese American, a Cuban American, an African American, a Mexican American, and a Chinese American have all proudly earned medals for our country. The United States is truly a melting pot among nations. It makes me wonder why some other countries cannot accept ethnic diversity but revert to civil war among themselves.

National pride is running high in the United States. We have been accused of being a nation of flag wavers. I take that as a compliment. It has not always been so. Flag Day, June 14, 1998, passed without one mention of that special day in our local newspaper. Apparently no one even gave it a thought. I was saddened and wrote an article about Flag Day and the seeming indifference toward our nation's symbol. The *La Crosse Tribune* published my article on July 12, 1998, under the title, "Respect for flag shows respect for nation." It must have struck a nerve, because I received many cards, letters, and phone calls from people agreeing with me.

Three years later, in the June 13, 2001, issue of that same newspaper, there was an article entitled, "Flag Day event will be 'quite a ceremony.'" It tells of all the ceremonies and observances of Flag Day that would take place the next day and also states, "This will be the third time in recent history that La Crosse has had a formal Flag Day ceremony." I would like to think that maybe, just maybe, my editorial in June of 1998 had something to do with that.

# Remember
## *Terry Smith*

Remember the fallen—
spirits of heroes, this is their story.

Remember the fallen—
years of training, moments of glory.

Remember the fallen—
into harm's way, they rushed to save.

Remember the fallen—
so quick, so brave.

Remember the fallen—
whose families search for sanity.

Remember the fallen—
no longer with us but in memory.

Remember the fallen—
pure innocence in their flight.

Remember the fallen—
their silence awakened, they rose to fight.

Remember the fallen—
sent early to their graves.

Remember the fallen—
taken from us in the first waves.

Remember the fallen—
with no more visions of their tomorrow.

Remember the fallen—
hearts forged in steel, eyes of sorrow.

Remember the fallen—
souls lifted high beyond any doubt.

Remember the fallen—
first in, last out.

Remember!

SECTION 10

# REVIEWS (BEFORE & AFTER 9/11)

London Bridge, transported and rebuilt at Lake Havasu City, AZ, 1997, by Barbara A. Pauls.

## Bridging the Gap
### Reviewer: David J. Marcou

**150 Years of Photojournalism**
*(Jahre Photojournalismus, ans de photos de presse)*

Part I edited by Nick Yapp; Part II edited by Amanda Hopkinson.
Koln, Germany: Konemann, 2000.

Most non-Europeans have never heard of London's Hulton Getty Picture Collection, but many people have seen famous photographs from it—for example, those in this superb one-volume history, including Korean War refugees, by Bert Hardy; President Lincoln posing with spectacles in hand, by Alexander Gardner; General Robert E. Lee, sitting, posed between two standing Southern officers, by Matthew Brady; Churchill, FDR, and Stalin seated at Yalta, by an anonymous photographer; and Queen Victoria reading at a desk, by W. & D. Downey. Advertised as one of the largest picture libraries anywhere, the Hulton Picture Collection merged with Getty Images in recent years, and Hulton Getty now owns more than thirty million images. PBS-TV's *Masterpiece Theatre* series *Shooting the Past* was based on it. (*Note:* The two-volume hardcover set was published by Konemann in 1995.)

Published by Konemann, in Koln, Germany, this large-format, mainly black-and-white book draws all of its photos from Hulton Getty, and includes images from Roger Fenton's Crimean War (1853-56) work, which won him the title "first photojournalist." Photography was invented around 1839, simultaneously in Britain and France, but it's British photography, from 1850 on, that gets the lion's share of attention here. There are few U.S. photojournalists in the book, but many U.S. subjects, and many rare photos are also included. That few foreign photographers are represented even though Hulton Getty owns many photos from around the world is a weakness, just as is the scarcity of photographers from anywhere but America and Europe in George Eastman House's *Photography, from 1839 to Today*, published in 1999 by Taschen, also in Koln. Still, it's nice to see so many "new" images used well. Part I (1850–1918) includes sections on Street Life, Entertainment, Empire, Aviation and Railways, World War I, the Russian Revolution, and New Frontiers. Part II (1918–present) includes sections on Nazism, War in Europe, Cinema, the Changing Role of Women, the Sixties and Seventies, Civil Protest, Disasters, and Sport.

The "Hulton" in Hulton Getty derives from Sir Edward Hulton, who founded the groundbreaking *Picture Post* magazine (1938–57)—first edited by Stefan Lorant, then by Sir Tom Hopkinson, the co-editor's father—which gave rise to the Hulton-Deutsch Picture Library in 1947, which became the BBC-Hulton Picture Library, now Hulton Getty. "Getty" is Mark Getty, a leading entrepreneur. The collection's core comes from photos taken for *Picture Post*, which retained copyrights on all of its photos. Greats like Bert Hardy, Kurt Hutton, Felix Man, Grace Robertson, Robert Capa, Cecil Beaton, Leonare McCombe, and Bill Brandt took pictures for that magazine, and writers like James Cameron, George Bernard Shaw, J. B. Priestley, Dorothy Parker, and William Saroyan helped accent them.

*150 Years* focuses on key social, political, economic, military, transportation, entertainment, sports, and cultural history. Striking are photos of Adolf Hitler reviewing troops in a tuxedo; Thomas Edison in his micrography lab; Buffalo Bill and Annie Oakley, seen separately, in full costume; Nagasaki, post-A-bomb; Neil Armstrong and Buzz Aldrin on the moon; gymnast-phenom Olga Korbut performing; an Aztec couple in Western-style regalia; the fully equipped dining room at the London International Exhibition in 1862, and, a century later, Britain's response to the Beatles; Jesse Owens; Martin Luther King Jr.; Nelson Mandela and F. W. de Klerk; James Dean, with attitude; Greta Garbo, with style; Korea and Vietnam; Jerusalem and Mecca; the Sharpeville Massacre; Arthur Miller with then-wife Marilyn Monroe; members of the British Women's Institute dancing; Sarah Bernhardt at sixty playing opposite Mrs. Patrick Campbell; and racecar driver Graham Hill at home. The collection's contents are monumental, as this book suggests.

# The *Spirit* of America in a Book

### Reviewer: Aggie Tippery

Reprinted from the **Houston County (Minnesota) News**, with permission.

September 11th, 2001—Terrorists destroy the Twin Towers of the World Trade Center in New York City and the Pentagon in Washington. These acts were aimed at destroying the spirit of America, and they will never be forgotten by the citizens of this coun-

*Quills and desks, 1990s, Independence Hall, Philadelphia, PA, by Gerald A. Bonsack.*

try. However, the terrorists failed in their efforts to destroy our spirit; in fact, they have drawn Americans closer together.

Coincidentally, a book, *Spirit of America*, went to the printer shortly after September 11th, 2001, here in the Coulee Region. It is a collection of essays and poetry written by local writers.

From the book's cover, I quote: "This is the America that speaks in many voices: colloquial and professional, religious and secular, fictional and reminiscent, verse and prose, all of them heartfelt, direct. It is the America that counts its blessings and shoulders its burdens, struggling and dying in far places, stretching out a hand at home to needy neighbors or eccentric visitors. It is the America that its countless friends abroad remember and love."—John H. Whale, author, former teacher and journalist.

The book was produced by the Western Wisconsin Technical College Writing for Publication and Photography classes taught by David J. Marcou.

I am happy to announce that I have three writings in the book. I have been a member of the writing class for three years and have thoroughly enjoyed meeting the other local writers, getting to know them, and hearing their weekly contributions read in class. Most of these writers also have stories in the book.

I was going to write a review of the contents of the book, but there are so many wonderful stories in it that I couldn't possibly tell you about them. Instead, I read the biographies of the contributors and decided to tell you about them.

Telling where they were born, what they have done, and where they have lived will impart to you why this book is so remarkable. It is the spirit of these people that flows from the pages as you read their pieces.

They all have ties to the Coulee Region (of west central Wisconsin and southeastern Minnesota), and a great many were born in this area. Others are from many states and lands around the world. They were born in Arkansas, California, Colorado, Delaware, Georgia, Illinois, Iowa, Kansas, Kentucky, Massachusetts, Michigan, Minnesota, Mississippi, Missouri, Nebraska, New York, Pennsylvania, South Dakota, Washington, England, France, Germany, India, Latvia, and Western Australia.

Their occupations include homemaker, engineer, teacher, student, librarian, probation officer, copyeditor, social worker, midwife, salesperson, surgical technician, farmer, photographer, artist, nurse, architect, attorney, mayor, postmaster, landscaper, pharmacist, priest, and computer programmer. There are also many retired persons.

They have traveled, worked, or were educated in Ireland, Germany, Spain, Greece, Australia, New Zealand, Mexico, Egypt, Israel, Jordan, Italy, Canada, England, Korea, Kosovo, Norway, Alaska, Samoa, Mexico, and Russia.

Their hobbies include traveling, reading, sewing, knitting, fishing, tennis, hiking, computer work, swimming, basketball, foreign languages, family gatherings, skiing, good clocks, quilting, spinning, gardening, soap-making, playing pool, canoeing, biking, Indian beading, and writing.

They have lived and worked in the largest cities of the world, in mid-size cities, tiny towns and hamlets, and on farms or ranches.

They are immigrants or sons and daughters of immigrants of other countries, who left their native land to find a better life. Some are third and fourth generation Americans and Native Americans.

Several have served their country in the armed forces, in wars from World War II to the Gulf War. One author was a prisoner of war in Germany for nineteen months.

From the minds of this diverse group of personalities come stories and poems of family and nature, personal experiences both humorous and tragic, stories of love, and excerpts from true life chronicles and fictional novels.

David Marcou added the last essay in the book after September 11th. In it, he reinforces our beliefs in the spirit of the heartland and America.

Marcou and members of his photography class took most of the photos in the book. They depict life in America in many ways. There are a Muslim wedding, an Amish clothesline, family portraits, a picture of the Marcou family reunion, the *American Queen* steamboat at La Crosse, Del Ray Harbor Marina in Los Angeles, bicyclists on the Great River Trail, a sunset in La Crosse, the Gerber family Christmas tree, and many other pictures that tell a story of their own—of our American way of life.

*Some of the group responsible for producing* **Spirit of America** *and* **America's Heartland Remembers:** *Front (L–R): Matt, Rose, and David A. Marcou; (Back) David J. Marcou, Charles and Christine Freiberg, and La Crosse Mayor John Medinger, at Pearl Street Books signing for* **Spirit of America,** *2001, La Crosse, WI, by Louise Randall-Winger.*

## To Love—Or Not
*Barbara A. Pauls*

Slowly, cautiously,
we remove the scars,
from the surface of
our bruised and tender hearts.
Like unfurling tendrils
of a delicate flower,
we allow our feelings
freedom to live again.

To take a chance
at love and life.
Remembering well
pain, anguish, and strife.
To love is to live.
To not love
is as death,
tho we live.

## Great Day Coming: Civil Rights before the Movement

*Reviewer: David J. Marcou, for* **The Milwaukee Journal,** *January 1, 1995*

### Speak Now Against the Day: The Generation before the Civil Rights Movement in the South,

*By John Egerton. Alfred A. Knopf*

Ralph McGill, the late syndicated columnist and a progressive Southerner, told a University of Kentucky audience during the civil rights crisis in 1959: "There comes a time when you must stand and fight for what you believe, for what you know is right and true—or else tuck tail and run."

John Egerton has not tucked his tail and run in *Speak Now Against the Day*. He has, instead, fought for what he believes in: the righteousness and the truth of civil rights in this country.

But why, one might ask, fight for civil rights any longer in the United States? Surely, Oprah is worth a billion dollars, and nearly everywhere one goes, black Americans have their civil rights. Both of these phenomena may appear true, but the civil rights movement was about something more than the color of a person's skin. It was about equality for all human beings, black or white, red or yellow. It was about the greatness of the American nation.

In this detailed, thoughtful, and provocative study of the years immediately preceding the civil rights movement in the United States, when a black Gandhi—Martin Luther King Jr.—was in the making, Egerton rehearses the defeats and triumphs for equal rights in the America of the 1930s, '40s, and early '50s, when most citizens were struggling mightily with their prejudices.

Here, Egerton comments painstakingly on the role of New Dealers in bringing the issues of equal rights and "separate but equal" methods of achieving those rights into play—before the landmark *Brown vs. Board of Education* Supreme Court decision of 1954—the same people who forgot about anti-lynching bills when America went "reactionary" in 1938.

*Aasam and his kids, 1980-82, Columbia, MO, by David J. Marcou.*

But Egerton does not stop with the New Dealers. He goes on to outline the early efforts by blacks to organize successful self-help and interracial groups during the 1930s, such as the Southern Tenant Farmers Union.

He notes the efforts of people in many walks of life to make the whole United States a better place to live: clergymen like Martin Luther King Sr.; social organizations like the YMCA and YWCA; education leaders like Mary McLeod Bethune and Benjamin Mays; sports figures like Jackie Robinson and A. B. "Happy" Chandler; writers like Langston Hughes, Richard Wright, and James Weldon Johnson; President Harry Truman; and ordinary working folk in the South, both black and white.

The author takes his title from Nobel laureate William Faulkner's warning to his native South: "We speak now against the day when our Southern people who will resist to the last these inevitable changes in social relations, who, when they have been forced to accept what they at one time might have accepted with dignity and good will, will say, 'Why didn't someone tell us this before? Tell us this in time?'"

*Speak Now Against the Day* is a first-rate history of the people and events that made civil rights crucial to America. Egerton and his subject deserve our attention and our thanks.

# In Vietnam He Took His Stand

Reviewer: David J. Marcou, *The Milwaukee Journal*, May 1, 1994.

### The Last Klick

*By Robert Flynn Baskerville.*

Robert Flynn has a way with words—telling, taut, vital, frightening words. His tale of life and death during the Vietnam War may or may not become a classic of modern war literature, but because it ends with one of the most dramatic conclusions I have ever read, it should become clear to those who read it that there was something great and noble about the Vietnam War as well as something sadly and brutally ironic about it.

Sherrill O'Connell is a professor/author in search of the truth and perhaps a little adventure. He decides to leave his wife, Jennifer, at home in Texas (daughter Marie has died) and works out a deal with *Real Magazine* to write stories about the war.

At first, O'Connell stumbles along among the press corps with lackluster results. Then, one day he protects his group by picking up a rifle and killing three Viet Cong, which turns him into an instant hero back home.

However, his feelings about how far the war should go—all the way to Hanoi or into Cambodia—put him at odds with the antiwar opposition stateside. He carries a rifle into more combat situations, becomes a fixture in the pages of *Real*, and begins to lose his wife's admiration and trust.

Mobile Vietnam War Memorial Wall. The name of Robert Arnold, U.S.M.C., the only military person from Centerville, WI, to die in that war (on April 18, 1966), is highlighted. 2002, Arcadia, WI, by Steve Kiedrowski.

He meets up with some rugged Marines, writes a few good stories that are taken out of context by *Real* and others, and tries to come to terms with the lack of objectivity among the press corps, as well as with Marie's death.

After committing the greatest mistake of his Vietnam tour until then—making love to "The Commie Fox," Norela Cook—he sees his honest concern for a young girl turn into charges of pedophilia. He spends the rest of his time trying to prove that the war should be fought by the Americans—with different strategy—and that he never molested anyone.

Just before he is to go home, in a last attempt to prove the value of U.S. military involvement (in infantry talk, the last "klick," or kilometer) he steps on a land mine and is immortalized by a television journalist.

Because O'Connell's wife has done an about-face on him since hearing of the pedophilia charges, his only comfort in his extremity is the knowledge that the hero he has been creating in a new novel about the Korean War has really become himself. The author of his own fate, O'Connell demonstrates his courage, which is indeed "beautiful," as he says.

Robert Flynn wrote for *True* magazine during the Vietnam War. His fiction here is filled with the awful horror and feverish splendor of that war. His view of the press shows that it alone did not rescue America from the debacle it contributed to creating. Flynn uses words to reveal a true literary Texan—Sherrill O'Connell.

# At Centennial, Steinbeck's Easy Reading Still Draws

*Geeta Sharma Jensen,* **Milwaukee Journal Sentinel** *books editor*

John Steinbeck was fired from the *New York American* in 1925 because his news stories didn't stick to the facts. His fictional reality, later showcased in such celebrated American novels as *The Grapes of Wrath, East of Eden,* and *Cannery Row,* earned him the Nobel Prize for Literature in 1962.

Today, thirty-four years after his death, and in his centennial year, he is as popular as ever—despite the cold shoulders of some academics who see his socially conscious fiction as somewhat sentimental and not worthy of full inclusion in the Western literary canon.

But Steinbeck is in the American psyche as much as Twain or Faulkner or any other writer who has told the story of America in the nineteenth and twentieth centuries.

If Fitzgerald wrote about the rich in America, Steinbeck gave us the life of the ordinary man. If Hemingway wrote about emotional brawn, Steinbeck wrote about the moral center.

Readers continue to flock to Steinbeck. He has never been out of print. Viking, his longtime publisher, sells around two million paperback copies of his books each year.

Paperback sales of *Of Mice and Men,* his 1937 story of two close friends pursuing the American dream in the farms of California, reached about 450,000 copies last year, nearly as many as the 500,000 or so copies of a title Oprah can sell by picking it for her TV book club. And *The Grapes of Wrath,* Steinbeck's Pulitzer Prize-winning novel of Dust Bowl migrant workers in the 1930s, sold 250,000 copies last year.

"Steinbeck's sales indicate he's widely read and appreciated and certainly taught a lot in schools," says Michael Meyer, a De Paul University English professor who recently completed a Steinbeck bibliography. "He's definitely being written about. Over a fourteen-year period, I found more than four thousand entries about him and his work."

Steinbeck was born on February 27, 1902, in Salinas, California. Celebrations have been going on since August to observe his centennial.

More than two hundred events are planned nationwide this year, among them a three-day conference next month at Hofstra University in New York.

Viking also has brought out handsome new paperback editions of six of his novels. They are being sold individually or as a boxed set along with a new hardcover collection of Steinbeck's nonfiction *America and Americans,* edited by scholar Susan Shillinglaw and Steinbeck biographer Jackson Benson. The reissues are selling well, said Michael Millman, a Penguin editor.

Yet, amid all of this adulation, there's a fault line in academia.

Steinbeck's popularity has ebbed and flowed in the higher-level literature classrooms of universities. While *The Grapes of Wrath* always has been studied in one university course or another as a defining novel of America's social history, Steinbeck's other novels have found more consistent favor in high school courses.

California, for instance, requires third-, eighth-, and eleventh-graders to read Steinbeck. His easy language and his strong, visual style make him accessible to younger students, some teachers said.

"Oh, he still has considerable appeal. At the same time, he's not so fashionable or hot —at least at our university," says John Goulet, professor of English at the University of Wisconsin-Milwaukee. "But I think his books are worth looking at carefully [at universities], and were I to teach a course on the American novel from 1900 to 1950, I would certainly strongly consider teaching him."

Shillinglaw, director of the Center for Steinbeck Studies at San Jose University, says Steinbeck has always been relevant and popular.

He's certainly being taught more in college, she notes, now that humanities and cultural studies are so much a part of English departments. Even such areas as environmental studies read Steinbeck, she said.

"He suffered at the hands of New Critics after the war," she said last week. "They began to look for ambiguity and symbolism in a text, so modernist texts like Faulkner and Joyce, which seemed to be the most complicated and different, got more attention —and [realist] texts like Steinbeck got little attention."

The divide seems to be between those critics and academics who side with Harold Bloom—a Yale University humanities professor who's come to be seen as an authority on the Western literary canon—and other academics, Californians and Midwesterners among them, who view Steinbeck as complex, working on many levels, artistically as well as socially and morally.

Bloom recently told *The New York Times* that Steinbeck "couldn't get Hemingway's music out of his head."

He dismissed *The Grapes of Wrath* as a politically correct book. Yet, less than two years ago, he had termed *Grapes* "the authentic American novel of the now-vanishing twentieth century," whatever its aesthetic flaws. He also included it in the appendix of his water-roiling 1994 book, *The Western Canon*, in a list he called "A Canonical Prophecy."

"[Bloom] has been dismissive of Steinbeck," observes Meyer, who will lecture on Steinbeck at the Hofstra University conference later this month. "Academia tends to think of Steinbeck as bourgeois or too sentimental, too appealing to the masses. He's not considered intellectual enough for those who think you have to be highbrow to be literary.

"But it's strange how we have given permission to these Eastern scholars to tell us how to read and what to read."

Bloom, a purist whose aesthetic sense springs from Shakespeare, is automatically suspicious of art that's hijacked for social criticism—art that smacks too much of political correctness. For him, the criteria is an amalgam of literary originality, figurative language, cognitive power, knowledge, and exuberance of diction, among others. Yet he also acknowledges that the freedom to be an artist arises out of social conflict.

Meyer and about seventy others scheduled to speak at the Hofstra conference are ready to take the argument to those quarters: to Steinbeck's works and what the Nobel committee called his "sympathetic humor and keen social perception"; to his honest representation of a changing America and the troubles and disillusionment of rural labor and the downtrodden; to his literary experimentations; and to his clean prose, which, though clear and spare like Hemingway's, also contains its own rhythms and patterns.

Shillinglaw says Steinbeck can be read on several levels. Steinbeck himself said there were five levels to *Grapes*, and four to *Cannery Row*—and if people reread Steinbeck with care, they will see him as a major social critic, artist and environmentalist.

In *Cannery Row*, for instance, Steinbeck's depiction of the tide pool, where Doc and the aimless local denizens muck about for biological specimens, can be viewed as a human tide pool—a place where connections are made.

"It's about the whole, the humanity, and it stretches to the metaphysical," Shillinglaw said.

Meyer and company opine that an American writer doesn't have to be part of the Paris pack to produce good literature.

Steinbeck said he didn't have the funds to live and travel in Europe, as so many American writers, including Hemingway, were then doing. He stayed home and wrote about what he knew. And what he knew gave his work heft. It was only in his later years, after the success of his novels, that he began to travel extensively. He moved to New York City in 1945, when he was forty-three.

**A Modest Beginning**

Steinbeck, the only son of the manager of a flour mill and a former school teacher, lived in Salinas and summered in the family's cottage near Monterey. The family was of modest means—his father had a few work-related setbacks—but he grew up in a home filled with books and developed a love for Mark Twain and Jack London.

He started writing stories in junior high school, studied literature and writing at Stanford but left in June 1925 without a degree. He then moved East, where he held a string of odd jobs, including one as a laborer in Madison Square Garden. He tried his hand at journalism, then returned to California the following year to write fiction. His first novel, *Cup of Gold*, was published in 1929.

"Migrant Mother" (revealed decades later to be Florence Thompson, who said she once lived beneath Steinbeck's Bakersfield Bridge), a 1930s icon, by Dorothea Lange, courtesy of the Library of Congress Prints and Photographs Division.

His recently published nonfiction collection, *America and Americans: And Selected Nonfiction*, reveals his broad reading, his love for intellectual talk with friends, his irony and dedication to his work, and his decency. He brought a journalist's eye to his fiction; his nonfiction was enriched by his narrative strength. He noticed those whom society usually didn't. In a 1956 newspaper column on the national political conventions, he noted a hot dog seller whose arms had been burned repeatedly by lifting the hot dog steamer.

Bloom believes it takes at least two generations to determine whether a writer is canonical. Steinbeck's long-term staying power, then, remains to be seen. But this much can be said now: He is a writer who can be read on many levels, and if you grow up in this country, you will read him at some point.

Steinbeck endures.

Copyright 2002, Journal Sentinel Inc. All rights reserved. This review is reproduced here with proper permission.

## Heart Home
### Barbara A. Pauls

Home is where the heart is,
but you must first feel at home
in your own heart.
Then you are home,
no matter where you are.
(After traveling Europe, 1996)

# SECTION 11
# AMERICA'S HEARTLAND REMEMBERS (AGAIN)

*Eagle flying high near tree, circa 2000, western Wisconsin, by Lori Peterson.*

# Wings of Freedom
## Terry Smith

From the powerful "Mighty Miss" to the meandering "Black River Bliss," these masters of uplifting thermals command the pristine skies over what many call "God's Country." Here, in the heartland of America, our national emblem, the American bald eagle, patrols our numerous waterways, searching for its favorite meal of fish. These giants of the blue, proud and majestic, glide effortlessly over wandering valleys and hidden coulees, between the magnificently carved bluffs of a long-in-retreat Ice Age.

Now, starting in early February and sliding into March, it's prime time in western Wisconsin for watching the fishmasters of the sky as they put on an aerial display that rivals the Blue Angels. As they soar high above Mother Earth, their keen eyesight can pick out a fish from up to a mile away. Then they dive at speeds of up to a hundred miles per hour, even faster than a falling share of Enron stock. They level off and sweep in, snatching a fish out of the water with their vise-like talons. Most of the time, here on the Black River, they drop out of a tree or lift up off the ice and approach their prey in a shallow glide, then drop quickly with a splash, although they usually miss.

Usually, bald eagles migrate in the winter, but if fish are plentiful, they group up and hunt side-by-side along the rivers. Our rivers must be healthy here, because the bald eagles are out in forces of hundreds again. On the Black River, along the Interstate 90 and Highway 35 corridor, the eagles have lined up, wing to wing, like penguins on an Artic ice cap. In their white caps and dark suits, the eagles take over all the ice edges and polka-dot the trees from La Crosse to Onalaska, Wisconsin. This grand performance by the Barrymores of the stratosphere has been breathtaking to the multitudes of people lucky enough to witness it.

What has to be one of the best spots to observe this natural wonder in our own backyard is the Embers Restaurant at Highway 35 and George Street in La Crosse. Located right off the Interstate and directly across from Shopko Bay, it's like a hot tree stand during rut in a Wisconsin deer-hunting season. You can sit at a table in front of the bay windows and watch the eagles through binoculars provided by the restaurant. You can dine on a fish sandwich while scoping them out as they dive for their lunch.

Many people observe this display from the parking lot, while others brave their way across four lanes of highway to the guardrail along the river. There, they line up like paparazzi at a Britney Spears concert, with binoculars and cameras, some on tripods, all the while trying to keep their rear ends from getting clipped off by traffic coming from the Interstate.

Even in the backwater sloughs, from the Black River to the Mississippi, bald eagles control the water, trees, and sky. The whole river basin area is alive with these birds of greatness, these birds of history.

Driving across the Interstate can even be an exciting experience. While my wife and I were driving back to Wisconsin from Minnesota one day, we suddenly had a near miss with a huge bald eagle with a seven-foot wingspan. It glided across the front of our car at rooftop height. It was a formidable sight, and at that moment, it looked bigger than our car. We thought it was coming through the windshield. I was sure there would be claw marks on the roof. So much for deer and cows being Wisconsin's only large-animal driving hazards.

Eventually, back at the water's edge, things were starting to get tight in the eagle lines as they jockeyed for top position. This was looking more like opening night at *Lord of the Rings*. Every now and then, an eagle got bumped into the river. Quickly, it jumped back onto the ice with a frenzy of flashing talons till tempers cooled down. Now, due to warmer temperatures, good ice is at a premium. This forces many eagles to soar over La Crosse's north side looking for food. Their large outlines, sweeping across the neighborhood sky, cause every bird, rabbit, and squirrel to race for deep cover. Even a mother mourning dove leaves her nest in a flight for life.

As sunset quickens its pace, eagle activity begins to slow down, though a few can still be seen against the beautiful backdrop of the Minnesota bluffs on the western horizon. The flight of the great bald eagle tends to freeze you in your tracks, mesmerizing your thoughts and visions. Several years ago, as I canoed down the Black River to North Bend Landing, a few eagles had just that effect on me. My wife and I were awestruck looking up at one perched proudly above us in a tree, as we slowly floated under it. It was at this point that we accidentally crashed into some friends in another canoe, who were crossing over in front of us. Their canoe promptly rolled over into the shallow river, much to their disdain. As much as I tried not to, I couldn't stop laughing. Somehow, they're still good friends.

The bald eagle has been the national emblem of the United States since 1787, when it was put on the Great Seal. Nowadays, you can find it on everything—coins and stamps, pottery, clothing, company logos, on state seals, and even in our music. In fact, a carving of a bald eagle is on the lid of first President George Washington's casket at Mt. Vernon. The great bird has even made it to the moon. Remember? "The Eagle has landed."

The American bald eagle represents the spirit of freedom. As our skies continue to fill with the returning eagles in growing numbers, their graceful shadows are cast throughout the valleys, ridge to ridge. They are the essence of our great country; the "Wings of Freedom."

## Safe Harbor
*Barbara A. Pauls*

A ship is safest in the harbor,
but that's not what
ships are made for.

## A Balanced Reassessment of the Life of the Late Junior Senator from Wisconsin
*David J. Marcou*

**Author's Note:** *This essay was inspired by a former teacher of mine, John Whale, who told me he wondered why Joe McCarthy hadn't been mentioned in* **Spirit of America**, *the book I co-edited with LuAnn Gerber in 2001. This essay was written in early 2002, the 45th anniversary year of McCarthy's death, and sums up a sad chapter in U.S. history, while* **Spirit** *is a positive comment on America, generally. This essay answers John Whale's query.*

The eighteenth-century French philosopher Jean-Jacques Rousseau wrote in *The Social Contract,* "It is impossible to live in peace with those we believe damned; to love them would be to hate God who punishes them; we positively must either reclaim them or torment them." Impossible as it seems, this essay will neither seek to wholly reclaim nor torment the soul of the late junior senator from Wisconsin, Joseph McCarthy. Instead, it will reassess his life with a balanced eye, inspired by the unconventional, yet balanced enough, view of him by Arthur Herman in his recent book, *Joseph McCarthy: Reexamining the Life and Legacy of America's Most Hated Senator.*

First, some of the McCarthy myth needs fleshing out. Since his name was given to a famous "-ism" ("McCarthyism," the practice of making accusations of disloyalty, especially of pro-communist activity, often unsupported or based on doubtful evidence) that is still reviled today, it needs to be said that McCarthy, who may very well have been the victim of bipolar disorder, not to mention alcoholism, was not wrong about everything. The Kennedy family, in fact, thought him a noble, if flawed, Irish Catholic crusader throughout his political career. Its patriarch, Joseph Kennedy Sr., was so enamored of McCarthy that that former ambassador to Britain even pushed hard enough that son Robert was hired by McCarthy as his minority counsel on the Senate Subcommittee on Investigations in 1953. (And Bobby Kennedy admired McCarthy enough to choose the senator as godfather to his first child.) When Bobby left that subcommittee a few months later, it was not because of any falling out with the senator, but due to his aversion to the tactics of lead investigator Roy Cohn. Brother John felt less affection for the senator, but still empathized with McCarthy's anti-communism. The Wisconsin senator even dated Eunice Kennedy, the sister of JFK and Robert and the mother of NBC newswoman Maria Shriver. Bobby also attended McCarthy's funeral, in 1957, asking a *Milwaukee Journal* reporter who recognized him (despite his sunglasses) to keep his presence secret, which the reporter did until recently. In fact, the Kennedy-McCarthy connection deserves a book of its own, if there isn't one already.

Second, although McCarthy knew there were communist sympathizers and spies in the U.S. government in the fifties and that they would be a threat throughout the Cold War, what he did about them was tragically flawed in its effects on both sides. In his famous 1950 Lincoln's Birthday speech in Wheeling, West Virginia, his list of 57 (some sources say 205) "security risks" in the State Department eventually proved inauthentic. During the direction of Congressional testimony, he made countless charges against government employees and others. Few were substantiated, and many of his methods were shown to be fraudulent and malicious. Thousands of people lost their jobs and several committed suicide as a result of his tactics.

And yet some of McCarthy's arguments remain persuasive to historians. For example, many historians still think Alger Hiss was a communist spy, no matter the effort the *Nation's* then-editor Carey McWilliams made to prove Hiss had been framed. *National Review* founder William F. Buckley Jr. has debated about Hiss, too, and has written a book about McCarthy. In fact, Hiss's role as counsel for the Nye Committee in the 1930s —which attacked the U.S. munitions industry for pushing America into World War I—used some of the same methods McCarthy would use in the fifties.

When chief counsel Joseph Welch asked McCarthy during the Army-McCarthy hearings of 1954, "Have you no sense of decency, sir, at long last? Have you left no sense of decency?" the country had to decide: Was McCarthy good or evil? There seemed no middle ground. When McCarthy was a teenager in the Fox Valley of Wisconsin in the 1920s, he dropped out of high school (later to return, then graduate from Marquette Law School, and serve in World War II, hence "Tail-Gunner Joe") and raised chickens. After a political career marked by overzealous publicity-seeking, McCarthy met his match in Welch in 1954, when that majority counsel got the best of him on the day Welch let loose with stunning aim. But McCarthy may have warranted that key rebuke, not only because the hearings he directed had lost their ethical focus generally, but also because he had just broken a promise to Welch not to mention a former Welch staffer, who had once been a member of a communist-front organization, in exchange for Welch's promise not to mention that Roy Cohn had dodged the draft. Welch, who'd taunted McCarthy often during the hearings, finally lowered the boom. To liberals, the damage had been done to McCarthy by himself already, in Wheeling; to conservatives, McCarthy had bitten the big bullet for their cause as he sat next to Welch and tried to respond. Soon after, McCarthy was censured by the Senate, led by then-Texas Senator Lyndon B. Johnson. Ten years later, the Vietnam War began for Americans, led by then-President Johnson, who hated communism as much as McCarthy.

The McCarthy debacle was the main attraction in Washington in the early 1950s. And McCarthy's extremist haunting of communist spies (arguably correct) and innocent noncommunists (painfully wrong) would disable U.S. anticommunists for decades, due to liberals' hatred of McCarthyism. Due to his grandstanding, rumor-mongering, alcoholism, and sheer incapacity to prove many of his charges, McCarthy's career went from top to bottom in near record time. He died in 1957, and his medical records are still a secret. But what McCarthy died of was not a physical ailment (even though he may have suffered from cirrhosis of the liver) so much as a spiritual one. He was loved by some and damned by others—including perhaps God Himself. Where once he might have laughingly shouted "More weight!" as did Giles Corey, the antihysterical, "anti-McCarthy" character in Arthur Miller's *The Crucible*, by 1957, all the weight in the world had been brought to bear on the former junior senator from Wisconsin, and he could stand no more. Joe McCarthy died defeated—from a broken heart. His wife, adopted daughter, and close friends knew that final fact all too well.

Was McCarthy right about the communist threat? Generally, yes; specifically, no. Ends don't always justify means. Is there a threat today? Well, if it's from communism, the communists are wearing fundamentalist clothing.

# The Adventuresome Summer of 1941

## Sam McKay

During the summer of 1941, I was nine years old. It was the summer between the fourth and fifth grades for me. In 1935, my father had bought a little hobby farm up in Hampton Falls, New Hampshire. We spent every weekend there, and my father had a huge garden in which we all toiled. My grandmother was gone all summer, making candy in the candy shop she and her sister ran in North Conway, New Hampshire. During the week, my father took the 8:06 train into Boston to work and returned on the 5:36. Consequently, he never took my brother and me anywhere. My brother was four years older than I, and, being the first born, went anywhere he wanted, when he wanted to, even though Mother stayed at home.

After school let out that summer, I became friends with a neighbor boy named David Benson, who lived several blocks from me and was a year behind me in school. I got to know his whole family. We used to play in the vacant lot next door to his house, acting out our favorite comic book characters: Bat Man and Robin, Superman, Captain Marvel, etc. On rainy days, we played on their sun porch. His mother, who was paralyzed from the waist down and confined to a wheelchair, made us cinnamon toast, which we had with ginger ale. She could manage quite well and did most of the housework. They had a small elevator that ran between the first and second story of the house. David had three or four sisters who were quite a bit older than he, which, on reflection, leads me to believe that he was an afterthought.

I can't remember whether David's father was retired or not. He was home a lot that summer. He was really considerate of his wife, and they liked to go on sightseeing trips to get her out of the house. They always took David with them, and, consequently, after I got to know them, I would go, too. My mother was happy to get me out from under foot and knew I would be in good hands with them.

On one such trip we went up to Salem, New Hampshire, which was just over the Massachusetts state line, where there was a horse racetrack. Of course, I'd never been to horse races. It was really exciting and colorful. David's father asked me what my favorite number was, and I said five. He disappeared, then soon reappeared with tickets in his hand. He gave me one, and it was a bet on horse number five. The race started and I cheered wildly for number five. The horse came in third, and I was really disappointed. David's father disappeared again, but returned with a fist full of dollars and gave me some. He said that I'd bet on the horse to show. I didn't know what he was talking about, and later, when I told my parents about it, they weren't too impressed.

*Trees and waterway, 1990s, United States of America, by Barbara A. Pauls.*

On another trip, we went farther north in New Hampshire to a tourist attraction called Benson's Animal Farm. This was, I guess, what you would call a private zoo. I don't think it exists anymore. It also was a place my parents would never have gone to. There were collections of monkeys, zebras, elephants, lions, and tigers, to name a few. The largest collection was of Mr. Benson's favorite, snakes. There were many varieties and sizes. But the exhibit that left me with the greatest lasting impression was a huge stuffed gorilla, which had been a featured attraction at the farm during his lifetime and was still attracting crowds. When they stuffed him, they preserved everything and did not cover his private parts. That was my first lesson in anatomy.

The summer was winding down, but the major event was about to take place. For years, going back almost to the formation of the American Baseball League, the New York Yankees and the Boston Red Sox had been great rivals. Every game was sold out, no matter how the teams were doing. David's father informed us one day that he had tickets to the upcoming game between the two teams at Fenway Park. I'd never been to a game. My brother used to sneak off and go with his buddies. The kids used to take the train into Boston and the subway out to the park. I said that I would have to ask my parents. They reluctantly gave me permission. We had pretty good seats, up several rows behind the Yankee dugout, on the third base line. The place was packed, and there were kids perched in the rafters trying to get a good view of the game. It was the top of the Yankee batting order. A tall, lanky, handsome man got up to bat for the Yankees. The crowd cheered wildly, but when the pitcher took his windup, it hushed. The pitch came in, and with a mighty swing he missed the ball. The crowd let out a deafening "OOOOOOH!" The next pitch was hit foul into the stands. The third one was hit high and long, but was caught by the center fielder. The dejected hitter turned back from first base and walked with his head down toward the dugout. The crowd stood up and cheered anyway. They stretched their necks to get a better look at him. Just as he was about to enter the dugout, he stopped, took off his cap, flashed a big grin, and waved to the crowd.

At this time, I didn't know much about baseball. (My brother sometimes had it playing on the radio, and once in a while I listened to it. David didn't know much about it, either.) I was afraid to show my ignorance, but David unabashedly asked, "Who was that guy, Dad?"

"Why that was Joe DiMaggio," his dad answered, looking askance at us. "He is breaking the record for hits in consecutive games this year. He's got over fifty of them."

Indeed, the Great DiMaggio went on that summer to hit safely in a record fifty-six consecutive games. There was another player in the game that day who became one of my heroes a few years later. He also broke a record that summer. He finished the season with a batting average of .406. He, of course, was Ted Williams. Many experts say they were the greatest left- and right-handed hitters, respectively, of all time. Both of their records from that season still stand today.

# The Red Cake

## *Anene Ristow*

Many handed-down recipes became favorites for my children. My son, Neil, was especially fond of the red Waldorf Cake. The recipe came out in about 1962. The story goes that a couple visited New York City and dined at the Waldorf Astoria Hotel and for dessert ordered the red Waldorf Cake. The lady was so impressed with this scrumptious cake that she asked if they would share the recipe. The waiter agreed, she gave him her address, and shortly after returning home she received the recipe and a bill for $300. Key ingredients included two ounces (four bottles) of red food coloring, and a not-so-sweet butter-cream frosting.

I happened to be at Neil and Tamara's home in Springfield, Illinois, on his birthday in March 1993. Neil wanted me to make the red cake. After looking around in Tamara's cookbooks for the recipe, I finally found one. Then I took off to the grocery store and bought the ingredients called for, which included the four bottles of red food coloring, about $4 worth.

After returning home, I mixed the batter and poured it into two round cake pans. Their stove was new, so Tamara watched as I set the temperature for 350 degrees, and also set the timer. The knob that sets the numbers for temperature when the "bake" button is punched also sets the minutes when the "timer" button is punched. Then I made one additional adjustment to the timer.

After a few minutes of baking, I noticed a burned smell and commented, but Tamara said something had cooked over in the oven a couple of days before and she had not cleaned it. She was sure that was what I smelled. We discovered we needed something else from the store for the dinner, so I volunteered to go. But still noticing the smell, I peeked in the oven to see the progress of the layers. About ten minutes were left on the timer. When I opened the oven door, out poured billowing black smoke with a burned-to-a-crisp smell, and the cake layers were black! Tamara, shocked and surprised, said, "My oven has never done this!" She looked at the temperature setting and blurted out, "No wonder, it's set on 580 degrees!"

We were both astonished, and burst out laughing. The smoke alarm went off. We opened all the doors and started fanning the smoke alarm to stop the awful, screeching noise. I guess I must have messed up the temperature setting when I made that one last adjustment. It was going on 4:00 P.M. now, and Neil would be home shortly after five o'clock. I quickly took off for the store again and got four more bottles of red food coloring, while Tamara aired the house. When I returned, I immediately started the batter for the second cake. This time Tamara did the settings on the stove. I didn't want to go near them, but we were still laughing.

We had been thinking of some kind of prank to do, so Tamara decided we should cut a slice of the burned cake, frost it, and serve it to Neil. Their three daughters were included in the secret plan. After dinner, and after the candles were lit and blown out and Neil made his secret wish, Tamara took the cake to the kitchen to slice, then returned to him with a scrumptious looking slice completely covered with frosting. Neil, longing to delve into his most favorite treat, took one bite, and with a look of surprise began spitting it out, yelling very loudly, "That's burnt!" The room rocked with laughter as we told him the whole story. Tamara then served him a slice of the good cake—that one turned out very nicely.

What to do with the burned cake? The bird feeder on the back deck was frequented by birds and squirrels, so we decided they would enjoy it. I cut up chunks and also crumbled small pieces and put it all out for those yard animals. Neither the birds nor the squirrels would touch it! After two days, every smidgeon of cake was still there, so Neil decided the stray dog that always came around looking for food scraps would eat it, and he put the cake out for it. We watched as the dog came sneaking around, looked at crumbs and pieces, smelled the mess, and walked away. All of it lay on the ground for a few more days, until we finally tossed it in the garbage. Neil, of course, had his camcorder out and recorded the several-day journey of his burned birthday cake and the final outcome.

As we reminisce now about favorite dishes and recipes, or whenever Neil's birthday rolls around, we still laugh about Mom's disaster with the stove and the red Waldorf Cake that the birds wouldn't eat and the dog turned away from!

### Red Cake

| | |
|---|---|
| 1½ | cups sugar |
| 1 | cup shortening |
| 2 | eggs |
| 2 | tablespoons cocoa |
| 2 | ounces red food coloring |
| 1 | teaspoon salt |
| 1 | teaspoon vanilla |
| 1 | cup buttermilk |
| 2½ | cups flour |
| ½ | teaspoon soda |
| 1 | tablespoon vinegar |

Cream together sugar, shortening, and eggs. Make a paste of the cocoa and red food coloring and add to the creamed mixture. Add salt and vanilla to the buttermilk with the cake flour. Mix the soda with the vinegar and fold it into the batter (don't beat). Bake in two 8-inch pans at 350 degrees for thirty minutes. When cool, split both cake layers to make 4 layers. (As you split the layers, follow the knife with wax paper between the layers so they can be moved more easily.)

### Filling

Cook 1 cup milk and 6 tablespoons flour over low heat until the mixture is the consistency of oatmeal; cool. Cream 1 cup butter, 1 cup sugar, and 1 teaspoon vanilla. Add the cooled flour mixture and beat until it looks like whipped cream. This amount of filling will frost the top and between the layers (so the red cake will show between the layers of filling). If you want to frost the entire cake, increase the amount of filling. Any remaining can be kept in the refrigerator.

# Jeanne

### *Barbara A. Pauls*

Words, gifts, material things
cannot express
my heartfelt love for you,
my sister, my friend.
You came to my wedding, my friend.
Lipstick on the ceiling, only you
could share the memory.
Hair dyeing in basement black,
psychology courses to improve
our mental state. Ironic, then,
the divorces came.
Birthday dinners, pooling money,
calls from Kresge's phone booth.
Only to a friend who cared
and did not care why.
Grandchildren, diets,
dinners, diets,
husbands, or lack thereof,
his kids, her kids, our kids.
Surgeries, illnesses (some we've
never heard of), aches, and pains.
Still, we smile, laugh, and love
the friendship that we've shared.
May we have many more birthdays
and memories,
my friend, my sister in love,
always.

## My Son, My Friend
### Barbara A. Pauls

You are more than a son,
you are also a friend.
A comfort to know,
if the chips are down,
without a negative sound,
you're steadfast by my side.
A hat, a shirt, a vest, or tie,
are things we sure can buy.
But all the money in the world,
cannot buy you by my side.
How do I express my love for you?
In your joys, your pains,
your ups, your downs,
my heart bears them with you.
I laugh, I cry, I share with you,
because I care so much.
My heart and soul, I care, I care.
I'm proud, and love you so.

## The Rocket Scientists of Butterfield Valley
### Tom Tippery

**Editor's Note by Aggie Tippery:** *This story was first printed in the* **Houston County (Minnesota) News**. *After reading Homer H. Hickam Jr.'s book about the "Rocket Boys," our son Tom recalled the rockets from his boyhood in Butterfield Valley. This episode took place at our former home, currently occupied by the Johnson family.*

Dad. He bought a farm. Though he was not a farmer, he could do two things at once. He learned how to farm and he taught his boys the joy of that life in the country. He sawed wooden slabs for heat in the winter. Through all the complaints and not understanding why, we had to help throw the wood into the basement and stack it in the corner. We had bad winters, with snow so high that we had to tunnel into the chicken coop. He would fire up that old Allis-Chalmers and clear the driveway with it, because it had a bucket. Not the right machine for the job, but it was all he had, so he made do. His boys were watching from inside, and although they did not know it, they were learning from him that sometimes you have to make do with what you have to get the job done. Winter is the hardest time of year in Minnesota, but it can bring out the best in people. It did in my dad. In retrospect, I don't think he enjoyed a minute of those 1950s winters on the farm, with the exception of coming back inside the house to see his caring wife and his boys, knowing that, for now, he had at least beaten back the winter for another night.

Dad is not a school-educated man, but his thirst for knowledge is not lacking. I remember that I was able to buy a couple of model rocket engines. I don't remember asking to buy them, but when I got them, he was excited and interested in them. I did not have the knowledge or the skills to hook them up and get them to work, but with a lot of help and working with what we had, we had fun. With a coat hanger that was covertly taken from an upstairs closet, hoping that Ma did not notice, he fashioned a counterbalance-style mobile for this rocket engine. The experiment took place in the basement next to the wood furnace. Ma thought we were working on something really important to keep the house warm. At least that's what we tried to make her think. The mobile was built, the rocket was mounted, and it was ready to fly. By the way, the rocket had a gasoline-fueled engine. Fueled and ignited, the rocket, shooting flames, started the mobile spinning. The more its temperature increased, the faster it spun, until it was out of control and, with a "Look out!" from Dad, it went flying into the wood pile, and we all scrambled to get it out. With a smile, Dad said, "Don't tell Ma."

We were excited by that experiment, and he saw that in us, so he took the experiment to the next level and mounted *both* engines onto the coat hanger. He built the hanger stronger, fueled the engines, and fired them up. The first experiment had been fast, but this one was unbelievable in speed, and yet the result was the same—the holder broke and flew into the wood pile with a pre-emptive "Look out!" warning. What a blast! There was more scrambling to remove it before the wood caught fire. At the end of the experiment, Dad again said, "Don't tell Ma," and with that, the rocket engines were put away—I think in order to keep us from performing our own unsupervised experiment. Another subliminal lesson learned by the Rocket Scientists of Butterfield Valley: Lee, Tom, and Bob, by the best of all teachers: Dad.

*Thanks, Tom, for the story and for "not telling Ma" until now. Over the years, there were many other projectiles rocketing through the air at our house (including youngest son Jerry). I saw the results, but I still don't know the details, because of the "Don't tell Ma" rule. Once someone was playing with a glow plug engine from a defunct model airplane, turning the propeller until it started the engine. It flew out of the perpetrator's hands and across the top of the room, knocking several holes in the ceiling. Another time, a hole appeared in the big window in the living room, but to this day, I have no idea who (man or boy) was responsible for that one. Or the hole in the basement door?? Keep writing your memories, Tom. Eventually, I might get answers to these riddles.—Mom.*

## The Soda Fountain in Fountain City
### *La Vonne Woodhouse Mainz*

My sister Shirley and I had taken a sightseeing trip along the Wisconsin side of the Mississippi River from Onalaska to Fountain City. Our objective was to see the huge thirty-plus-ton boulder that had become dislodged from one of the hills on the east side of Fountain City on April 24, 1995. It had rolled down the steep slope and slammed into Dwight and Maxine Anderson's house, coming to rest in their bedroom.

Fortunately, no one was hurt. Mrs. Anderson had been in the bedroom just moments before, taking pictures of the newly redecorated room. She had just returned to the kitchen when the boulder crashed into the house. It filled the bedroom and protruded through the roof, and it is now quite a tourist attraction in Fountain City. The Andersons have opened their home to sightseers. Mrs. Anderson described the frightening experience and gave us a tour of the house.

After viewing the boulder that came to rest atop a smashed bed and tracing its destructive path down the hillside, Shirley and I decided to find a place where we could quench our thirst on that warm summer day in 1995. We found much more than just a cool drink.

As we walked through the door of Lettner's Corner Store, we entered into a slice of the city's history. An amiable lady named Fran Lettner operated the store, which was located on the corner of Main and Liberty Streets. Her energy and liveliness belied her seventy-three years. Fran, who also was an on-call obstetrical nurse, had been the proprietor since 1986. When we commented about the uniqueness of the store, she was happy to tell us about the history of the building.

The building was constructed in 1866 and was originally used as a general store. In 1884, it became a drugstore that at one time included a doctor's office. Part of the old building was now a coin laundry, and Fran operated an antique store and soda fountain in the other half. Because she is an avid antique collector, all sorts of interesting antiques line the walls and fill every available space in her store. Her business card called it "Antiques, Collectibles & Junque."

The soda fountain was installed in 1926. It still has the original marble counter and high, turning stools, each with a unique footrest. As I sat on my stool and sipped the most delicious chocolate soda I had ever enjoyed, followed by a wonderful old-fashioned fountain Coke, my eyes caught a handwritten sign posted on the old, ornate, mirrored soda fountain wall. It read, "If you are grumpy, irritable, or just plain mean, there will be a $10.00 charge for putting up with you." It was signed "Fran."

I was sure that if a person with a grumpy, irritable, or mean attitude came into the soda fountain, Fran's sunny disposition would quickly melt it away. Fran told me that every morning a group of ten or twelve senior citizens came in to sit at the fountain, enjoy some old time treats, and reminisce. Fran said that she was open for business six days a week, from nine to five, and that she was thinking about staying open Sundays, too. She said that the tourist business had picked up since the huge boulder had rolled down the hill into the Andersons' house.

While visiting with Fran, I glanced up and noted that the decorative pressed-tin ceiling was painted royal blue and trimmed in gold, with a gold phoenix occupying each corner. Above the door was an impressive thirty-by-sixty-inch stained glass panel of an eagle that was made by Leonard Alcamo, a local artist. "Fountain City, WI, Founded in 1839" was inscribed on the glass. It was a beautiful piece of art.

The well-maintained exterior of the building was a tribute to its devoted owner. Fran, who is part Irish, was flying an Irish flag atop the building below the American flag. She told me that the half of Fountain City north of Highway 35 is known as Germantown, while the part south of the highway is known as Yankeetown. Just to be a bit controversial and as a conversation piece, she had decided to fly her Irish flag.

The ice cream and soda fountain was the subject of an article in the *Saint Paul Pioneer Press* a few years ago. In the May 14, 1995, issue of *The New York Times*, the fountain was included in a commentary of interesting places to visit between Red Wing, Minnesota, and Prairie du Chien, Wisconsin. *The New York Times* article mentioned that a steady stream of schoolchildren bring in their pennies for Fran to bank for ice cream and candy. They, too, enjoyed the delights of yesteryear.

Sadly, because of bad health, Fran Lettner had to close her ice cream and soda fountain in 2000. I am so glad that I had a chance to meet her. My sister and I sat at her antique soda fountain and enjoyed sipping on those delicious sodas, just as fountain customers would have done more than three-quarters of a century ago.

# The Carpenters

### *Barbara A. Pauls*

"Was the worst they'd ever seen!"
when they arrived on the scene:
Two previous relatives, hired as
 carpenters.
Insulation was hanging, wires were
 dangling.
Birds were banging inside on the
 windows!
They cared and they shared,
they joked and jawed,
while they hammered and sawed.
And the sound of saws ringing
was better than any singing,
to a weary homeowner's lament.
James, me man, leader of the pack.
Quiet, sure, proud of work,
which shows itself in the crew he
 picked.
Steve seems shy or eccentric.
Maybe it was the electrical
that lifted him more than once.
Tho he talked gruff, of women and
 stuff.
Inside he really isn't so tough,
even if he says fish is more his dish.
Bob talks sort of rough and tough,
but he worked just as hard.
Al, carpenter, jack of all trades.
Any piece of wood, any piece of
 board.
He could make it fit.

John, young John, good,
 hardworking.
Carved new steps to look old, always
 thinking.
Almost went for a swim on ice on the
 pond
retrieving a tarp. Always there to
 help,
proud to help, wherever needed.
In the dawn's early light
their trucks pulled in
and they arrived with a friendly grin.
Even tho they talked so gruff
the light in their eyes showed
a caring they could not deny.
In their giving, without a word,
was a gift of love on a special day.
A birthday gift of giving to finish a
 home.
For to a woman, home is her heart.
A priceless gift I'll never forget
from this crew of men with hearts.
Bigger than big hearts, caring hearts,
hearts showing what words did not
 say.
You go on to other jobs, my men.
I may not see you again, but
just know, your kindness to me
lives forever in my heart.
I will never forget that morning
when the trucks pulled in.

# My Latvian-American Mother

### *Anna Muktepavels-Motivans*

She never saw her home again.
She died in exile,
grateful to the people
who sheltered us and

the country of our refuge
that gave us hope.
May God grant her Eternal Light!

# Bedtime for an Old Woman
## La Vonne Woodhouse Mainz

A soft bed beckons the tired old woman.
The multicolored quilts, the eiderdown cushion,
comfort her pain, as whispered prayers
are quietly spoken.
The hushed, still night descends low
to close the portals of this day
and open them for the morrow.
A flood of memories holds sleep at bay.
Unfettered and unbound, remembering when
the little girl within
ran barefoot through the glen
and the pastures of her youth.
She feels the cool of a crest-filled brook
on her toes, while frogs leap in
and crayfish look.
She smiles and sleeps, content within.

# Grandpa's Corncob Pipe
## Robert (Bob) Smith

Prior to World War II, the American family was a viable unit, held together by loving, concerned parents. There was also a strong, steady, positive influence from grandparents. During my early years as a youngster on the farm, we grew up sharing everyday life with wonderful grandparents. Grandmas and grandpas were not sent off to some old folks home. They generally remained on the farm their entire lives and were always a very important part of family structure.

My grandfather was a very special person to my brothers, sisters, and myself. For me, a day never passed that was not shared in some way with my grandpa. He taught me how to fish, hunt, set live traps, and harness a workhorse. He also taught me how to saddle and safely ride a fast horse. He demonstrated the technique for shoeing a horse, for dehorning a mean cow, for milking cows and goats, for using farm equipment safely, for cutting and chopping wood, and for mending the barbed-wire fence across the back forty. Along with manners and respect for others, he also taught my siblings and me how to relax and enjoy life. I could go on forever describing the values and grass roots education and experiences Grandpa taught us every day.

Grandpa sat by the hour with us on the open front porch during the warm summer evenings. For hours, we watched the endless flight of a thousand fireflies. We sat very silently as he identified all the country night voices. He knew the sounds of the different owls, bobwhite, and whippoorwill. He identified the croak of a frog, the shrill sound of a tree toad, and sounds of the many insects occupying the night air.

Occasionally, we listened intently to the clear sound of a yipping fox or a neighbor farmer's coon hounds racing through the hills in fast pursuit of some unlucky night creature. Sharing this precious time with Grandpa was a great learning experience. I am sure my siblings and I have all benefited from this throughout our lifetimes.

Grandpa had but one vice, and he shared it with his grandchildren. This daily habit provided him with the opportunity to enjoy one of his handcrafted corncob pipes. Locating the right size corncob from the corncrib, Grandpa cut out a piece from the center of the cob. Next, he took his razor-sharp hunting knife and very delicately carved out a perfect cylinder, approximately two inches deep, inside one end of the cob. The next step was to locate a certain type of hollow reed. The reed he needed could be found only down by the creek bank. Once he'd found the right reed, he then could craft a stem for his pipe.

The country was then experiencing a long, devastating depression. Many experts, including my grandpa, believed it was the worst period in America's history. Money and jobs were almost nonexistent, so seniors like our grandparents had to survive without any source of real income, such as retirement pensions, Social Security benefits, government handouts, or welfare. Grandparents found themselves totally dependent on their families.

Without money, the only real pipe tobacco Grandpa ever enjoyed was a package or two he'd receive for Christmas or some other special occasion. Most of the time, he had to settle for the next best substitutes available. What he smoked was cheap, plentiful, and easy to locate. He smoked and enjoyed dry corn silk, which he pulled out of dried, field-corn cobs. For an extra special treat, he opened his small leather pouch of sweet-smelling alfalfa chaff and gently filled his trusty pipe. I shall always remember how much I enjoyed the sweet aroma of smoke that filled the air when Grandpa lit up a pipeful of fresh alfalfa chaff.

Eventually, Grandpa's sight and hearing began to fail. Many years of hard farm labor had worn him down physically, taking a toll on his back, hips, and knees. Painful arthritis attacked his hands and fingers. I knew how much these physical problems plagued him, and yet, with a friendly smile and that familiar gleam in his warm, blue eyes, he always felt he had at least one pleasure in his life . . . his faithful old corncob pipe.

# The Whale House
## *Jim Solberg*

To a child, the world is full of fantastic wonders. Some we figure out for ourselves, others we depend on our elders to explain to us. I loved it especially when my grandfather explained things to me. He lived over a hundred miles away, an unimaginable distance to a child, so any time spent with Grandpa was treasured. In addition to everything else that made him so special, his ability to tell stories and explain things endeared him to me. He seemed so responsive and so patient that I thought of him as a deep source of wisdom. Whatever he said, I felt, was pure truth. That's how I learned that the City of La Crosse, Wisconsin, had a strange way of keeping its whales.

One day, when Grandpa drove my brothers and me to visit Myrick Park and Zoo in La Crosse, we noticed a little brick building on the edge of the park. "What is that little house for?" we asked. It had a little door and what seemed like a little window, and I even thought I saw a cute little chimney. Grandpa had previously told us stories about tiny elves and fairies, gremlins, and trolls. These were about the only kinds of creatures we could think of that could possibly be living in there. Imagine our surprise when Grandpa told us that the city kept a whale in there! Just the opposite of what we expected —and it wasn't even near the other animals. My brothers were apparently too young to be really shocked by his strange and unexpected answer. Maybe they didn't even know what whales were, or at least how big they are.

But my little mind was reeling with confusion. "How . . ." I finally braced myself to ask, "How can they get the whales in there?" Grandpa looked puzzled at first, probably a little surprised by his grandson's precocious curiosity about engineering and municipal water supply, but he forged on with a perfectly sound explanation of how and why the city kept a "whale" in the little brick enclosure. I heard his sage references to "deep whales," "water tables," and "aquifers," but I really had no idea what he was talking about.

I wanted to pursue the point further but his satisfied expression had made it clear that a perfectly good answer had been given, and by asking more, I feared that I would only make myself look like a very dull child, indeed—perhaps even rude. So I let it slide and eventually even suppressed the whole event—not wanting to admit to myself that I couldn't understand how the city workers managed to keep a whole whale in that tiny place. Especially after my grandpa had gone to the trouble of thoroughly explaining it all to me.

It wasn't until years later that I finally realized why I felt slightly uncomfortable every time I saw La Crosse's "whale house." Subconsciously, I was still wrestling with a feeling that there was some sort of vague impossibility going on in there—one that I was just too dumb to understand. One day, clean out of the blue, it dawned on me—*Well houses? . . . Whale houses! Ohhhhh!* And then I recalled Grandfather's patient but misunderstood explanation to me. The memory refreshed for me the innocent and unquestioning faith of a child in the ones they love—and the power of the spoken word, whether understood or not. The little brick house is still packed overfull, but now with nothing more than rich memories for me— reminders of someone whose wisdom and love I dearly miss.

"Whale House," 2000, National Zoo, Washington, D.C., by David J. Marcou.

## Ode to Archie
### Barbara A. Pauls

To have "Archie" David Wolfe
as family, friend and carpenter
has been a blessing to us all
throughout the past seventy-four
    years.
Pole buildings, pump sheds,
houses big and small.
Electric, board, or plumbing,
he can do it all.
Winter, summer, fall or spring,
he works throughout it all.
Stocking cap when it's cold,
bare back when it's hot.
"What do ya need, Archie?"
"Where is that shopping list?"
"It's written on that board!" he'd roar
with a grin from ear to ear.

He can be quick of wit—
make sure you don't get bit!
But he still gets presents . . .
like pheasants.
Years of family memories:
hunting trips, venison feeds,
cranberrying and craziness,
roasting and toasting,
even pig nests! (He knows the rest!)
Years have come and gone
for "Archie" David Wolfe.
He's a man to be proud of,
from stocking hat to workman's
    hands.
We've surely been most blessed,
as we've nothing but the best.
Because Jesus, who was a carpenter,
knows Archie's passed his test!

## Forgotten Heroes
### William Kulas

*Editor's Note: This essay might have been placed earlier in this book, but once you've finished it, you will understand why it's here.*

People treat calendars like any other household item. Except for the special days, each day seems as ordinary as the next. Only when history thrusts a catastrophic event upon us does a date assume special significance. Such is the case with September 11th, 2001. All people living then will probably remember what they were doing when they heard the news of the terrorist attacks. That tragic day will be elevated to the status shared by other significant dates: the bombing of Pearl Harbor, the dropping of the A-bomb, and the assassinations of John Kennedy, Bobby Kennedy, and Martin Luther King Jr. Children will listen to parents and grandparents talk about that terrible day.

    My account probably differs little from others. The day began like any other day. Once I'd heard two people at the post office talk about the events, I went home to watch the television. By then, the two airplanes had crashed into the Twin Towers, and rumors peaked about more attacks. As I watched and listened, frantic reporters discarded the formality of poised reporting. The whole event became like a giant tarantula, engulfing me in its web. As much as I wanted to turn off the television, I could not disentangle myself from its sorcery or the silence of the anchorperson as the Twin Towers came crashing down in replay. My stomach seemed pummeled by it all. After what seemed like an endless pause, the commentary returned to its mesmerizing spell. But the words seemed meaningless; the pictures told it all.

Suddenly the thought crossed my mind: I must face my parishioners. After years of their hearing me preach of a loving and merciful God, how could I explain this horror? To compound matters, reports surfaced about the suicidal zealots who carried out the attack. Now a new element entered my mind. *How could I reconcile the cries for revenge with the gospel of turning the other cheek?*

As a pastor and police chaplain, I have faced crises before; many have been far more personal. With the same suddenness as September 11th, I find myself thrust into such crises. By the time I arrive, the emergency technicians, police officers, or firemen are already working on the victim in a titanic struggle to wrestle the person's life away from the grip of death. My job is often to provide information and comfort to the agonizing loved ones. Often, the seconds and minutes drag the tragedy into an endless drone.

Sometimes, these soldiers of life wrench the person back to life. Yet the anxiety only diminishes—it's not quelled. Death has been beaten back, but not destroyed. The loved ones still dwell in fear of its ruthless return. Sometimes, death conquers. The violent pounding, the frantic running, the intense muscle flexing—all dwindle to a sad realization of death's terms of surrender. Like a conquered army, the technicians must now face defeat as death howls in laughter at their futile attempts. Now they must face a new struggle—telling the relatives of their loss. They always speak in the kindest of terms: "We did everything we could. But we lost him." They bow their heads in quiet resignation, and return to gather the remnants of their lifesaving weapons. Now, I must try to make sense of this loss. Every member of the clergy in this position faces this daunting task: how to assure the relatives of the presence of a loving God and of an unexplainable purpose in this death. Bandages can stop bleeding, water can quench flames, but clergy carry few healing tools. The Scriptures, prayers, and words can help, but they still do not soothe the dark fear of the loss.

At that point, clergy feel very helpless. Their words seem inadequate, their readings seem hollow, their prayers seem useless. Nothing can restore the life so brutally ripped away from the loved one. The trust in the fatherly care of God seems eternally broken. Often clergy can only sit in silence. Presence means so much to loved ones as they wander through the thoughts of their minds. Just being there means so much to them.

Such was the occasion on September 11th. No words could really help. Many sought answers for questions that I could not explain to myself, let alone them. I could only hear the words I heard many years before: "I saw Satan laughing with delight." I would not add to his gloating with cries for revenge. The tinge of Vietnam colored my vision. I could only cry out for forgiveness.

Whether the current response will parallel the great triumph of World War II or the defeat of Vietnam remains to be seen. We cannot tell if we are following the trail of the Soviet Union to its demise. Time has reserved that secret to itself, and no force in nature can pry open its message before its time.

The emergency personnel earned great glory, and rightly so. Why must it take a national tragedy to bring us to honor these warriors of life? Should they not receive greater reward? However, they often need healing themselves. For many, the source of their strength is a word of reassurance from their chaplain. In the midst of the triumphant parade of the heroes, hopefully, people will not forget the forgotten heroes, the beacons of hope in the midst of great need—the clergy.

## A Thankful Gift to a Pastor

*Yvonne Klinkenberg*

A Thanksgiving and Christmas gift
given by me—
You brought back the trust
of a church, you see.
This is to say
thanks to my Lord above
for the family I have
that's filled with love
and my family in church,
with prayers that we share,
just for that moment
we show we do care.
If we believe we take them into our
    home,
to strengthen our faith,
from our Savior (we try) never to
    roam.

## World Peace Flag

*Steve Kiedrowski*

With American flags flying as high as our patriotism these days, another flag may join the fold. Jim Brush of rural Galesville, Wisconsin, has designed and is marketing a world peace flag.

Jim said, "We don't have a world peace flag—a universal symbol of peace. I thought of the idea before the September 11th attack. It inspired me to go ahead with the flag."

The flag has seven stars (one for each continent), five colors (at least one color from every country's flag) and hands joining together in peace. "World Peace" is printed at the top and "United States of America" at the bottom. Since final modifications, the lower line is interchangeable with other countries' names, a business name, or even a family name.

"It's important to know that this flag doesn't replace any flag, but is to be flown next to it," Jim said.

However, Jim's dream is not just a world peace flag, but also a world peace foundation—a nonprofit organization that would promote peace around the globe, help students with scholarships, and start fund raisers for the less fortunate.

Jim stated, "We've created the World Peace Foundation, Inc. and have our own web site. We want to go into schools and help students, to have academic banquets, create talent contests, and have benefits. Of the money generated, seventy-five percent would go back to the school or other organization and twenty-five percent would go to the foundation. The web site is www.Theworldpeacefoundation.com"

Assisting Jim in this project is his wife, Cindy, who said, "It would be exciting to make this foundation more than a dream, to make it come true. We want to do wonderful things for kids and [help with] other worldwide needs."

Jim has hired a public relations director and someone to design web sites and do promotions.

He also has a little political help. Ron Kind, U.S. Democratic Congressman from Wisconsin, is campaigning for the World Peace Foundation. He gave one of the first world peace flags to President Bush, to be flown over the White House.

There is even talk of getting the Pope to bless some of the flags and then auction them off for charity.

*Jim and Cindy Brush and the world peace flag Jim designed, before final modifications (see final version on back cover), 2002, Empire Screen Printing, Onalaska, WI, by Steve Kiedrowski.*

Jim smiled. "It's a dream, but the idea and timing are right. We certainly need a world peace flag now."

Besides being president and founder of the World Peace Foundation, Inc., Jim is also owner of the Brush Trophy Room Museum in Centerville, Wisconsin, and owns Empire Screen Printing of Onalaska, Wisconsin.

He plans to expand the flag design into jackets, hats, t-shirts, cups, decals, and jogging apparel.

Right now, the flag is flying in front of Empire Screen Printing. The decals, t-shirts and some of the related items will be produced right at Empire.

Some day, Jim would like to see the world peace flag carried into the Olympics, with athletes wearing outfits fashioned after the flag.

The foundation is trying to find a way for other corporations to support the flag. Companies like McDonalds, Subway, or Hardee's, could have promotions where they hand out collectible decals of countries and states with a meal.

The La Crosse's Boys and Girls Club is interested in displaying the world peace flag, too.

Cindy Brush said, "I would like to see the flag fly all over the world."

The flag can be purchased in just about any size, with a customized inscription on the bottom.

Jim wants his foundation to work with other foundations to help raise funds for research into cancer and muscular dystrophy. He feels it's the patriotic thing to do.

Jim states, "My ultimate goal is to have a world peace foundation in every country. To make the flag so known, so that people from all over the world would look at it and say, 'That's the world peace flag.' We even hope to open an office within the area of the Twin Towers in New York City. We just want to promote world peace."

*"Freedom Is Not Free," 2000, part of the Korean War Memorial, Washington, D.C., by David J. Marcou.*

# AUTHOR BIOGRAPHIES

*Editor's Note: Many of the contributors to this book have ties to the La Crosse, Wisconsin, area. Thus, locations like La Crosse, Onalaska, the University of Wisconsin (UW), and Western Wisconsin Technical College (WWTC) are abbreviated for easier reading.*

**Emma Bader** was born in La Crosse and graduated from La Farge (Wisconsin) High School in 1991. She also graduated from the UW-Eau Claire with a B.A. degree in Psychology and Criminal Justice. Currently, she works for the Wisconsin Department of Corrections as a probation and parole agent. In addition to photography, Emma's interests include art, playing pool, and playing tennis.

**Helen Bolterman,** now retired, was employed as an administrative assistant for the Onalaska School District for more than twenty years. Born in Omaha, Nebraska, she has lived most of her life in the La Crosse area. She and her husband, Wesley, have three living children: Rodney, Janet, and Jean. In addition to writing—she has been published often in *Good Old Days* and also has published her autobiography, *Memories*—Helen enjoys traveling all around the United States and to Norway, her ancestral homeland.

**Gerald Bonsack,** a professional engineer, was one of thirty-five hundred photographers selected worldwide to shoot for the *Dawn of the Millennium* book project. Three of his photos were used there. His photographs have also been published in other books, calendars, newspapers, and brochures, have been used on TV, and were even used on a text panel at the Carnegie Science Center. He was the featured artist in the premier issue of *Kaleidoscope Review*. Jerry has traveled extensively and lives in Onalaska. He has two grown children, Jason and Dee.

**Monica Chiu** is both mother to two-year-old Ellie and an assistant professor of English at the University of New Hampshire. She graduated from La Crosse Central High School in 1983, eventually earning her Ph.D. in English, specializing in Asian-American Studies, at Emory University in Atlanta. On weekends, when she is not grading papers, Monica and her husband, Brian Locke, spend hours with Ellie, Play-Doh, and books at playgrounds and toy stores.

**Ursula Chiu** was born in Germany, where she taught high school French and English. After immigrating to America, she taught in the Chicago and La Crosse school systems. She raised three children with her late husband, Alec Chiu, a professor from China. In her retirement, Ursula enjoys reading, writing, gardening, and woodcarving. Also, she recently completed the manuscript for her book of memoirs, concentrating on her childhood in pre-World War II Germany.

**Joyce Clason** was born in Burlington, Wisconsin, where she graduated from St. Mary's High School (now called Catholic Central High School) in 1951. In 1954, she married Ralph Clason, and they have six grown children and eight grandchildren. The Clasons own an auto dealership in La Crosse and are very active in the community. They were Commodore and First Mate for that city's 1991 Riverfest. In addition to socializing and writing, Joyce enjoys canoeing, cross-country skiing, and traveling the world.

**Alice Cook** was born in Ponca, Nebraska, and graduated from Ponca High School. She has been director of the Harry J. Olson Senior Center in La Crosse for one year. She is married to Earl Cook, and they have one son, Kevin, who is married to Peggy, and that couple has four boys. Previously,

Alice was a legal secretary and also helped out with the family tavern in Stevenstown, Wisconsin, near Holmen. She hadn't done much writing before penning her poem, "Thoughts," but one month after 9/11, she decided she had to write something about the terrorist attacks, came home, and turned out her poem in fifteen minutes. It's very worthwhile writing.

**Father Robert Cook, O.S.F.,** has been pastor of St. Joseph the Workman Cathedral in La Crosse since 1991. Previously, he was chief of staff for Diocese of La Crosse Bishop John Paul. Born in La Crosse, he attended Cathedral Grade School and Aquinas High School there. He graduated from Holy Cross Seminary in 1961 with a degree in Philosophy, and from St. Francis Seminary for Theology in 1965. He was ordained soon after. He is chairman of the Franciscan Skemp Foundation and a member of the Aquinas Foundation Board, the United Way Board, and the Rotary Club. He has four brothers, Arthur, Richard, Gary, and Kevin. Father Cook is a 2002 winner of the Pope John XXXIII Award (Viterbo University), Bishop John Paul Award for Distinguished Alumni (Aquinas High School), and the Silver Beaver Award (Boy Scouts of America). In addition to pastoral care and writing, he enjoys fly-fishing.

**Joyce Crothers** moved from Freeport, New York, where she was born, to the La Crosse area thirty-five years ago. Married to Bill, she is the mother of four and grandmother of five. She has been published locally, and is currently transcribing her great-grandfather's Civil War diary. In addition to writing, Joyce's interests include soap-making, quilting, knitting, spinning, printing, camping, and gardening.

**Mary Claire Fehring** was born in Rockford, Iowa and graduated from high school there and from St. Theresa's College in Winona, Minnesota. With her late husband, Bob, she has three sons and one daughter, as well as six granddaughters and one great-granddaughter. Mary is a retired dietitian who does not like to cook. In addition to writing, she enjoys reading and knitting.

**Denise Havlik-Jensen** was born in La Crosse in 1961. She graduated from Aquinas High School in 1979 and from WWTC with a personnel technician degree in 1981 and an R.N. degree in 1992. She works as an R.N. for the Hillview Health Care Center in La Crosse. Denise is married and has one daughter. In addition to photography, she enjoys travel and other outdoor activities, especially in northern Wisconsin.

**Elizabeth (Betty) Holey** has always been a storyteller. She took a year of creative writing at the University of North Carolina–Chapel Hill and has earned two university degrees, a bachelor's from the University of Missouri in Home Economics and a master's in Nutrition from Chapel Hill. She intended to write professionally, but instead got married and raised a family with her husband, Jim, and worked as a nutritionist. Betty is retired, but still likes writing, and also very much enjoys spending time with her family, especially her Chinese granddaughter, Anna Li.

**Ida Hood**—no biographical information was available for her when this book went to press.

**Donna Huegel** grew up on a farm near New Hampton, Iowa, and now resides near La Crescent, Minnesota, with her husband, Len. They have two grown sons, Eric and Ryan. She attended Mount Mercy College and the University of Iowa. Formerly an editor for the *Tulsa World Herald*, Donna has also authored *Many a Grove* and *Orchard—The Story of John S. Harris*. Currently, she writes historical articles for the *Houston County (Minnesota) News*, enjoys doing artwork, and is active in the local historical society and her church.

**Grant Huntington** (1955-1997) was a well-known commercial photographer in California who specialized in architectural, culinary, and agricultural photography. His Huntington family roots extended back east to Lebanon, Connecticut, a town famous for its association with the

Revolutionary War. In 1996, Grant made his first visit to the hometown of his ancestors to help photograph for a book on the history and architecture of the town, *Around the Lebanon Green*, published by the Town of Lebanon. This was his last major work before his untimely death from cancer in 1997.

**Geeta Sharma Jensen** was born in India and earned an M.A. in English there, as well as an M.A. in Journalism from Marquette University in Milwaukee. A journalist for more than twenty years in Racine and Milwaukee, her beats have included the courts, government, business, and education. She has been books editor for the *Milwaukee Journal Sentinel* since 1999. Geeta is married, and she and her husband have three children.

**Lucinda Ann Kane** was born in Shelby, Tennessee, in 1959. "Lucy" was raised mainly in San Diego County, California, where she was an active member in the 4-H and Future Farmers of America during school. After graduation, she worked for Hewlett-Packard for more than twelve years in manufacturing, technical, and personnel operations. She married John Gray in 1991, and they have three children, Samuel, Angela, and Ian. Lucy has been involved in children's ministries for more than ten years. She and her family relocated to western Wisconsin recently, where she serves as an assistant administrator to her church's Children's Director and as secretary to her local Parent Teacher Organization. Besides writing, she finds pleasure in people, plants, and pets.

**Steve Kiedrowski** is an artist and writer from Trempealeau, Wisconsin, who has two sons, Ryan and Andy. He studied Commercial Art at WWTC and works for Empire Screen Printing in Onalaska, Wisconsin, as an art inspector and has also done public relations work there. In addition to serving as a contributor and publicist for this book and for *Spirit of America*, he is a feature writer for the *Winona (Minnesota) Post*. Steve also devotes time to political cartoons and has illustrated numerous books as a freelance artist. He has appeared in the movie *Intersection* as well.

**Doris Kirkeeng** was born in Wauwatosa, Wisconsin, and graduated from Horicon (Wisconsin) High School and from St. Mary's School of Nursing in Milwaukee; she also completed graduate courses at the UW-La Crosse. She has traveled to Guam, the Philippines, and Europe. Her interests include coin, plate, and periodical collecting; oil painting; and writing. Doris has four married children and eleven grandchildren.

**Yvonne Klinkenberg** was born in Rochester, Minnesota, quit school at sixteen, and married Amos Klinkenberg in 1947. She has six sons and three daughters. At sixty-four, she earned her GED and high school diploma, and at seventy-three, she still loves to learn. Best known as a poet, Yvonne enjoys writing about any subject that springs to her mind, and she is capable of writing a poem to suit any occasion with just a moment's notice. In addition to writing and her family, she enjoys travel and photography.

**Father William Kulas,** a Diocesan priest for the Catholic Diocese of Winona, Minnesota, is pastor of both St. Joseph's Parish in Rushford, Minnesota, and St. Mary's Parish in Houston, Minnesota. He was born and raised in Dodge, Wisconsin, and although his father is deceased, his mother is still living, as is his married brother. Father Kulas's degrees include a B.A. from St. Mary's University in Winona in Classics, Philosophy, and Social Studies; an M.A. in Theology from St. John's University in Collegeville, Minnesota; a Specialist in Educational Administration degree from Mankato (Minnesota) State University; and a J.C.L. in Canon Law from Catholic University in Washington, D.C. In addition to pastoral care and writing, his interests include playing golf, woodworking, reading, and computers.

# AUTHOR BIOGRAPHIES

**John H. Leisgang** was born in La Crosse, where he graduated from Cathedral Grade School and Aquinas High School. He retired from the UW-La Crosse Academic Computing Department in 1997 after more than twenty-five years there. He had worked at Allis Chalmers Manufacturing Company previously. John has been active in the Boy Scouts for more than fifty years, and he is a lifelong member of the Cathedral of St. Joseph the Workman Parish in La Crosse.

**Nelda Johnson Liebig** has taught elementary school in Wisconsin, Alaska, Montana, American Samoa, and Russia. She has seen many of her children's stories published, and her first novel, *Carrie and the Crazy Quilt*, received a Distinguished Service Award from the State Historical Society of Wisconsin in 1997. Her *Carrie* trilogy is based on events surrounding the Peshtigo fire of 1871. In addition to writing and travel, Nelda enjoys hiking and spending time with her family.

**LaVonne Woodhouse Mainz** lives in Onalaska. She and her late husband, John, raised five children, Karen, Lois, Richard, Robert, and Randy. At age fifty, she studied art and has won awards for her oil paintings. She served on the state board of Wisconsin artists. She is also a published writer and poet and has written, illustrated, and published five *Grandma Bon's Coloring Storybooks* dedicated to her grandchildren. She has written and published a children's novel, *The Pinkelton Girls: The Mystery of the Gold Box*. La Vonne has contributed writings to six other books, including *Spirit of La Crosse* and *Spirit of America*.

**David J. Marcou** was born and raised in La Crosse, where he graduated from St. James Grade School and Aquinas High School. He also graduated from the UW-Madison (B.A.-History); University of Iowa (M.A.-American Studies); and University of Missouri (B.J.-Journalism). He has directed the group that produced this book and six others, including *Spirit of America*, which he also co-edited. And he has published eleven books of his own, including three photo books, two with his son, Matt. In addition, Dave has lived and worked as a journalist in London, Seoul, Missouri, and Wisconsin. He enjoys reading, writing, photography, and travel.

**Matthew A. Marcou** was born in 1987 and raised in La Crosse, where he graduated from Cathedral Grade School and Aquinas Middle School. He is currently a freshman in high school and has been taking pictures since he was three and one-half years old. Many of his photos have been published, including those in two photo books with his dad, Dave, and his first poem, "Snowman," was published when he was eight. In addition to his photographic and literary contributions to *Spirit of America*, Matt typed the entire manuscript for it, and performed similar duties for this book.

**Tom and Joy Marcou** live in the Washington, D.C., area and work for the U.S. Department of Defense. Tom is Dave's brother, and he was born and raised in La Crosse. Joy (Dycus) grew up in Texas. While Tom was serving in the U.S. Air Force, he earned his bachelor's degree in Accounting, and Joy did the same while she was working on the Air Force bases where they were stationed. Tom has one son, Stephen, who lives and works in Illinois. The couple's interests include house decoration, computers, travel, fine cuisine, movies, and photography. They have lived in Britain, on both U.S. coasts, and in Colorado and Texas while Tom was in the military.

**Bernard McGarty, O.S.F., S.T.D.**, a priest of the Diocese of La Crosse, is Visiting Scholar for Ecumenical Studies at Viterbo University in La Crosse. He earned a Doctor of Sacred Theology from Angelicum University in Rome, writing *John Donne as a Persuasive Preacher*. Other publications are *Meditations for Lenten Weekdays* and *Biking and Canoeing in Western Wisconsin*. Father McGarty has served as pastor and assistant pastor in many western Wisconsin parishes including in La Crosse, Wausau, and Eau Claire in addition to having been editor of the diocesan newspaper, the *Catholic Times*, then known as the *Times Review*.

# AUTHOR BIOGRAPHIES

**Sam McKay** has lived in the La Crosse area since 1973, and retired to Chaseburg, Wisconsin, in 1987. Born in Salem, Massachusetts, he came west to attend the UW-Madison, where he graduated in 1954 with a bachelor's degree in English. Following his service in the U.S. Army, he became a retail bookseller. Sam has always wanted to write and be published, and he's working on two book manuscripts, one dealing with his military experiences and the other with a cross-country car trip with his family in 1948.

**Anna Muktepavels-Motivans** was born in Latvia and received her primary education there. Her high school education was in a displaced persons camp in Germany. She earned her B.S. degree from the Butler University School of Pharmacy. Until her retirement, her life's work was analytical chemistry and hospital pharmacy. Her hobbies include reading, writing her memoirs, weaving, spinning, knitting, nature walks, and traveling. She and her late husband, Joseph, have six children and twelve grandchildren. Anna lives close to the bluffs and the beautiful Mississippi River in La Crosse.

**Charles Nierling** grew up in rural northeast Iowa, where he attended Waukon Senior High. Following graduation as valedictorian in 1993, he went on to study at Yale University. In 1997, he received his B.A. in Political Science. Charles moved to New York City in 1999. He is listed with the NASD as a Registered Representative, Uniform State Agent, General Securities Principal, Registered Options Principal, and Registered Equity Trader. On September 11th, 2001, he was working in the New York Mercantile Exchange on the Hudson River, just west of the World Trade Center.

**Virgene Nix Oldenburg** grew up in a large family on a southern Eau Claire (Wisconsin) County farm. She is the product of a one-room schoolhouse. After graduating from Eau Claire Regis High School and attending the St. Francis Hospital School of Nursing in La Crosse, she became a registered nurse and married Doug. "Nixie" enjoys her husband, their seven children and nineteen grandchildren, letter-writing, reading poetry and short stories, and golf—not necessarily in that order.

**Barbara A. Pauls** was born in Chicago, Illinois, and raised in Mosinee, Wisconsin. She was employed by the Wisconsin Department of Revenue before starting and managing an assessing firm now owned by one of her sons. She feels her greatest achievement was raising her four children, Sheila, Lisa, Todd, and Ted, and seeing them all receive college degrees. Her greatest happiness is having the love of her children, grandchildren, and friends. In addition to seeing her family and friends, Barbara enjoys world traveling, reading, writing, socializing, and outdoor activities, including sailing and playing golf.

**Lori Peterson** was born in La Crosse as Lori Ann Smith. She grew up in Onalaska, where she now lives with her husband, Mike. She is currently employed by La Crosse County as a 911 emergency dispatcher. She enjoys spending time off with her husband at their cottage near Hatfield, Wisconsin. They spend their summers boating and water-skiing on area lakes and rivers. She has many hobbies, including making frames and matting her own photos. Lori is Mark Smith's sister.

**Louise Randall-Winger** was born on the Upper Peninsula of Michigan. She graduated from Blue Island County (Illinois) High School, and, eventually, from WWTC, with a Personnel Technician associate degree. She spent twenty years in the U.S. Navy after high school and currently is employed by WWTC. In addition to photography, Louise enjoys line-dancing, eagle-watching, and wildflower identification.

**Anene Ristow** was born in State Line, Mississippi, and graduated from Clarke Memorial Junior College and the Baptist Memorial Hospital R.N. program in Memphis, Tennessee. A registered nurse for thirty-five years, she later supervised the eight-hundred-bed facility from whose nursing school she had graduated. With her late husband, Glen, she has four children, seven grandchildren, and five step-grandchildren. Anene has published the story of her husband's battle with lymphoma, *Cancer: A Different Trip*. In addition to writing, her interests include church work, reading, and public speaking.

**Jim Rodgers,** a native of Oklahoma, is a professor of Political Science at Saint Mary's University of Minnesota in Winona. He received master's and doctorate degrees in Political Science from Idaho State University. Jim has taught at SMUMN for twenty-one years and specializes in courses on political and social thought. He is co-author of a text on domestic terrorism, *Facing Terror* (2002), with Tim Kullman.

**Rick Romell** has been a reporter since 1976, first for the *Milwaukee Sentinel* and then for its successor, the *Milwaukee Journal Sentinel*. He is fifty-one years old and a native of Milwaukee, where he lives with his wife, Kathleen Zinner, and their daughter, Emma. Rick holds degrees in Journalism from the UW-Milwaukee and Northwestern University.

**Mary Lou Ryan** was born in Austin, Minnesota. She earned a B.S. degree in Education from the University of Minnesota, and taught in the St. Paul public school system. She and her husband, Jim, a peripatetic professor, and six children lived in Detroit, Reno, and St. Paul before settling in La Crosse in 1968. Writing has been an off-and-on pastime for Mary Lou since grade school. She was co-editor of her high school paper and a feature writer on her college paper. She has edited newsletters for the League of Women Voters of La Crosse County and the Alliance for the Mentally Ill.

**Sharon Swenson Schmeling** has roots in Iowa and Wisconsin. She and her husband, Ken, have enjoyed the Coulee Region since 1997, when they began renovation of her great-grandfather's Norwegian log farmhouse, circa 1872. Her interests include reading, writing, and child welfare. She attended the UW-Whitewater as an Elementary Education major, was instrumental in the founding of two community theatres, and has co-published a children's musical. She is the mother of four grown children and one dedicated Australian shepherd.

**Sue Silvermarie** was raised in Wisconsin and earned her M.S.W. from the UW-Milwaukee. Her work has run an interesting gamut which includes gerontology specialist, mail carrier, and certified poetry therapist. She has driven a catering truck, tutored prison inmates in creative writing, and had a massage therapy practice. Recently, she worked in a Mayan community in Guatemala as a human rights observer. Her book *Tales from My Teachers on the Alzheimer's Unit* is available from Manticore Publishers.

**Mark Douglas Smith** was born in La Crosse and grew up in the Onalaska, Wisconsin, area. He currently lives in La Crosse, where he has been employed for almost fifteen years as a firefighter. Mark and his wife, Jean, have two children. Their daughter, Bobbie, is in her second year of school at UW-La Crosse. Their son, Jesse, graduated with the class of 2002 at Central High School. Mark has many hobbies, including scuba diving, trapping, hunting, and fishing. Sometimes he even finds time to write.

**Robert (Bob) Smith** lives in La Crosse with his wife, Bonnie. He retired in 1993 from an exciting newspaper career, which included his time as general manager of the *Chicago Daily News* and work in the business department of the *Des Moines Register*. He currently enjoys writing, volunteering, and visiting with his two children (Terry and Cindy) and five grandchildren. Bob was one of the first U.S. GI's to climb Mt. Fujiyama after World War II. In May of 2000, he had successful heart valve surgery, and he dreams of climbing mountains again someday.

## AUTHOR BIOGRAPHIES

**Robert (Terry) Smith** was born in La Crosse and raised in Waukegan, Illinois, Meridian, Mississippi, and Des Moines, Iowa. He graduated from Waukegan High School and attended the College of Lake County (Illinois) for 2½ years, and also received a Floral Design degree in Chicago. He has worked as a photojournalist and a floral designer for his parents' businesses (he is the son of Bob, another author here, and Marcilee). For twenty-one years, he worked for the Onalaska Water Department and for twenty-two years was a volunteer firefighter, also in Onalaska. In addition, he served as Director of Emergency Government there. Terry has been married to Cheryl for twenty-five years, and they have one daughter and three grandchildren. Among his interests are golf, fishing, writing, and photography.

**Jim Solberg** is a La Crosse native who graduated from Aquinas High School in 1964 and received a B.S. degree in Secondary Education at UW–La Crosse. He taught junior high science at Holy Trinity School in La Crosse and worked for several years as a drafter and survey manager at Solbergs' and Associates Surveying and Drafting. He also traveled the country as a representative for Sun Photo, an aerial photo firm. He recently received a Masters of Public Health degree from UW–La Crosse and does respite care for disabled adults. He has pursued his interests in writing and photography in the last few years and has had his works published in the *La Crosse Tribune*, the *Galesville Republican*, the *Country Gazette*, *Badger Sportsman*, and *MidWest Outdoor News*. He loves outdoor activities and especially enjoys time spent with his children, Peter and Sarah.

**Blaine R. Thorson** was born on French Island in La Crosse County, Wisconsin, in 1935. He is one of eight children and graduated from Logan High School in La Crosse. He spent twenty-five years in the U.S. Navy, working in telecommunications. He was the associate dean of San Diego (California) Community College for ten years, as well. Apart from writing poetry, Blaine has a great love for hunting and fishing. He now lives with his wife in Brice Prairie, Wisconsin, and has two children and four grandchildren.

**Agnes (Aggie) Tippery** lives in southeastern Minnesota with Ivan, her husband of more than half a century. She graduated from St. Peter's High School in Hokah, Minnesota. Ivan and Aggie have five sons, five grandsons, and one granddaughter. After retiring from a technical writing job, she worked for twelve years at a local hospital. Retiring from there, she began writing a weekly newspaper column and volunteering in Hokah. In 2001, she put her stories of that community into a book, *Stories of Hokah from Aggie's View*. She teaches a "Writing Your Life" class to senior citizens and others in the area. Her other interests are sewing, cooking, and traveling.

**Thomas (Tom) Tippery** was born in Iowa and moved with his family to rural Minnesota at the age of two. He hated English class but loved science while in school. He served three years in the Intelligence Branch of the United States Army Security Agency. While in Germany, Tom married his childhood sweetheart, Nadine. They live near the farm he grew up on, in rural Minnesota. He is an electrician, and besides writing, his hobbies are woodworking, winemaking, electronics, and ham radio operation.

**Frances (Nina) Valiska** and her husband, Jim, live in Mosinee, Wisconsin. They both enjoy photography and fishing. They also enjoy visiting their children and grandchildren. Nina and Barbara Pauls are sisters.

**Karmin Van Domelen** was born in Belvedere, Illinois, and raised in Oconomowoc, Wisconsin. She graduated from the UW–La Crosse in Sociology and Community Health Education. She also has a degree in Culinary Arts. She worked for the S.C. Johnson Wax Company in Racine, Wisconsin for fourteen years. Karmin is married to Gary, and they have a seven-year-old son, Sean. In addition to writing, she is interested in cooking and crafts, including mosaics and jewelry.

# AUTHOR BIOGRAPHIES

**Evelyn (Phelps) Wilhelm** was born and raised on La Crosse's north side. She graduated from St. James Grade School and Aquinas High School (1952). She is the mother of ten children and has, at last count, sixteen grandchildren. Her interests include spending time with family and friends, playing golf, reading, and taking classes like basic computer and writing. Evelyn has traveled to Italy, Israel, Jordan, Greece, Egypt, and many places in the western and southern United States.

**Richard Wood,** forty-seven, has been a staff photojournalist for the *Milwaukee Journal Sentinel* since 1978. He graduated from the Indiana University School of Journalism. He has photographed many difficult stories in difficult places. On 9/11 he photographed the collapse of the World Trade Center from six blocks away. Rick has won many national and regional awards for his work on poverty in Iraq, North Korea, Somalia, Haiti, and Brazil. He is one of fewer than two hundred Americans who have been allowed into North Korea since 1953. Other assignments have included the 1998 Winter Olympics in Nagano, Japan, and the 1997 Superbowl in New Orleans.

**Jennifer (Choua Yang) Xiong** was born in Namu, Laos, in 1976. She graduated from Eau Claire (Wisconsin) North High School in 1995 and graduated cum laude from the UW–Stout in 1998 with a B.S. degree in Human Development and Family Studies. In 1999, she received an M.S. degree in Guidance and Counseling. Jennifer and her husband, Michael, have been married for eleven years and have five children. She currently works for the Wisconsin Department of Public Instruction as an Education Specialist with the Gear Up Program, working with economically disadvantaged students. In the 2001 Scott Thompson film, *My New Voice*, she played a Hmong mother.

*Billboard in front of a telephone pole cross, 2002,*
*Copeland Avenue, La Crosse, WI, by Steve Kiedrowski.*

# Over Lake Arbutus, Forever
*Mark D. Smith*

Soft white wings in a blue black sky.
I stand silent in the darkness, and watch them
    go by.
The season is pushing the cold and the snow.
Somehow, they always seem to know
    when to go.
Small flocks of tundra swans.
Like the Mississippi, south they flow.

Communicating to each other, in their
    haunting tone.
Moving at night, for reasons unknown.
In the darkness, they appear, like ghosts
    in the sky.
Wings outstretched and broad
    as gracefully they fly by.

Long necks silhouetted against a backdrop
    of stars.
They navigate the sky on their journey afar.
From the blackness they emerged;
    into the blackness they've gone.
I won't see them again
    until winter is gone.

*Composite photo of swans flying over Lake Arbutus, circa 2000, western Wisconsin, by Lori Peterson.*

ORDER FORM FOR

# *America's Heartland Remembers*

Number of books to be mailed within the United States
at US$25 per book (including tax and shipping) _____

Number of books to be mailed outside
the United States via Airmail
at US$30 per book (including tax and shipping) _____

Total payment enclosed via International Money Order
or cashier's check in US$ _____

Name _____

Address _____

City/State/Country/Postal Code _____

Phone _____

E-mail address (optional) _____

Please send this form along with your payment, made payable to:

**David J. Marcou**
c/o: 1720 Prospect Street
La Crosse, WI 54603, USA

Tel. 608-784-2796
E-Mail: wordpic@hotmail.com

Normally, you will receive your book/s
within two weeks after your payment is received.

*Thank You!*